Scalded to Death by the Steam

Scalded to Death by the Steam

AUTHENTIC STORIES OF RAILROAD DISASTERS

AND THE BALLADS

THAT WERE WRITTEN ABOUT THEM

Katie Letcher Lyle

ALGONQUIN BOOKS

For Paul M. Shue

ALGONQUIN BOOKS
P.O. Box 2225, Chapel Hill, NC 27515-2225

© 1983 by Katie Letcher Lyle.
ISBN 0-912697-01-6

Words and music to "The Wreck of the C & O No.5," "The Wreck
of the 1256," "The Wreck of Number 9," and "The Freight Wreck
at Altoona" copyrighted by MCA Music, 445 Park Ave., New York,
N.Y., 10022. "Billy Richardson's Last Ride" printed by permission
of the copyright owners, Jerry Vogel Music Co., Inc., and MCA
Music. Words and music to "Ben Dewberry's Final Run" and "The
Wreck of the Virginian No. 3" are copyrighted by Columbia Pictures Corp., and are reproduced by permission of that company.

Music Examples by Helen Jenner

Contents

Introduction   1

The Wreck of the Old 97   14

The Wreck on the C & O   34

The N & W Cannonball Wreck   50

The New Market Wreck   57

Billy Richardson's Last Ride   68

The Hamlet Wreck   77

The Guyandotte Bridge Disaster   83

The Wreck of C & O No. 5   92

The Wreck of the 1256   102

The Church Hill Tunnel Disaster   116

The Freight Wreck at Altoona   125

The Wreck of the Royal Palm   132

The Wreck of the Virginian Train No. 3   141

Three in Kentucky   150

The Wreck of the Sportsman   163

Spikes on the Rail   173

The Wreck of Old 85   182

Others: 188

The Wreck Between New Hope &
Gethsemane; The Wreck of the Flyer,
Duquesne; The Wreck of No. 3; The
Wreck of the 444; The Fate of Talmadge
Osborne; The Powellton Labor Train
Explosion; The Ride to Hell

Bibliography   205

Index   208

Scalded to Death by the Steam

Introduction

I

The city council met last night; the vote was four to three,
To tear the home town depot down, and build a factory,
To take that strip of history, and tear it off the map,
To take old Engine Number Nine, and melt her into scrap . . .

("Blue Water Line," Anonymous)

In my grandparents' house where I spent some years as a child in the mid-forties, there was an old wind-up Victrola with packets of needles and a cabinet full of old records. There was also a delicate lady's guitar with one frizzled string.

On rainy days, I played the Victrola. One of the first records I discovered was Vernon Dalhart's

(Photo on opposite page) Building the C & O Railroad, 1873–74. This heavy cut in the mountains was typical of the herculean task that the railroad builders confronted. Note the tipple, possibly for coal, alongside the track, and the lone figure, possibly a track inspector. *Cook Collection, Valentine Museum.*

"Wreck of the Old 97." I listened to it over and over, thrilling to the words. "The Wreck of the 1256," "The Wreck of the Virginian No. 3," "The Wreck of the C & O No. 5"—all these I loved and learned. My grandfather was something of a train buff, and encouraged my singing. Among his frequent homilies was the story of the brave engineer Billy Richardson who had been tragically killed on duty. He urged me to remember, perhaps sensing that the railroad, at least as he knew it, was dying.

Lexington had once been a fairly busy rail terminal. By the tracks that ran down behind my grandparents' house I stood every day in summer, making friends long-distance with the nameless engineer who backed the only slow C & O freight engine into Lexington each morning around eleven, then took it out again a while later, this time headfirst. Soon it would stop coming altogether.

One day Andaddy had business in West Virginia,

and I rode along with him in his 1926 Model T. Ford, which he called his "confounded machine." I still remember the spring morning, "the sunlight piercing the leaves," as one of the songs went. By the side of the road beyond Covington there was a sign: JERRY'S RUN. I knew the *cities* in the songs existed, like Washington and Charlottesville, but it took that tiny landmark to convince me of a deeper truth. "From Covington to Jerry's Run, old number five did roll. . . ."

"Is there really an Allegheny Tunnel?" I asked, anticipating the next line: "Through the Allegheny Tunnel with the crew so brave and bold. . . ."

There was, up a treacherous rutted railroad access lane, where we got out of the car and walked amid poison ivy and hawthorn, following the track around a bend. There it was, a black arc in the mountainside! "Little Sweetheart," he said, for the millionth time, "remember this."

I date my passion for train songs and the stories behind them from that moment, near my sixth birthday. For it was at that moment that I saw the stories as true, about real people, who had suffered and died.

Eventually I got four strings for that old guitar and learned to play it ukelele style, but it had not been cared for and was warped and dry and would not stay in tune, so for my eighth birthday I got a beautiful Favilla tenor ukelele, bigger than an ordinary uke. I sang barbershop songs, Hawaiian songs, train wreck songs. My mother commented that she thought I'd collected every horrible song ever written. But what could you expect from a Mozart fan?

When, in 1949, a radio station went on the air in Lexington, I never missed a chance to sing on it. During the week my down-hill neighbor John Starling (late of the Seldom Scene) and I would sometimes sing and play together, but each Saturday at noon we would scowl at each other across the stage of the Kiddies' Karnival and vie for the $3.00 grand prize, which was won by getting the highest rating for the day on something called an "applause meter." Sometimes one of us even won.

In philosophical moments I pondered the stories of the wrecks, wondering as much as I could bear to about the suffering of the men who were scalded to death by the steam. That year I prevailed on my father to take me to Danville to see where Old 97 had crashed. The field trip was a disappointment. Stillhouse Trestle was gone, the ravine partially filled to create Highway 58, and not a sign of the excitement.

It was only after I'd finished college, when the "urban folk renewal" movement of the early 1960s started, that I began to realize the value of my music. I was lucky enough to sing professionally off and on for five years between college and marriage, for three years at Peabody's Bookshop in Baltimore, and later at some places in Nashville. Along with other ballads I sang like "Three Drowned Sisters" and "Roane County," I still wondered what truths lay behind my all-time favorites, the wreck songs.

I had two great railroading friends in those days. A B & O westbound train left Baltimore around suppertime, arriving at Shenandoah Junction, West Virginia, about eleven, where "Happy" Myers and Charlie McCrory were the night dispatcher and relief agent-operator. The connecting N & W train "up the valley" of Virginia (southward) to Buena Vista didn't leave until three or four A.M., so deep in the night I would sing Happy and Charlie train songs. Soon I began to alert them ahead of time of my coming, and they would be waiting for me with ham biscuits and hot coffee.

I went on to life's other things: marriage, teaching, mothering, novel-writing—with train wrecks very much on a back burner. Once in those years I came upon a poem by Whittier which went in part,

CONDUCTOR BRADLEY (always may his name
Be said with reverence!) as the swift doom came,
Smitten to death, a crushed and mangled frame.

Sank, with the brake he grasped just where he stood
To do the utmost that a brave man could
And die, if needful, as a true man should.

Men stooped above him; women dropped their tears
On that poor wreck beyond all hopes or fears,
Lost in the strength and glory of his years.

What heard they? Lo! the ghastly lips of pain,
Dead to all thought save duty's, moved again:
"Put out the signals for the other train."
John Greenleaf Whittier

Excited to be reminded, I actually began a paper on the train wreck songs. I think the reason I quit was that I could not imagine a journal that would be interested in such a "study."

In January of 1982 I was asked to write this book. I was skeptical, knowing, when I got right down to it, nothing about trains, and not a lot about American popular poetry. I thought there would not be enough material for an entire book.

Finally I agreed to spend a few months on the project, still doubtful about the saleability of such a topic, even if the material could be found.

What has developed is a book about train accident songs, and the wrecks or mishaps that the songs record. I began with the songs, then researched the events. The songs included cover a time period roughly from the Civil War to the First World War.

If one marked every spot on a map of the lower forty-eight states where a wreck that had a song composed about it occurred, a heavy cluster would form west of the Blue Ridge and east of the Ohio River, north of the Smokies, and south of the north fork of the James River. Though there are certain notable exceptions, clearly it is Appalachia where the strongest tradition of ballads about railroad disasters developed. In studying these ballads and their stories, interesting people have emerged from the mists of the past, and this is a book, it turns out, about some brave men, and some fools.

Where the wrecks were: according to Robert Shaw's *A History of Railroad Accidents, Safety Precautions, and Operating Practices*, here are the states where the major steam railroad accidents in the United States happened, between 1890 and 1933.

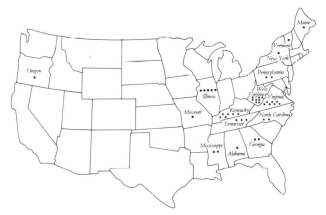

Where the songs were made: the dots show only the state in which an accident occurred that had a song or songs made about it, not the location within the state. Several wrecks cannot be located geographically.

Paul Shue, 1982. *Photo by Katie Lyle.*

II

Oft when I feel my engine swerve
As o'er strange rails we fare,
I strain my eyes around the curve
For what awaits us there.
(*Cy Warman*)

For just about a century, steam railroading in America flourished. On Christmas Day, 1830, the first regular passenger service began. Scarcely a century later, competition from automobiles, buses, trucks, and eventually airplanes, had already begun to effect the slow choking death of the most romantic mode of land transportation ever devised. Yet Paul Shue, whom you will meet often in this book, likes to quote David Morgan: "If any man has invented a mechanism with just fifty percent of the steam locomotive's solid spiritual satisfaction, he hasn't applied for a patent yet."

Steam engines are now part of the past. But, like fossils, they have left inerasable traces on our psyches and in our language. We speak of being "on the track" or "off the track," of "making the grade." An "engineer," once exclusively in America someone who drove a train locomotive or engine, is now the operator of almost any piece of equipment. We who cannot remember steam locomotives still speak of going "full steam ahead."

Yet railroads were and are metaphors of the future. Possibly nothing else characterizes modern man better than rapid transportation. The "saga of the iron horse" symbolized the change, progress, and novelty which the American dream has always embodied. An English lady, Mrs. Houston, in *Hesperos, or Travels in the West*, which was published in London in 1850, commented, "I really think there must be some natural affinity between Yankee 'keep-moving' nature and a locomotive engine."

There were few accidents in the early years of railroading. Trains ran slowly, and there were not very many of them. For a long time they were not allowed to run at night or on Sundays. But nineteenth-century America was more concerned with growth for its own sake than with quality of growth, and technology soon got ahead of itself. Railroad historians agree that in our haste to cover the land with a network of tracks for trains to transport goods and passengers quickly and cheaply, errors were made. Contractors built the railroads at a previously agreed price; the faster they could build and the less they could spend, the more money they could make. Track was laid hastily and carelessly, by whatever labor could be got cheap. Often roadbeds were poor, tracks flimsy, bridges unstable, grades steep, tunnels unshored. Timber and brush used as fill did not last, for long.

As for the trains themselves, early schedules were nightmarish, as each locality declared its own time and each railroad was a law unto itself. This situation invited collisions. The boilers on steam engines were poorly gauged, and were in constant danger of exploding. Add to this that crew members were no more infallible judges of the capacities of their machines than we are today infallible judges of our automobiles. Dispatchers too often sent out erroneous information, further compounding the possibility of accidents.

And so, as early as the 1850s, accidents were becoming epidemic. Engines could go fast enough to be dangerous. Some tracks were twenty years old, and some bridges already rotten. Equipment and rights-of-way were poorly kept up. Switches were faulty. In mountainous country, landslides were an ever-present danger. Engineers often drove their engines too fast. Leon Beauvallet, a Frenchman touring the United States in 1855, called the railroads "a miracle of headlong carelessness." Tom Dixon, whose impress appears often in this book, recalls that traveling salesmen always tried to get berths in the middle of the middle car of a train, the spot farthest from a head-on crash or a rear-end collision.

The phenomenon of actually staging wrecks as a spectator sport emerged around the turn of the century. For example, at the official opening of Buckeye Park in Ohio on Memorial Day in 1896, an "immensely successful" train wreck was had on the Columbus, Hocking Valley and Toledo Railway, which drew, in spite of heavy rains, twenty thousand onlookers.

III
Now railroad men, take this warning:
Heed your orders well,
For how soon the Lord may call you,
No human tongue can tell.
(*"The Wreck of the Virginian No. 3," Roy Harvey*)

The South, and especially Appalachia, responded to the inroads of industrialism as it had always responded to things, with music. Bill Malone, the Lomaxes, and other folklorists have observed that the rhythms of the railroad are evident in much southern popular music. Syncopation and counterpoint imitate the clicking of the drivers on the rails. "Breakdowns" possibly grew out of an imitation of train sounds. The beat, in blues, boogie-woogie, and jazz, behind all of the notes, echoes the sound of trains.

Among the thousands of American songs about railroads are the wreck songs I have always loved. As Shelley put it, "Our sweetest songs are those that tell of saddest thought."

What are these songs like?

As a body, they may comprise a sort of white folk-epic. Their diction is "formulaic," in Albert Lord's term; they employ repeated "epic phrases" such as "receiving his train orders, he climbed in the cab to ride," and "when I blow for _____, they will surely know my call." Norm Cohen, commenting on the concept of "plagiarism" in folk composition, points out that "there is nothing original in our words, but we expect groups of words to be original. The unit of

The Wreck Between New Hope and Gethsemane

Arr. by
Nick Manoloff

By Karl & Harty
and Doc Hopkins

1. Once two trains with might-y power run-ning six-ty miles an hour 'Twas a
2. Ster - gin the en-gin-eer was brave, saw his train he could not save Saw a
3. When the morn-ing light it came all a-round the burn-ing train Ma-ny
4. Ma - ny lives of men were lost and most fear-ful was the cost That the

fear-ful speed be - tween mid-night and day _____ Ster-gin must have been a -
head-light 'round the curve like light-ning flash _____ An-other train was head-ing
friends and ma - ny loved ones gath-ered there _____ Fast be - neath that burn-ing
L and N Com-pa - ny did sus - tain _____ 'Twas the dark-est hour that

sleep Passed the point he had to meet And it caused an aw - ful
on He soon saw that he was gone And they came to - geth - er
train They saw their friends they could not save So they turned a - way al -
night Peo - ple gath - ered to that fright But they could not save them

wreck a - long the way. _____
with an aw - ful crash. _____
most in sad des - pair. _____
from that burn - ing train. _____

Dark was the night Men

worked with all their might In that wreck a-bout two o'-clock or

three _____ 'Twas a morn-ing in No-vem-ber long to be re-

mem-bered That wreck be-tween New Hope and Geth-sem-a-ne. _____

creativity in a folk culture . . . is significantly larger than in a literary culture." Wreck songs generally begin with calling the listener's attention to the setting: "Just after the dawn of the morning"; "On a cold and dark cloudy evening"; "Far away on the banks of New River. . . ." In effect these formulaic openings describe the background against which the action will occur.

- The disastrous wrecks, in terms of lives lost, were generally not written about. Mass tragedy has probably never been as interesting as the death of one or two individuals.

- In the years covered by these songs, Americans were looking for heroes. Literature is made, I believe, in response to the question, "How is a good man to behave?" These songs of brave engineers provide at least some answers to that question. The action of a lone man caught under the reverse lever and scalded to death by steam is raised to a higher level: it is a symbolic story of a hero, representing all of us. Thus each song becomes a lesson in how we should act under stress, providing occasion for a warning of cosmic significance and an example of the fragility of man in the hands of a seemingly whimsical deity.

Brave, young, and true, the sung-about engineer certainly qualifies as a prototypical American epic hero. He was in the forefront of industrialism, running his machine that ran the world. He was also self-reliant, restless, and on the move. His engine was his sidekick, mistress, and wife—always "she." His life of "rugged individualism" provided him unfettered access to new people, places, and things. And the railroad itself, an object of life familiar to everyone, is often seen as symbolic of eternal truths, as in "Life's Railway to Heaven":

You will roll up grades of trial; you will cross the bridge
  of strife;
See that Christ is your conductor on this lightning train
  of life . . .

James McCague, in the foreword to *The Big Ivy*, writes movingly of engineers; his sentiments are typical.

It used to be that whenever an old main line hogger was laid away, they'd time the ceremony so that [the train] would whistle a requiem in passing . . . and the smokestack would lay a rolling pall of smoke across the land, and the long mourning of the whistle and the rolling rumble of steel on steel would drown out the minister's last few words. And the mourners would be reminded then that their departing brother was one who had regularly, through most of the days of his life, lived on terms of easy intimacy with danger, surrounded by the thrashing pound of iron massively fashioned, breathing live steam, hurtling across the miles at his command faster than lesser men ever went their whole lives long.

It somehow set him apart. The machine age brought few enough heroes, and he was one, and if he had too often partaken of the fiery waters, to the detriment of his family's happiness and the public peace . . . If his conversation had been studded with casual blasphemies, his will had been stubborn beyond belief, and his temper habitually carried a short fuse . . . Well, what did all that amount to, against the fact that he had been a man among men?

This portrait points out an important fact: though he may have been badly flawed, an engineer was somehow magical. It may not be fair even to bring up accuracy when one is speaking of this type of literature. The raw truth is that most of the engineers who died in the songs in this book wasted their lives. Billy Richardson died because he was careless, Ed Webber because he did not heed sound advice. "Steve" Broady, F. C. Scheline, Harry Covington, and Homer Haskell all died because they ran their trains too fast.

Yet I think this did not much matter to those who loved these songs. Generally, as today, the *facts* were not important: the man was not required actually to be glamorous or heroic or even good, though it is certainly an American trait to heroize men who

In this original lithograph by W. L. Shepherd, from *Harper's Weekly*, February 10, 1872, the figure out in front of the train is signaling it to stop. In the center, the brakeman turns the brake wheel. In front of him is the woodbox; the older engines ran on wood. The engineer peering out of the right side of the cab grasps the throttle with his left hand and the Johnson Bar, or reverse lever, with his right. *Courtesy L. P. "Pick" Temple.*

show "gumption." The process of fiction was all that was needed in a headlong spurt of national growth that forced the country to create instant heroes in answer to the need for an identity. Even today we make heroes quickly and foolishly: James Dean and Elvis Presley should be examples enough. Almost always, in the songs that this book is about, the trainman is elevated to hero merely by the fact of his death. American ballad sentimentality thrives on stories of untimely death, and finds in the stories not just the excitement for its own sake that the Scots and British found in stories of disaster, but, as has been often noted, occasions for moralizing. Epics, being national models, are always concerned with the matter of order. A train wreck disrupts the natural order, yet offers an excuse to contemplate a man's life in terms of justice and morality. I expect this is why the facts in wreck songs are not very important; the story is all. Pick Temple, folklorist and former television star, has written, "I think one of the things that attracts me philosophically to folk music is our innate belief that there is dignity in the least of us. Some might say, some dumb guy did one more stupid thing and lost his life. So what? Well, we in our country, at least, *care* about the loss of even a single life. We care enough to mourn the dead by singing the ballads that were inspired by the event."

That the nineteenth century in this country was more concerned with growth than refinement is evident in the train wreck songs. Many are of appalling quality, often factually inaccurate, carelessly written, emotionally unrestrained, and literarily unsubtle. They have their share of the gore that was a journalistic commonplace of the American Victorian era. G. Malcolm Laws defends "the sincere tenderness of the stories," and "America's sympathy for the victims of tragedy," yet he admits the songs are "not skillful," but "the natural product of a people who respond generously whenever disaster strikes." Of course, mediocrity has always been the norm in the popular, mass-market music field. Certainly the newspapers and magazines of this same period are full of the most appalling verses, on myriad subjects.

Predictably, the more popular a song became the less accurate it tended to be. Certainly, the earlier songs, the anonymous "Wreck of the F.F.V." and "The Wreck of the Old 97," are the most inaccurate of all. The folk process is, of course, a rather inglorious combination of "artistic" changes, forgetfulness, mishearing, illiteracy, and other factors. Later errors in the composed ballads must be laid at the doors of careless composers, like Andrew Jenkins. In both his ballads discussed in this book— "Ben Dewberry's Final Run" and "The Wreck of the Royal Palm"—he has got the essential facts wrong or omitted important information. Cleburne Meeks, on the other hand, was as accurate as he could be, failing only in the ultimate interest of art. (In each of his songs discussed, the disaster is preceded by an imagined conversation which foreshadows the tragedy.) The songs written and recorded commercially, often within months or even weeks of a disaster, then distributed throughout the country, stayed pretty much the same as originally written.

Epics, often based on some distant event (like the Trojan War), are not necessarily true to history, but they are true to the ideas of order and morality. Similarly, moral tags adhere to the end of nearly all wreck songs, as they did in much nineteenth-century American "fireside" poetry. The moral tags point to the uplifting side of the tragedies, the nobility of the human spirit, the American concern for our fellowmen, and our commitment to Christian belief.

IV
My heart is warm with the friends I make,
And better friends I'll not be knowing;
Yet there isn't a train I wouldn't take,
No matter where it's going.
(*"Travel," Edna St. Vincent Millay*)

To say that I could not have written this book alone is an understatement. I knew virtually nothing about trains. It is railroad policy to destroy out-of-date timetables and records. Official wreck pictures are hard to come by, since no railroad is anxious to publicize its failures. Newspapers were thrown out, along with old zinc plates and glass negatives, when microfilm came in, and time has destroyed emulsion negatives. I am not a folklorist, and had never done much research. I had to lean heavily on Royster Lyle, then on friends; and finally on strangers.

Eventually I sent letters to twenty-nine papers in the vicinities of the wrecks I was studying, asking for information and pictures. I was delighted and gratified at the scores of responses I got. I had no idea of the generosity, trust, and kindness that I would find, in the responses to my letters and in the many people whose help I asked along the way. I cannot possibly introduce or thank all the people who made this book happen, but here are a few.

My dear husband Royster, of the George C. Marshall Foundation, who is an old hat at research (*The Architecture of Historic Lexington*, University Press of Virginia, 1977), deserves my first thanks for his help from beginning to end, but primarily for his sublime tolerance in the face of frozen food and frequently abandoned children. I could not have completed this project without his support. Cochran, eleven, deserves formal thanks, too, for his babysitting prowess and original phone messages: MOM: ONE OF YOUR TRAINRECK BOYFRIENDS CALLED. CALL HIM BACK AT _____. CAN I HAVE A MT. DEW? Jennie, four, has my gratitude for her genuine interest: "Mommy, sing the 'Wreck of the Sportsman.'" "What's a 'junction on the line'?" By the end of the project, she had learned the lyrics of several of the songs by heart.

Paul Shue, of Staunton, Virginia, retired post office employee and radio announcer (WSVA, WTON, WAYB, and Armed Forces Network) has collected railroad songs, especially wreck songs, and has been a railroad buff since childhood. His weekly radio program, "The Poet's Window" (1944–1973), often dealt with steam railroading. When I first went to see him in March 1982, he turned over to me without hesitation his entire collection of books, scrapbooks, and tapes. He introduced me by mail to Pick Temple and Ron Lane. Since then, he has often accompanied me in search of material, spending hours recording songs, going through card catalogues and boxes of old photographs, and tolerating sweltering hours in the car. "It's no fun to have something if you can't share it," he says. I cannot go to visit Paul and his wife Lois and come home without a plant, or a new tape, or some tomatoes. Along with Willard Kibler, we have organized "The Broken Rails," and sung already at public functions. It gives me great joy to dedicate this book to Paul.

Mr. Ben P. Knight enjoys his retirement from forty-one years with the C & O, the last ten as Assistant Superintendent of the Clifton Forge Division. I am sure he never expected to be called on at this late date to remember how engines were named and numbered, what "dropping a pin" means, and a thousand other bits of information that a greenhorn needed to write a book about trains. He and his wife Jean have both been unfailingly kind and generous, even when I called or dropped by almost daily for months. He even knew what an "angel cock" was.

Lafayette Parker "Pick" Temple, II, of Sun City, Arizona, an old friend of Paul Shue's and an avocational folklorist, hosted from 1948 to 1962 a popular TV show for Giant Food's Heidi Baked Goods. In these years, more than 250,000 Washingtonians between the ages of three and sixteen signed on as Giant Rangers, including Nixons and Kennedys. "Pick" is a painstaking and formidable proofreader, whose notes and suggestions are always valuable and witty.

E. Sterling "Tod" Hanger of the C & O Historical Society works at the Greenbrier, is an active member of the Alderson, W. Va., fire department and rescue squad, but breathes railroads. Major Thomas W. Dixon, Jr., also of Alderson, president of the C & O Historical Society, is stationed presently in Saudi Arabia, but deeply involved with the C & O. Both, despite the many other demands on their time, have lent me photographs and other graphic materials, suggested textual changes, and offered great support. Bill Wheatley, Lloyd Lewis, Everett N. Young, and Bob Gifford of the COHS have also been most helpful. In fact, the C & O Historical Society just may be made up of the nicest guys in the world.

Ron S. Lane of Columbus, Indiana, is another C & O buff who has lent photos and information which he has worked hard to gather, especially his study of the Alley family. A man of enormous interests, talents, and energy, whose letters are nothing short of delightful, he has published many articles about C & O wreck songs and produced a slide show on the subject.

Maureen Worth, Ph.D. in Psychology, my backdoor neighbor, colleague, and friend, has acted as navigator, confidante, and boon companion on several overnight trips to West Virginia and Kentucky. She has listened with good humor as I interviewed someone, cheerfully searched overgrown graveyards with me for long-dead engineers, always tolerating the heat and long hours with her easy grace and intelligence.

Robert Chapman spent a sizzling July day chauffering Maureen and me all over Huntington to take pictures and has spent much time looking up and xeroxing information for me in the Marshall Library there.

Bob Moore of WCHS in Charleston, another railroad song buff, taped songs and sought information for me from the Collis P. Huntington Branch of the NRHS, to which he belongs.

Kinney Rorrer of Ringgold, Virginia, who teaches history and government, airs "American Bluegrass" on radio WDVA in Danville, and collects old records, has taped songs for me and collected information beyond the call of duty.

G. Howard Gregory of Danville, Virginia, has turned up, in addition to his fine book on Old 97, information and photos of several other wrecks.

Wylma "Sis" Davis and the staff of the VMI library have been more than accommodating in helping me to find microfilm and rare books. The staff of the W & L library have also been extremely helpful.

Norm Cohen, author of the fascinating and impressive tome, *Long Steel Rail*, kindly sent me tapes and xeroxes of songs I could not find elsewhere. Everywhere from the Library of Congress to Princeton, West Virginia, I have trod more easily on paths which he blazed.

All of these I thank warmly.

I am, as always, grateful to Janet Cummings, the world's best and fastest typist.

Lowell Cooper, my friend and colleague at Southern Seminary, prepared the musical examples for this book. In many cases, all he had to work from was a terrible tape of an old record, or even my own rendition of a tune. Being unable to read music myself, I decided to ask him to transpose all tunes to the key of C major, to facilitate learning them. Thus the musical novice should be able to "pick out" the notes on the piano or other instrument without undue difficulty. Once the tune is learned, it may then be easily transposed into another key.

I want to say a special word of thanks to my dear old friend and professor, Louis D. Rubin, Jr., of the University of North Carolina, who thought up this book, then provided me with the editorial leadership I needed to write it.

There are many other people who answered letters from a stranger, entrusted family photographs to a woman they never met, answered the phone to a stranger's voice, then took time to answer her questions or dig up information. Many of these people have on their own time sought further to help me, and are mentioned at the end of the individual chapters with which they helped. If I ever entertained the thought that the world has become too busy for people to help each other, I was mistaken. Writing this book has proved it. I wish I could write about all these remarkable people. They have my deepest gratitude: Jane Roth Baugh; Bari Ballou; Nelson Benyunes of the Danville, Virginia, newspapers; Edmund Berkeley, Jr., of the Alderman Library, University of Virginia; Marvin Black, Robert B. Claytor, Michael Bickham, and Aubrey Overstreet of the N & W; Betty F. Boswell; Franklyn J. Carr and Marie Drumheller of the C & O; Charles B. Castner of the L & N; Mike Collingwood and the staff of Andre's Studio; Jim Comstock; Jimmy Costa; M. Ellwood Cridlin; Dan Daniels of Grumbacher Paints; Charles H. "Sandy" Davidson, IV; William Hughes Dean; Jim Dedrick and the staff of the Lexington, Va., *News-Gazette*; Alan Fern of the National Portrait Gallery; Fred Glazer and James Waggoner of the West Virginia Library Commission; Gary Grant of the Danville, Va., Historical Society; Jerry Hess of the National Archives; Jill Huntley of the Southern Seminary Library; Barbara W. Ingram; Jack R. Johnson; Joyce Kachergis; Ben Kline; David and Linda Krantz; Bob Kulp of the Bluegrass Railroad Society; Ken Lane; Elizabeth Leonard; Deborah Noxon of the Norfolk-Southern; Bruce Poundstone; Helen Rowland of the American Association of Railroads; Hobart Scott, Sr.; Vern Scott; Sarah Shields of the Valentine Museum; John White of the Smithsonian; Sally Wiant of the W & L Law Library; Waverly K. Winfree of the Virginia Historical Society; and Myra Ziegler of the Summers County, W. Va., Library. I also thank the staff of the Yellow Brick Road for keeping our daughter Jennie happy and safe while I wrote all summer.

The Wreck of the Old 97

*They were goin' down grade making ninety miles an
  hour,*
When the whistle broke into a scream,
He was found in the wreck with his hand on the throttle
Scalded to death by the steam.

On a hot autumn day, September 27, 1903, one of
the world's fastest mail trains (some say *the* fastest),
number 97 on the Southern Railway, wrecked on the
outskirts of the city of Danville, Virginia. "Old" was
merely an adjective of affection, for 97 had been in
service only a year. The wreck occurred just before
3:00 P.M., though the watch of the engineer, found
in the mud of the creek into which the engine and
all four cars crashed, had for some reason stopped
at 2:18.

Of all the railroad disasters in American history,
that of Old 97 has no peers except perhaps "Casey
Jones." One reason for its almost immediate re-
nown, certainly, was that it involved not merely a
fast train, but one carrying the mail. From their beginning, mail trains had taken the fancy of the
American public. A song, "Fast Mail," was popular
just after the turn of the century. Stewart Holbrook
tells us in *The Story of American Railroads* that the
"thought of a special train, devoted wholly to written and printed communications of one kind and another, was cherished by the people. The picking up
of mail pouches from the stanchions of way stations,
while the cars fled past, was dramatic." Railway
mail clerks became minor romantic figures in the
public mind, and at least one private county school
was established to teach the art of the railway mail
clerk—by correspondence, of course. Pick Temple
recalls ads in magazines even then with large headlines: BE A RAILWAY MAIL CLERK!

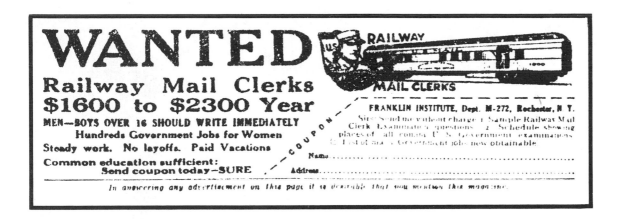
Holbrook tells us that serious hazards to all mail trains were accidents and wrecks. "In almost every wreck, the postal car, being up forward, was derailed or smashed, and often burned. From 1876 to 1905, there were 9,355 accidents to trains carrying postal cars. In these collisions and derailments a total of 207 clerks were killed, 1,516 others seriously injured, and 3,764 more slightly injured. That adds up to 5,280 casualties, or more than one casualty to every two accidents."

In 1902 the Southern Railway was granted an annual appropriation of $140,000 to haul the mail between Washington and Atlanta, on the New York to New Orleans line. The first run of Old 97 was November 2, 1902. The idea was to move the mail fast; as an incentive, the railroad had to pay cash penalties if the mail was late, $100 for every thirty minutes' delay.

An undated article from the Atlanta *Constitution* points up the glamour of this train. About four months before the fatal crash, in the spring of 1903, Old 97 made an emergency concession, agreeing to hook the French actress Sarah Bernhardt's private heavy steel car onto the train and haul it from Atlanta to New Orleans so she could be on time for a Sunday afternoon performance. John McWaters was the engineer. The heavy car dragged the mail train's usual running time down by fifteen minutes. At Opelika the engineer, trying to make up the lost minutes, told the dispatcher, "If we're not at Montgomery at 3:17, send the wrecker to the foot of Notasulga Hill." They made Montgomery on time, running the sixty-six miles from Opelika in sixty-four minutes!

The Southern Railway's main line ran from Washington to Danville, along the eastern slope of the Blue Ridge, and good time could be made on the long stretches of straight track through poor piney land in between the curves. Fast mail trains, according to the railroad book of rules, had the right-of-way over everything but passenger trains. Double tracks were rare in those days, so there were frequent sidings for passing trains to go and wait, necessitating accurate traffic control. To this end, telegraph lines for communications between the stations ran alongside the tracks. Old 97, as did most trains by then, had Westinghouse airbrakes, and of course a steam engine fueled by coal.

The locomotive number did not correspond with the train number. No. 1102, the engine pulling train 97 on September 27, 1903, was a ten-wheeler, or a 4-6-0 locomotive, weighing approximately 160,000 pounds. 1102 was known as an unpredictable engine, the wooden cab having caught fire once a year before. For an hour past its normal departure time in Washington, train 97 waited, that September 27, the engine stoked up and ready, held up by a late mail train from the north. Once the mail was aboard, it left quickly. The crew changed over in Monroe, Virginia, a division point just north of Lynchburg, an hour late there also. On this particular day the regular crew, probably because of the delay, had been ordered to another train. When Joseph A. "Steve" Broady of Saltville, Virginia, took over as engineer, he was stepping into a possibly dangerous engine on a relatively unfamiliar run, with the train already an hour behind schedule. Broady had been with the Southern only a month, having been employed previously on the Norfolk & Western. He had operated a train on this run only once before.

With him in the cab was fireman Albion G. "Buddy" Clapp, of Whitsett, N.C., and a second fireman, a black apprentice whose name was Robert Dodge, an "extra" to help him increase his speed and make up some lost time.

Of Broady, we know fairly little. He was thirty-three, a bachelor, affectionately regarded by his family. A surviving photograph shows a narrow-faced, clean-shaven man, his hair thin on top. On the day of the wreck, Postal Inspector B. B. Webb was waiting on a dusty siding in Chatham, Virginia, aboard a train going the other way. Broady was a stranger to him on a familiar run; as 97 rushed by, Webb turned to a friend and asked, "Who's the bearded engineer?" So that detail of Broady's appearance is known, at least for the day of his death. Although mustaches were common in 1903, beards were not; perhaps Broady wished to stand out as different from other men. Or maybe he thought the beard would distract from his premature balding. He was nicknamed "Steve," almost certainly after the famous daredevil of the day, Steve Brodie, who had some time before jumped off the Brooklyn Bridge on a bet and survived. The nickname may have been pure circum-

Joseph Andrew "Steve" Broady. *Courtesy Tom W. Totten.*

stance, or it may have indicated that his fellow railroadmen regarded Joe as a bit of a daredevil himself.

He had 167 miles to cover between Monroe and Spencer, North Carolina, and it was the worst part of the run. The normal running time was four hours and fifteen minutes. The Southern mail train had an average speed of thirty-seven and a half miles per hour, including stops, a remarkable pace under the existing circumstances. Under ideal conditions 97 sometimes reached a speed of ninety miles per hour. At any rate, impressed by the importance of getting the late mail to Atlanta on time, "Steve" Broady clearly intended to make up some lost time. It is recorded that he opened the throttle and moved out of Monroe at a good clip.

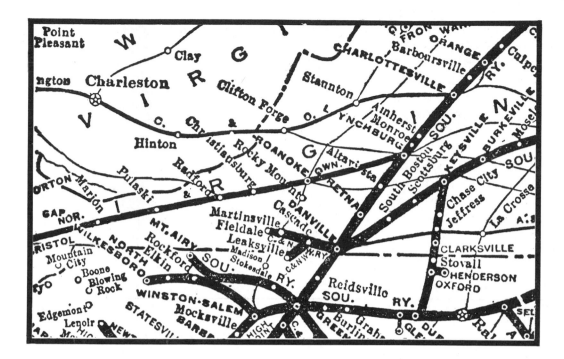

From there it was only 6.8 miles to Lynchburg. Just a few minutes later, Broady eased the train across the James River Railroad Bridge north of that city. When he pulled into Lynchburg's Union Station with its stylish mansard roof, a young man swung on board. He was Wentworth Armistead, a seventeen-year-old express company employee whose job was to come aboard each passing train to check the safe locks as a security measure. Another youth, twelve-year-old Ralph Thompson, planned to debark at Lynchburg. He had come on Old 97 from Washington to visit relatives. He was "deadheading," riding free, which was his due as the son of a railroad employee. His father was John Thompson, one of the mail clerks on the train. Neither youth had time to get off the train, so suddenly and swiftly did Broady take off. They would have to ride on down the line, therefore, and come back on the next through train.

Danville, sixty-four miles away, was the next scheduled stop. The train was due at 1:40 P.M., and it was already past one. The way was through red clay country, and the fields along the tracks would have been starred with autumn asters of white and purple. In 1953, Jennings J. Dunlap, a mail clerk who escaped without injury, recalled that passing through Franklin Junction they could "scarcely see the countryside, so fast was the train going." David Graves George, the Franklin Junction telegraph operator, recalled later that his "hand trembled" as he wired ahead to Danville the time of 97's passing. Supposedly, one of the two youths who had been trapped on the train at Lynchburg got off at Franklin Junction. It was not a scheduled stop, but sometimes 97 stopped there to replenish the water for the boiler if it was low. Most sources say 97 did not stop that day at Franklin Junction. One account says it did. Ralph Thompson, who was seen leaving Lynchburg, yet was not on the train when she wrecked in Danville, "turned up" the next day in Franklin Junction. The most probable explanation is that, since he was supposed to be on the train and had family waiting for him in Lynchburg, he jumped off when 97 slowed for a curve near Franklin Junction, knowing the train would not stop until Danville. He could have figured on catching another train back to Lynchburg that was coming through Franklin Junction going north.

J. Harris Thompson of Lexington, Virginia, a survivor who was injured in the wreck (no kin to the boy Ralph), later explained in an interview that a rivalry existed at that time between the Southern, Atlantic Coast Line, and Seaboard Air Line in maintaining fast schedules and in delivering the mail on time. Although only two scheduled stops were made between Washington and Danville, at Monroe and Lynchburg, there were approximately fifty 'catch stations' where mail was put off and taken on without stopping the train. It was Thompson's duty on this run to take care of all the catch stations, but when 97 sped through Dry Fork just south of Chatham, the train was going so fast that he could not make the pickup from the mail crane, a wooden or iron affair projecting out over the track, from which the mail bags were hung.

Lima, Virginia, lay just north of North Danville on White Oak Mountain—not a proper mountain at all, but the highest rise in the otherwise flat scrub-pine landscape of Pittsylvania County. From White Oak Mountain, it was downhill all the way to the Dan River. A sign on the approach side said SLOW UP, SHARP CURVE AHEAD. The speed limit was posted at fifteen miles per hour.

Stillhouse Trestle, built in 1874 and demolished in 1935, was 325 feet long, gracefully curved, wooden, elevated, and precarious. It bore trains over Stillhouse Creek, a marsh and a ravine, down to the bridge over the Dan. This was an unusual piece of track; any train failing to slow down sufficiently before entering it would have been in trouble. What is clear is that Broady, who was new to the route, seriously underestimated the time it would take him to brake his locomotive for the trestle crossing. Afterwards, numerous persons reported that 97 was traveling at an appalling speed as it approached the scene.

Evidence seems to indicate that Broady tried to get the drive wheels into reverse. Eighty tons of iron negotiating the track with locked wheels could have accounted for the uncommon amount of road dust that eyewitnesses reported noticing. If Broady didn't jump, perhaps it was because he believed, until the last instant, that he would stop the engine in time.

Witnesses said Broady must have been going ninety when he approached the trestle, and his whistle was certainly screaming the warning: Runaway train! Yet some say he never even applied the air brakes. All we can know is that he ignored the warning sign, SLOW UP, SHARP CURVE AHEAD, until too late.

As the drivewheels of engine No. 1102 struck the curve, a flange on one of the wheels broke off. The careening steam locomotive jumped the track. It ran for some distance atop the wooden crossties, bumping along wildly at an impossible staccato pace, and then it plunged off the trestle at the beginning of the curve and fell seventy-five feet through the air down into the ravine, carrying with it the trailing cars.

Two small boys playing underneath the trestle were spared. They were thrown to the ground by the impact, but they were far enough away not to have been hurt. Pictures show that the engine came to rest on the bank of Stillhouse Creek, but then three cars came down, one at a time, on top of her and each other, imbedding the engine deep in the mud of the creek. The cars, of course, were reduced to splinters.

The first thing the shocked bystanders noticed was the deafening noise of the crash itself, and then, swiftly following that, an unreal silence. The final mail car remained fairly intact; it broke through the trestle last, then fell. Telegraph wires dangled uselessly, delaying communication. The cries and

A view from the north. Notice the brake wheel on the final car, and the twisted railing. Smoke obscures the scene, from the fires which broke out soon after the crash. A mill building is visible in the background. *Courtesy Norfolk-Southern Corporation.*

groans of victims began to rise from the splintered wreckage, mingled with the excited chirping of hundreds of canaries. On board 97 were six crates of them bound for Atlanta. The crates were partially destroyed by the impact. Eyewitnesses said that the hundreds of yellow creatures singing and fluttering amid the dark splintered wreck and the moans of the victims lent a particularly macabre touch to the scene. Later accounts averred that the canaries were around the area for several years afterwards, that they stayed and interbred with local sparrows.

Many people saw the disaster occur. People in Danville were taking the air on their porches following their midday Sunday meals. At least one woman fainted. Another reportedly miscarried.

The Danville ladies, in their shirtwaists and bustles, view the crash site from the ground, while the men dare to walk the high trestle to investigate the damage. The final car, which stayed somewhat intact, is in the center of the picture. *Danville Photo-Finishing.*

Within twenty minutes there were rescue workers on the scene. A U.S. mail clerk, B. R. Boulding, took charge of the scattered mail, which was government property. Many valuables, such as watches and rings, belonging to the victims, were recovered and secured from possible looters. Most of the mail pouches were intact and the mail in good condition, considering the extent of damage to the train.

Broady was thrown some distance from the engine, and his body was found face down in Stillhouse Creek. Conductor J. Thomas Blair was also killed outright, and his body, in pieces, was the first recovered from the wreckage. Four postal clerks were also killed, including J. L. Thompson, father of the boy who left Lynchburg but did not reach Danville, the fireman Albion G. Clapp, apprentice fireman Dodge, and the flagman, whose job it was to signal approaching trains. One dead body that could not be identified was at first assumed to be Ralph Thompson's, but turned out to be that of Wentworth Armistead, the other accidental passenger. Postal clerk Lewis Spies was critically injured, and died on October 6. The bodies, according to witnesses, were mangled and broken, and the skin and hair were flayed from the heads and chests of Broady and Clapp by the superheated steam from the crushed boiler, far hotter than boiling water and under great pressure.

In 1943 Warner Twyford recalled that at least seven injured people were removed from the wreckage and lay on the creek bank several hours before they could be taken to hospitals. During that time the "good women of Danville" tried to make the injured comfortable.

Mary Booth Vaden of Danville recalled the wreck

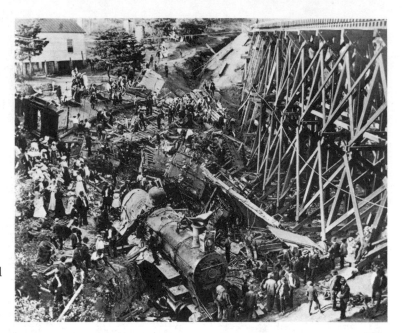

Old 97, after the engine was righted and a great deal of the splintered wreck removed. This view is from the south.

many years later to Adele Clement: "I can barely remember that day so long ago, but I was a child and did go and see it. . . . Father carried Mama and us children in the buggy to see if what they had heard was true. *It was*—the thing that impressed me most was the white sheets spread over the dead bodies. I could never forget . . . we were on a high hill on this side (Danville) of the wreck and looked far down at what had happened."

Grim as the situation was, it was not without its small touch of humor. A woman bringing water for the injured halted before one suffering man, who licked his parched lips as he gazed on the dipper with unconcealed longing.

"My good man," said the woman, hesitating, "are you a Christian?"

"I ain't a heathen, lady," he replied impatiently, reaching for the water.

One eyewitness, a Danville weaver named Chappell, remembered a Dr. L. L. Vann of Danville moving among the victims with a hypodermic needle administering morphine to the suffering. Chappell also

recalled that there was no fire at the scene, only dust and steam—great clouds of steam. But Chappell was remembering only the initial moments after the wreck; fire broke out later, say the news accounts, and the Danville fire department sent engines to the wreck.

Because the mail was so important, mailclerks from Charlottesville, Richmond, Greensboro, and Atlanta were rushed to Danville to assist in resorting the mail. Express manager W. F. Pinckney escaped with a few minor bruises. He regained his nerve immediately, and came out of the broken express car bringing his money box with him. He checked out all shipments and escorted them into the city.

The Danville *Bee* the next afternoon reported that "After nightfall, torches gleamed in the hands of the wrecking crew, throwing a red glare over the spectacle. An engine was drawn up as close to the trestle as was safe with its reflector on the horrible scene in the ravine 75 feet below."

In the following years there were many recollections published by witnesses and survivors of the wreck of the Old 97.

James Lester of Danville recalled that "train 97 was going so fast it straightened out the curve," plucking rails from the bridge on its wild journey.

In 1933, post office Inspector B. B. Webb of Richmond reminisced about the wreck to the Richmond *Times-Dispatch*. He was a veteran of the Washington mail service and the clerk who was usually on the Washington–Danville run, part of the crew that did not go that fated day. One of the clerks who survived Old 97 was Jennings J. Dunlap, and Webb and Dunlap were to survive another famous wreck a year later in New Market, Tennessee (see pp. 57–67). Wallace Phillips, writing in *The West Virginia Hillbilly*, March 30, 1968, relates that Broady had been "hanging around the chief dispatcher's office in Greensboro" in the early morning hours of September 27, and when a call came for a crew to deadhead to Monroe to pick up "Old 97" Broady bragged his way into the assignment from chief dispatcher Nolan, saying he "could take Old 97 for a ride!"

A dispatcher named W. E. McIvor seemed to remember that Broady remarked on leaving Monroe, "I'll get to Spencer on time or I'll sink this thing into Hell."

In January 1907, Old 97 was discontinued when Congress failed to renew its appropriation because, according to a Congressional spokesman, "the regular passenger trains get mail to the southern states fast enough."

On March 4, 1963, J. Harris Thompson, one of the last two survivors of Old 97, died at the age of eighty-two in Lexington, Virginia. On September 24, 1964, J. J. Dunlap, the last survivor, died, at age eighty-five, in Washington, D.C.

Paul Shue told me in March 1982 about a visit to Broady's grave at Saltville, Virginia. "One time a couple years back, I was on my way to Alabama to

Courtesy Paul Shue.

visit my son. I went off U.S. 81 at Saltville. At Crabtree's store the owner told me, 'Go back one tenth of a mile, and look up on the left, and you'll see a barn. On the hill past the barn is an outcropping of cedar trees, and it's in there.' Well, that hill was full of cedar outcroppings; I wandered around through cockleburrs and Spanish needles, and finally found this little graveyard. It was evidently a resting place for cattle. Almost at once I found the tombstone, knocked over, lying among cowdung and weeds, not even on its base. It made me so sad. I took some pictures and went on, because I couldn't lift it back up by myself. Two men could have done it. Later on, I contacted the Old Dominion Chapter of the National Railway Historical Society, and the Virginia historical marker association. They suggested I contact the Southern Railway. I tried the Saltville Ruritan Club. It seemed nobody cared. Finally I got in touch with Johnson, the landowner, and he was sympathetic. He said he'd been intending to put the stone back in place. I told him I'd sleep easier when I knew it was done, that it wouldn't cost him anything but a stamp to let me know. I never heard from him. I don't know whether he ever did it."

Ask anyone about railroad wreck songs, and he's likely to scratch his head, think a moment, and recall the "Wreck of the Old 97." He probably won't know the year, or the place, or the railroad, but he'll remember White Oak Mountain and Steve Broady, the young engineer scalded to death by the steam, his hand still gripping the throttle of his engine.

What accounts for this? The wreck was a relatively small one outside of Danville; many much more spectacular and grisly train wrecks have occurred that are not memorialized in song. And none was ever as popular as this one.

There are probably several reasons why "The Wreck of the Old 97" takes its place so firmly in American folklore. First, many photographs of this wreck were taken and distributed nationally, thus fixing the tragedy visually in people's minds. Second, it occurred in a part of the world with a tradition of keeping tragedy alive in song.

But perhaps most important, as Norm Cohen points out in *Long Steel Rail*, the song we have now was set to a tune already popular, and therefore easily remembered. It seems clear that all of the ballads about "Old 97" drew heavily on a long line of well-known songs, largely parodies of the very popular "Ship That Never Return'd," copyrighted in 1865. The moral tag is very nearly stolen whole from one of these, "The Parted Lover."

Bill Malone, in *Country Music, U.S.A.*, writes that "the 'Wreck on the Southern Old 97' had been subjected to the molding influence of oral traditions for over twenty years before it was first recorded in 1923; the 'finished' product, therefore, was probably the work of several people."

Norm Cohen agrees: "It is evident that half a dozen or more parodies on 'The Ship That Never Return'd' were in oral circulation in the southern mountains in 1903; several of them involved trains. It is not unlikely, therefore, that different persons should write ballads about Old 97, all independently using the same tune—even though such an occurrence would generally be taken to indicate that the different balladists borrowed from one another."

While no one agrees on exactly what a folk song is, it is safe to say that "Old 97" is apparently closer than most train wreck songs to a true folk composition. It seems clear that there were at least three, perhaps as many as a dozen, separate songs composed about the event which later, in the group folk process, sorted themselves into one fairly consistent ballad, which became, in the twenties, the equivalent of top song on the hit parade.

Aboard the first train arriving on the scene of the wreck from the north was the telegraph operator David Graves George of Franklin Junction. In 1927, when he learned that the song had made a lot of money, and that the author was being sought, he stepped forth and filed suit against Victor Records to reclaim some of the profits. The battle was to be a long one. After a series of appeals, reversals, and new rulings that lasted for five years, George was denied any payment.

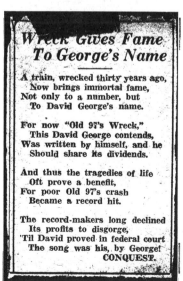

Wreck Gives Fame To George's Name

A train, wrecked thirty years ago,
Now brings immortal fame,
Not only to a number, but
To David George's name.

For now "Old 97's Wreck,"
This David George contends,
Was written by himself, and he
Should share its dividends.

And thus the tragedies of life
Oft prove a benefit,
For poor Old 97's crash
Became a record hit.

The record-makers long declined
Its profits to disgorge,
'Til David proved in federal court
The song was his, by George!
CONQUEST.

Courtesy C. C. Meeks.

THE WRECK ON THE SOUTHERN OLD 97

(SONG) WITH UKULELE ARRANGEMENT

By HENRY WHITTER

TRIANGLE MUSIC PUB. CO. 1658 BROADWAY

GRAND PIANO COMPANY Incorporated 30? S. JEFFERSON ST. ROANOKE, VA. "Everything Musical"

Henry Whitter was said to be an inspiration to many other hopeful musicians of his time. It was reported that he sang and played so badly that other young singers believed they certainly could do better than he did, and thus were encouraged to try their fortunes at music. *Courtesy David Krantz and Kinney Rorer.*

Malone says, "One individual who contributed to the song's structure and popularity was a well-known Virginia hillbilly singer named Henry Whitter, who kept the ballad alive through local performances in the Fries, Virginia, area. His recording was not only one of the very earliest in the commercial hillbilly field, its popularity also directly inspired the entrance of Vernon Dalhart (and others) into hillbilly music. His individual performances often had an unintended result. Many people were inspired to become performers because they were convinced they could do a better job than Whitter!"

"The Wreck of Old 97" is atypical of most train wreck songs in that there was more than one version. The wreck itself had been so discussed and written about and recalled by survivors that it was inevitable that a lot of information available would be wrong. For example, we are told that there was fire, that there wasn't; that Albion's nickname was "Clem," or that it was "Buddy"; Steve Broady's becomes "Pete," "Steve Brooklyn," or "Steve Brady." But when was truth ever at a premium in the creation of a legend?

The Wreck of Old 97

They gave him his or-ders at Mon-roe, Vir-gin-ia, Say-in', Pete, you're way be-hind time, This is not Thir-ty-Eight, but it's old Nine-ty Sev-en, You must put her in-to Spen-cer on time.

The text that follows is from a Vernon Dalhart record, Victor #19427-A, and is a fair representation of the variants remembered today.

WRECK OF THE OLD 97

They give him his orders at Monroe, Virginia,
Sayin, Pete, you're way behind time,
That is not 38, but it's Old 97,
You must put her in Center on time.

He looked round and said to his black greasy fireman,
Just shovel in a little more coal,
And when we cross that White Oak Mountain,
You can watch old 97 roll.

It's a mighty rough road from Lynchburg to Danville,
And a line on a three-mile grade,
It was on that grade that he lost his average,
And you see what a jump he made.

He was goin' down grade makin' 90 mile an hour,
When his whistle broke into a scream;
He was found in the wreck with his hand on the throttle,
And a' scalded to death with the steam.

Now ladies, you must take warnin,
From this time now and on,
Never speak hard words to your true lovin' husband,
He may leave you and never return.

Similar versions substitute "Steve" for "Pete" and "Steve Brooklyn said" for "He looked round and said." It is not difficult to see how this error came about. The line "And a line on a three-mile grade," is rendered variously as, "And Lima's on a 3-mile grade," which refers to the town of Lima, Virginia, through which 97 passed, and is accurate, or "And all on a three-mile grade," which seems a slurring of the former.

In general, truth is not so important as story in wreck songs. Heavily influenced by the popular American fireside poetry of the mid-to-late nineteenth century, these songs always promote the ones who died to the apotheosis of humanity. In the case of Old 97, "Steve" Broady was "the brave engineer" or "the brave, brave man that pulled 97."

Yet the Southern Railway did not conclude that Joseph Broady was a hero at all. The engine and cars were judged to have been in good condition, the track had previously been inspected and pronounced safe, and everyone else appeared innocent. Broady alone was blamed for the disaster. The Southern Railway eventually awarded ten thousand dollars each to the families of all the other men killed.

The ballad attributes words to Broady that cannot be ascertained, since all in the cab died with him. His fireman, whom the song calls "black and greasy" perhaps metaphorically, was actually a white man; of course the apprentice, Robert Dodge, was black. The song implies some marital conflict, but Broady was single. According to Pat Fox, Broady's sister years afterwards said that her brother had, at the time of his death, been engaged to a Bluefield, West Virginia, girl. But perhaps she was overprompted by folklorists, and this may be part of the family's romanticizing of the event. There are many minor variations, such as "whistle began to scream" in place of "whistle broke into a scream." More important is the frequent substitution of "air brakes" for "average." Actually, either makes equally good

---

"WRECK OF THE OLD 97"
September 27, 1903
Danville, Va.

On a cold frosty morning in the month of September
When the clouds were hanging low,
Ninety-seven pulled out of the Washington station
Like an arrow shot from a bow.

Old Ninety-seven was the fastest mail train
That was ever on the Southern line,
But when she got to Monroe, Virginia
She was forty-seven minutes behind.

Oh, they handed him his orders at Monroe, Virginia,
Saying: "Steve, you're away behind time.
This is not 38, but it's old 97
You must put 'er in Spencer on time.

Steve Broady said to his black greasy fireman,
"Just shovel in a little more coal,
And when we cross the White Oak Mountain
You can watch Old 97 roll."

It's a mighty rough road from Lynchburg to Danville
And the line's on a three mile grade.
It was on that grade that he lost his air brakes
And you see what a jump he made.

He was going down hill at ninety miles an hour
When the whistle broke into a scream—
He was found in the wreck with his hand on the throttle
And scalded to death by the steam.

Now ladies you must all take fair warning
From this time ever more—
Never speak harsh words to your true loving husbands
They may leave you and never return.

---

sense. It is probable Broady had "lost his average" or his air pressure all along the length of the train by speeding towards the curves and braking going around them, a practice known to railroaders as "whittling" and considered dangerous. "True loving husband" may stand in place of "true love and husband." Sometimes "Spencer" is mistakenly sung as "Centre" or "Center."

The line "This is not 38, but it's Old 97" refers to the relative speed of 97 over a slower, lower-numbered passenger train, dependable but not glamorous.

Broady was not, of course, found in the wreck "with his hand on the throttle," but rather, as we have seen, face down in Stillhouse Creek, his train watch in the mud nearby, stopped short at 2:18. "Life's Railway to Heaven," a popular song copyrighted in 1890, enjoins the hearer to "keep your hand upon the throttle, And your eye upon the rail." This song may have influenced the writer(s) of Old 97. A moral tag at the end of a poem or song was a chief characteristic of fireside poetry—here, as often, it has nothing whatever to do with the ballad itself, but is added as a sort of assurance that the audience of the songs will not fail to take away with them something uplifting and sobering.

The black apprentice fireman Robert Dodge, who had joined the crew to help the regular fireman keep the boiler steam pressure high and make up time, was also the subject of a ballad. As given by Pat Fox, it could, with effort, also be sung to the tune of "The Ship That Never Return'd." No source is given, but it is clearly a separate composition from the other.

THE BALLAD OF FIREMAN DODGE

His name was Dodge, Robert Dodge . . .
And he was black as sin.
But his heart was full of love and light,
Not sooty as his skin.

His home was in Catawba—
A red-bank railroad hovel,
And he earned his family's living
With his strong arm and a shovel.

He loved the shanty Gospel sings
And oft to church did go . . .
And never did he ever think
With Steve and Al he'd blow.

Singing as he threw the coal
To stoke the fires of hell,
'Mid the screaming of the whistle
And the clanging of the bell . . .

He was just a Colored fireman
But he reached the gates of Heaven
When with Broady and with Clapp that day
He pulled Old Ninety-Seven.

Ah, lonely there among the pines
His grave this day does lie;
The God of Heaven remembers him,
And men cease not to sigh.

For he put one word in legend—
Dodge, an ordinary name—
For he wrecked Old 97,
And undying is his fame.

Cohen gives one version of "Old 97," by the Arizona Wranglers, that seems to have an entirely separate origin, and may in fact involve at least a partial confusion of facts with another wreck. It is as follows, sung to the same tune.

THE WRECK OF THE OLD 97

Steve Brady kissed his loving wife,
By the rising of the sun;
And he said to his children, "May God bless you,
For your dad must now go on his run."

'Twas the twenty-second day of that November,
And the clouds were hanging low;
He took Old Ninety-seven out of Washington Station
Like an arrow shot from a bow.

I was standing on the mountain that cold and frosty
    morning,
And I watched curling smoke below;
It was steaming from Old Ninety-seven's smokestack
Way down on that Southern road.

Ninety-seven was the fastest mail train
Ever run the Southern line;
But when she reached into Richmond, Virginia,
She was twenty-seven minutes behind.

He received his orders at the Richmond station,
Saying, "Steve, you're far behind;
Now this isn't Thirty-eight, but it's Old Ninety-seven,
You must put her into Spencer on time."

When he read his orders he said to his fireman,
"Do not obey the whistle or the bell;
And we'll put Old Ninety-seven into Spencer on time,
Or we'll sink her in the bottom pits of hell."

He saw the brakeman signal and threw back his throttle,
Although his air was bad;
And the signalman said when he passed Franklin
    Junction
You could not see the man in the cab.

Steve looked at his watch and said to his fireman,
Just throw in a little more coal,
And when we reach those Cumberland Mountains,
You can watch Old Ninety-seven roll."

He went over the grade making ninety miles an hour,
And his whistle broke into a scream;
He was found when dead with his hand on the throttle,
And was scalded to death by steam.

When the news went in o'er the telegraph wires,
This is what the Western said:
That brave, brave man that was driving Ninety-seven,
Is now laying in North Danville, dead.

The people waited at the depot,
Till the setting of the sun;
It was hours and hours the dispatch was waiting,
For the fastest train ever run.

    (*Arizona Wranglers*)

Cohen notes that the November date in this and similar versions was first explained by Harvard folklorist Robert W. Gordon, who was called in as an expert in the lengthy years of litigation over the song's authorship. Gordon thought that whoever wrote this song might have had the wreck of Old 97 confused with another Southern wreck, that of Train 37, also southbound in roughly the same area, specifically ten miles or so south of Lynchburg, on a cold frosty morning, November 29, 1906. In this wreck Samuel Spencer, president of the Southern Railroad, was killed in his private car, along with several of his friends. This wreck, too, was widely publicized, with eulogies of Spencer appearing in newspapers all over the country. Spencer, North Carolina, named for him, was the site of the Southern's largest shops, and is, of course, where Old 97 was headed when she crashed. The engineer in that wreck, who was not hurt, was William Kinney of Spencer. One wonders whether he might have been nicknamed "Pete," but a 1954 reminiscence by Thomas O. Acree informs us that he was called "Bill."

In this wreck at Lawyers, Virginia, Samuel Spencer, president of the Southern Railroad, was killed, "on a cold frosty morning in the month of November." It is possible that whoever wrote "The Wreck of the Old 97" had it confused with this wreck, also on the Southern, near the site of Old 97's demise three years before. *Courtesy Norfolk and Western.*

In 1972, Paul Shue, in the true folk tradition, "put together" the following composite version, which has the advantage over the others of accuracy. It is sung to the usual tune.

THE WRECK OF OLD 97

1. 'Twas the 27th day in the month of September,
   The clouds were hangin' low,
   When Old 97 pulled out from Washington
   Like an arrow shot from a bow.

2. Well, the Old 97 was the fastest mail-train
   The Southland had ever seen;
   Well, she run the road from Boston down to
      Washington,
   Through Jackson, down to New Orleans.

3. Joseph Broady kissed his loving wife
   About the rising of the sun;
   And he said to his children, "God bless you all;
   Your father must go the run."

4. Yes, Old 97 was the fastest train
   To run that Southern line,
   But when she pulled in to Monroe, Virginia
   She was forty-seven minutes behind.

5. Well, they handed up his orders down in Monroe,
      Virginia,
   Saying, "Joe, you're way behind time;
   This is not Thirty-Eight, but it's Old 97—
   You must put her into Spencer on time."

6. Joseph Broady was the engineer—
   A mighty brave man was he;
   But many brave men have lost their lives
   To the railroad company.

7. Yes, Broady was the engineer
   On that fatal Sunday eve;
   And his fireman leaned out from the cab at
      Lynchburg,
   Just waiting for the signal to leave.

8. Well, they gave him the signal, and he threw back
      the throttle,
   Although the air was bad;

And the people said, when he passed Franklin
   Junction
You couldn't see the man in the cab.

9. He turned 'round and said to his black and dusty
      fireman:
   "Shovel on a little more coal,
   And when we cross that White Oak Mountain
   You're gonna see Old 97 roll."

10. Then Broady said to his trusty fireman:
    "Don't obey the whistle nor the bell,
    I'll pull Old 97 into Spencer, North Carolina
    Or I'll sink 'er in the bottom pits of hell."

11. It's a mighty rough road from Lynchburg down to
       Danville,
    And there lies a three-mile grade;
    It was on that mountain that he lost his air-brakes;
    You can see what a jump he made.

12. He was goin' down grade, makin' ninety miles or
       better,
    When his whistle broke into a scream;
    He was found in the wreck, with his hand upon the
       throttle,
    And scalded to death by the steam.

13. Yes, Old 97 was the fastest mail train
    The Southern had ever seen;
    But on that fatal Sunday evening
    Her death list . . . it numbered thirteen.

14. Well, the news came in on the telegraph wire,
    And this is what it said:
    "The brave, brave man who left Monroe, Virginia,
    Is lyin' down in North Danville—dead.

15. Now, all you ladies, you must take warning,
    From this time now and on,
    Never speak harsh words to your true lovin'
       husband—
    He may leave you, and never return.

Another verse, designed primarily to show the similarity between this song and "The Ship That Never Return'd," might be inserted between verses 14 and 15, and goes like this:

Did she ever pull in? No, she never pulled in,
And her time was due at one;
But for hours and hours the dispatch was waiting
For the fastest train ever run.

(Paul Shue, based on Tom Rush's version and information from the book Old 97 *by Pat Fox, October 1972)*

This song, obviously another version of the prototypical song, was sent to James Taylor Adams by H. J. Miller in 1940.

THE TRAIN THAT NEVER RETURNED

1. I was going round the mountain one cold December
     day
   A watchin' the steam boil up high,
   It was from a fast train, on the C and O railroad
   and the engineer waved good-bye!

Chorus
Did she ever return? No she never returned,
Tho' the train was due at one,
For hours and hours, the watch-man stood waiting,
For the train that never returned.

2. His sweet little wife came into the station
   Said last night my heart did yearn,
   I dreamed last night, and it's still in my mem'ry,
   I'm a-fraid she will never return.

3. "Goodbye sweet wife," said the jolly con-duc-tor,
   As he sig-nalled with his light,
   If the wheels will roll, and the en-gin-eer stays sober,
   we will all reach home safe to-night.

I have come across one curious explanation for the song's great popularity. According to Paul Shue, when Vernon Dalhart and Carson Robison went to New York to record "Old 97," they had an odd number of songs. They left 97 for last, and the Victor people said they should come back the next day with something for the reverse side. They went back to the Hotel Knickerbocker and that night wrote "The Prisoner's Song." It was this song, Shue says, that sold more records than any other song prior to 1930. He believes that "Old 97" "rode to fame on the back of 'The Prisoner's Song.'"

On September 11, 1946, an editorial in the Richmond *Times-Dispatch* reported that "The State Conservation Commission appears to be giving favorable consideration to a proposal for an official marker in North Danville on the site where, back in 1903, Southern Railway Train No. 97 plunged from a trestle, killing the engineer and eight others.

There is excellent scholarly precedent for the thesis that where a man or a woman has contributed something widely known to American life, the career of that person should not be ignored. Such was the principle on which the *Dictionary of American Biography* was compiled. The DAB incorporates sketches of such figures as "Christy" Matthewson, Walter Camp, Lydia Pinkham and Tom Thumb.

If these Americans are worthy of inclusion in the best American biographical reference work, then the spot where the "Old 97" plunged off its trestle should certainly have an official marker. . . . To the best of our knowledge the wreck of the "Old 97" is more familiar to the average American than the Battle of Bunker Hill or the Siege of Petersburg.

Though the scars are erased, the trestle gone, the ravine partially filled in and grassed over to support Highway 58 on the north shore of the Dan River, there is such a marker. As automobiles tear by, one stands by it and looks down from the side of the highway into the grassy valley at an impromptu baseball game, then out at the tarpaper roofs of the little houses, some of which must have been there in 1903, and tries to gauge whether it really goes down seventy-five feet. It looks more like forty, fifty at most. The track bed is gone, too, victim of time and kudzu. We must accept on faith that this is the spot where Old 97 crashed.

Photo by Katie Lyle.

NOTES

Howard Gregory discredits the Wallace Phillips story, saying Broady wouldn't have been in Greensboro, but Spencer, and that Nolan was not a chief dispatcher until 1905.

J. Harris Thompson lived and died in my home town of Lexington, but I had not the nerve to go and talk with him about the wreck, even when his daughter, Evelyn T. Law, my high school Latin teacher, urged me to do so.

Around 1975 John A. Duncan constructed a 4' × 8' model of the curved trestle and wreck. With a topographic map and 1/4" scale, he reckoned the distance from rail to creekbed as 43', not 70'.

Canaries were imported by the English in the fifteenth century from the tropical Canary Islands and domesticated in aviaries.

These clever finches became the rage among the upper classes of Britain, and, by the nineteenth century, among Americans as well. Also, canaries in cages were taken into coal mines with the miners. If they stopped singing or collapsed, it meant there were poisonous gases in the mines that might either suffocate the miners or explode; the delicate birds would react faster than the miners. Thus the phrase "the canary in the coalmine" came to refer to anything that portends disaster. It is a charming story about the canaries staying around Danville for years, though a Virginia ornithologist, Royster Lyle, doubts it could be true, as tropical birds could not survive the relatively harsh Virginia winters. Ben Knight suggests that Danvillians were perhaps mistaking goldfinches in breeding plumage for canaries!

Pick Temple recalls that J. J. Dunlap, when he died, was living in a nursing home in northern Virginia. Pick learned that most of the folks living there knew nothing of his background until the obituaries were published.

Works consulted were *The Wreck of Old 97* by Pat Fox; *Long Steel Rail* by Norm Cohen; *The Story of American Railroads* by Stewart Holbrook; "The Wreck of Old 97" by James I. Robertson, Jr., in *Virginia Cavalcade* (Autumn 1958); Paul Shue's private collection; the Richmond *Times-Dispatch*, 13 Mar. 1933, 16 Sept. 1938, 21 Mar. 1943, 27 Oct. 1943, 26 Sept. 1948, 6 June 1953, 27 Sept. 1953, 4 Mar. 1963, 24 Sept. 1964, 27 Sept. 1964; Danville *Register*, 30 Oct. 1957; *Country Music, U.S.A.* by Bill Malone; *The Folk Song Abecedary* by James F. Leisy; *The Frank C. Brown Collection of N.C. Folklore*, Vol. 2; *The West Virginia Hillbilly* 30 Mar. 1968, article by Wallace Phillips; "Engineers I Have Known" by Thomas O. Acree, in *Trains* 14 (July 1954). I came belatedly to Howard Gregory's *History of the Wreck of Old 97*. He writes that the second fireman was a white man, John Madison Hodge of Raleigh, based on research by Raymond B. Carneal of Winter Park, Florida, who in the sixties talked with Hodge's cousins and checked court records of the Wake County, N.C., Superior Court regarding the Southern's settlement with Hodge's estate. (Final Settlements, Book F, p. 551). "Stillhouse" is also spelled "Still House." I have accepted Gregory's spelling. The undated Atlanta *Constitution* article was sent me by Virginia Bird of Buena Vista, Virginia.

Here, briefly, are the particulars of the litigation over authorship of "The Wreck of Old 97." George sued Victor (headquartered in Camden, New Jersey) for royalties plus interest due him as author of "The Wreck of Old 97." In 1934, Judge John Boyd Avis of the Federal Court for the District of New Jersey handed down and signed a decree that George was the author of the song, and must be paid accordingly. No amount was stated. George's lawyer called it a final decree, but the court considered it interlocutory, that is, one that must be appealed within thirty days; a final decree has a much longer period of appeal. Victor apparently chose to regard the decision as final, not interlocutory, and waited longer than the thirty days to appeal, thus opening the question of whether the appeal was even legal. The Third Circuit decided that it was a final decree and that therefore they had jurisdiction and that an appeal was timely, and then determined that George was in fact not the author. He appealed to the Supreme Court. That Court, on the principle that "just because the kittens were born in the oven does not make them biscuits," reversed the Third Circuit Court decision on the basis that the circuit court lacked jurisdiction to designate the decision final instead of interlocutory, and that in fact the appeal was not timely. They never got around to the question of authorship. This forced the case back to the original district court which on September 15, 1938, repeated its original decree that George had written the song, and awarded him $65,295.56 plus six percent interest. Victor appealed to the Third Circuit again, saying George was not the author, and won.

George appealed three times to the Supreme Court, but each time they refused to grant his petition, so in the end George lost, receiving nothing—not even his attorneys' fees [*Victor Talking Machine Co. v. George*, 105 F.2d 297 (3d Cir. 1939)]. Terry P. Diggs, Attorney at Law, from Hot Springs, Arkansas, was extremely helpful in interpreting this information.

On September 24, 1982, at the Blue Ridge Institute, I came across an untitled manuscript almost identical to "The Prisoner's Song," that was sent to James Taylor Adams in 1940. The informant claims to have learned the song "about 35 years ago." Though folk-informants are not particularly reliable, that would date a version of "The Prisoner's Song" around 1905, a good twenty years before Dalhart and his record of "Old 97."

Finally, Kinney Rorrer adds this wacky note: in 1927, the Victor Records Book, distributed to music stores, listed "The Wreck of the Old 97" and other hillbilly songs under Languages, Foreign. About forty from the top, the "language" of country music was noted as "Southern."

The Wreck on the C & O

There's many a man has lost his life in tryin' to make
  lost time,
But if you run your engine right, you'll get there just on
  time.

The death of a handsome young engineer named
George Alley, on October 23, 1890, near Hinton,
West Virginia, inspired what is perhaps the third
most popular wreck song in America, after "The
Wreck of the Old 97" and "Casey Jones."

George Washington Alley, so heroically named,
was a member of a prominent railroading family. According to Ron Lane, C & O historian, his father,
Captain Leonidas Salathiel Alley, began a railroading
career with the C & O (at the time the Virginia Central) in 1852. He ran all types of engines in his long
career, and made the first run from Clifton Forge to
Hinton when that portion of the C & O main line
was opened in 1873. Captain Alley fathered six sons,
all of whom worked for the C & O, and three of
whom were involved in wrecks, though only George
was fated to die in one.

One of the memorable events of Captain Leonidas
Alley's life concerned a passenger run that he made
during the Civil War. He had brought a load of
Georgia soldiers from Jackson River Depot to Staunton one cold day in November 1861. What happened
then is related in a letter from A. H. Brentlya of Atlanta to Captain Alley in 1904: ". . . it was bitter
cold, and as the night closed in with flakes of flying
snow from the neighboring mountains, you grasped
your lantern—your work finished and well done,
you started for your home and the comforts that you
knew waited you.

Chesapeake & Ohio Ry.
Vestibule Limited.

BETWEEN
CHICAGO
ST. LOUIS
CINCINNATI
LOUISVILLE
OLD POINT
RICHMOND
WASHINGTON
BALTIMORE
PHILADELPHIA
NEW YORK

CHESAPEAKE & OHIO Route

THE

FAMOUS F.F.V. LIMITED
FAST FLYING VIRGINIAN

Has no equal between

NEW YORK and CINCINNATI

via

Philadelphia, Baltimore, WASHINGTON

and the

Mountain and Springs Resorts of the Virginias.

Vestibuled, Electric-Lighted, Steam-Heated.
All Meals Served in Dining Car.
Observation Car Attached.

COMPLETE PULLMAN SERVICE

TO

Louisville,   Chicago,   St. Louis.

"The Rhine, the Alps and the Battlefield Line."

The most interesting historic associations and the most striking and beautiful scenery in the United States are linked together by the Chesapeake & Ohio system. The line follows the banks of the beautiful Ohio and the mountain-circled Kanawha, lies through the wild and impressive canons of the New River and the celebrated Springs region of the Virginias, crosses the famous Shenandoah Valley, the Blue Ridge and the Alleghany Mountains, and passes over many of the most noted battlefields of the Civil War.

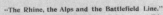

VIRGINIA.

Farms The choicest farming lands of the world, rich soil, perfect climate, reliable yields, no blizzards, best paying market of the country, finest forests, cereals, tobacco, peanuts and garden truck. The Garden Spot of America.

Homes Good society, good schools, good churches; all refining influences. Most delightful climate. Southern Europe is duplicated in Virginia; the balmy air of Italy and Spain in Springtime prevails here the year round.

Resources Coal and iron in abundance. Beautiful marble. Hard and soft timber. Superior water-power. Nutritious grazing lands. Extensive fresh and salt water fisheries. Best oysters in the world.

Industries Rich supplies of raw materials, cheap and rapid transportation to all the best home and foreign markets, make Virginia one of the most desirable sections of our country for manufacturing plants.

H. W. FULLER, General Passenger Agent, WASHINGTON, D. C.

Dementi-Foster Studios.

Lon Alley's C & O train No. 14 at Alderson, West Virginia, on April 26, 1981, just hours before it wrecked at Fort Spring, West Virginia. *Courtesy C & O Historical Society, Alderson, W. Va.*

"As you started, you met at the door of the telegraph office 4 or 5 soldiers who were seeking some place of shelter from the weather, all the public houses being filled to overflowing.

"You, out of the goodness of your heart took them home with you and gave them a hearty Virginia hospitality with all that it implies.

"Ah! How well I remember when we reached your house—you knocked on the door, and a soft, tender voice asked, 'Who's there?' 'It's me, Cassie, and I've brought some Georgia soldiers to spend the night with us.'

"My dear friend, have you forgotten her reply? I never have, and here it is: 'They are more than welcome if they are soldiers, it matters not from where they come.'

"Of the little squad of Georgia soldiers that sat at your table that November night I believe that I am the only one who has not passed over the river and to rest under the trees."

```
        Hinton West Virginia
            July 11  67
Dear Mr Lane I Will Try And give
you little Infermation 1 went to fireing
 1895 that was five years  after george
 alley got killed  it was still fresh in
Every Bodys  mind  you know george Aleleys
  father was engineer on a work train he had

 three sons all engineers lon  georg dick
 ( father   of them all ifired  two years

For lon on passenger  train  13 an 14
I Thought   bout Old Man Alley He Belonged
   At Richmond  But He Had Rights On All
 Div Is Any Where That work Train Went
  He Went With It He  Father Of All These
      Boys .I fired 5 years Ran and Eng
for 55 yrs  is am 93 yrs old
       MH. Maloney
```

The FFV Limited: the vestibule at the end of the car earned it one of its popular nicknames, the Fast Flying Vestibule. *Courtesy Ron Lane.*

The Alley family had a sterling railroad record. Lane's genealogical account of the family avers that "not one of the Alleys ever received a reprimand for negligence or poor service," and that the combined services of the Alleys on the C & O amounted to 279 years.

George Alley was born July 10, 1860, in Richmond, Virginia. When he was twenty-eight, the C & O inaugurated its first luxury name train, The Fast Flying Virginian, to run daily between New York, Washington, and Cincinnati, train No. 3 westbound, and train No. 4 eastbound. In Ron Lane's words, "the train itself was a revolution in passenger travel on the C & O. Functionally it featured solid vestibules, steam-heat, electric lights, water coolers, electric fans, and leather coiled-spring seats. Artistically it

was one of the most beautiful trains ever to be put on the tracks. The exteriors were painted a rich orange, with maroon bands over the windows which bore the railway name and PULLMAN in gold leaf roman capitals. The gay red wheels and silvered glass windows gave a striking effect in combination with the bright paint. The interiors were finished in mahogany, rosewood, and cherry with mirrors enclosed by nickel or brass plating.

"When Mayor Noonan of Cincinnati on an inspection tour declared that these coaches looked like the homes of the First Families of Virginia, the officials adopted the initials as the designation for the elaborate cars. The cuisine served in the dining cars was of the style and quality of the best metropolitan hotels, at a uniform price of one dollar." Other nicknames were attached to it during the early days. It was called the Fast Flying Vestibule, and, according to Ben Knight, Fuller's First Venture, Mr. Fuller being at that time a general passenger agent for the C & O. Cohen confirms this. Tom Dixon of the C & O Historical Society, in the *C & O Historical Society Newsletter* of December 1979, however, writes that "The name of the train was not actually revealed until its first trip when it was announced as 'The Fast Flying Virginian Vestibuled Limited' and was given a coat-of-arms in the form of an ornate shield design with the initials 'FFV' intertwined within. Almost at once this 'FFV' occasioned comment. The World Travel Gazette tells about travelers guessing as to the meaning of those initials, with the following results: 'First Families of Virginia. Fast Flying Vestibule. Fine Fast Virginian. Flying Fast Vestibule. Fuller's Favorite Vestibule. Fuller's Flying Vestibule.' The correct translation, however, is said to be 'Fast Flying Virginian,' a significant and appropriate title for the handsome solid vestibule trains. . . ."

George Alley had been a fireman for his father, and then a locomotive engineer in his own right, so he was a natural choice for engineer. George's regular run was from Clifton Forge to Hinton on westbound No. 3, returning to Clifton Forge on eastbound No. 4. It was on the early morning of October 23, 1890, that FFV Train No. 4 pulled into Hinton from Huntington, more than an hour behind time. At Hinton, Alley and his fireman Lewis Withrow were waiting to board Engine 134, an F-10 class 4-6-0, built by the New York Locomotive Works at Rome, New York, in July 1890, and pull it on to Clifton Forge. Clifton Forge meant the end of the run and home for both men. They must have been impatient. Also boarding at Hinton was another fireman, Robert Foster, who had been substituting for Withrow, and would now deadhead home.

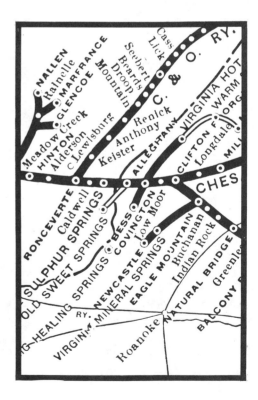

Alderson, West Virginia, in 1897. George Alley is buried in the Greenbrier Baptist Church cemetery, northwest from the center of the photo. *Photo by J. W. McClung. Courtesy Tom Dixon and the C & O Historical Society, Alderson, W. Va.*

It was rainy and overcast, and still dark when they left Hinton around five A.M. Of course an engineer was always eager to make up as much lost time as was safely possible, so there was every likelihood that Engine 134 was traveling at a faster speed than usual that morning. They were only a few minutes out, three miles east of Hinton, near the mouth of the Greenbrier River, when the headlight's beam suddenly picked up a huge boulder ahead that had fallen from the cliff above, a common occurrence in the mountainous and curving part of the line, particularly in wet weather or when freezing and thawing weakened and cracked the shale and limestone of the Appalachian mountains.

Alley, professional even in crisis, pulled on the brake with his right hand, and cried to Withrow to jump while he stayed in the engine and tried to bring the heavy tenwheeler to a halt. Foster, the deadheading fireman, jumped out of the window on the cliff side. Withrow tried to leap from the gangway on that side, but just as he did, the big locomotive slammed

into the boulder and turned over on its right side. Withrow, still in the engine, was sprayed with scalding water and badly burned. In the meantime, in the cab with his right hand on the brake level, George Alley was pinned tight by the reverse bar. His left arm and his right leg were broken, and, as there was nothing between him and the steam escaping from the damaged boiler, he was severely scalded. Behind him, mail and baggage cars were also derailed.

Rescue workers came from Hinton at once. For five long and agonizing hours, the young engineer lay there, in and out of consciousness. There is no record of whether they tried to move him. Constantly he asked for his family: "Are they coming? Are they coming?" His devotion to his family was made much of later in the press. Railroad officials and friends indeed tried to get Alley's wife and four children from Clifton Forge to the scene of the crash, but Clifton Forge is eighty miles from Hinton, and George died before they arrived shortly after 10:30 A.M.

The passengers had a "narrow escape"; if the train

The FFV train No. 3 wrecked again near Wiggins, West Virginia, on March 7, 1907, killing Engineer John Flannagan and Fireman Michael Quinn. Although the wreck was similar to George Alley's seventeen years before, Flannagan never reached immortality in legend and lore.

The white objects on the track in the foreground are the sheet-covered bodies of the engineer and fireman. *From W. R. Ford Collection; Mrs. Grace Bradberry; and C & O Historical Society, Alderson, W. Va.*

had not been slowed down considerably before the concussion, all the coaches would have gone into the river. Subsequent articles claimed that a watchman had passed the spot only a few minutes previous to the crash and found the tracks clear; others condemned the railroad for not having extra watchmen along the stretches of track where rockslides were most likely to occur, especially in periods of rainy or freezing weather.

Lewis Withrow, 1925, standing at the top of his gangway. He was at that time Chief Mechanical Inspector of the C & O. *From the collection of E. M. Whanger. Courtesy Thomas W. Dixon, Jr.*

Foster, the deadheading fireman, was not hurt seriously. For a long time it was thought that Lewis Withrow, burned on his neck, arms, and side, would not survive, but he eventually recovered. After four months, he was back on the rails, and became the regular fireman for George Alley's brother Leonidas, Jr., known as Lon. (However, the Alleys were unlucky for Withrow, for on March 26, 1891, according to Tom Dixon, on an eastbound run out of Alderson, West Virginia, while rounding a curve just before the Second Creek Tunnel, his train hit the rear section of a local freight that had come loose from the rest of its train. Both trains caught fire, and both Lon Alley and Withrow were injured. A Captain Clifford and all his crew in the caboose were killed instantly, along with two other brakemen deadheading on the train.)

George Alley was an instant hero, and tributes of praise and sympathy poured in from all over the country. George Alley had proven supreme dedication, and an unjaded age honored him as an exemplary citizen of his day, his country, and his profession.

The Clifton Forge and Iron Gate *Review*, on October 31, 1890, only a week after Alley's death, printed the following poem by an aunt of George's, Mrs. Alexander McVeigh Miller, of Alderson.

IN MEMORIAM

He is dying! Are they coming?
　　Will he hear their last goodbye?
Last night when he passed from them
Little did he think to die—
Die like this by dread disaster,
　　Ending his young life so soon,
Ere the morning of existence
　　Changed into life's fervid noon.

He is dying! Are they coming?
　　Ah, there is some strange delay!
And the iron horse lags hourly,
　　While his weak life ebbs away.

But the brave young martyr murmurs
Messages for home and wife—
Planning for their future welfare
  When he shall be done with life.

He is dying! Are they coming?
  Breaking hearts are on their way,
Will they speak the last goodbye
  Ere there dawns eternal day?
Anxious friends bend down and hear him
Whispering of his little girl;
They must leave unshorn those ringlets—
  How he loved each raven curl.

He is dying! Are they coming?
  Loved and loving ones from home?
Will they reach him ere death's darkness
  Fold him in its solemn gloom?
Pitying God, oh, speed the engine
  As it rushed o'er the track!
Nay, too late! the life Heaven gave,
  It has taken eternally back.

He is dying! Are they coming?
  George has tired and fallen asleep;

Drifted out of life so gently
  That they scarce knew when to weep.
But they told them when they came
  Of his patience and his love,
Of the kindly words he said
  Ere his spirit soared above.

He is dying! Are they coming?
  Yes, on Heaven's crystal shore
There were angels watching, waiting,
  Loved ones who had gone before.
They were ready to receive him,
  Mothers, sisters, kindred, friends,
And the Heavenly hosts gave welcome
  To that life which never ends.

The songs that George Alley's death inspired were numerous, and their history is not clear. "The Wreck on the C & O" has various titles: "George Alley," the engineer's name; "Engine 143," the locomotive's supposed number; "The FFV," which was the name of the passenger train, and even "George Allen," and the general title, "The Fatal Run."

The Wreck on the C & O

A-long came the F. F. V., the swift-est on the line, Run-nin' a-long that C and O road, just twen-ty min-utes be-hind; Run-nin' in to Su-ville, head-quar-ters on the line, Re-ceiv-ing their strict or-ders from the sta-tion just be-hind.

Folklore has it that the first song may have been composed by a black engine wiper who worked in the Hinton roundhouse. Norm Cohen says there seems no direct evidence of the song prior to about 1900.

No known photograph of the crash of the FFV in 1890 exists, but the photo on the facing page, dated 1890, shows a C & O wreck, and Tod Hanger of the C & O Historical Society, an expert on railroad architecture, confirms that the equipment pictured was in use at the time. He believes that the location is in the New River Gorge; thus this photograph may actually be of George Alley's wreck. *Cook Collection, Valentine Museum.*

There are at least eighty known variants of the song about George Alley, according to Ron Lane. This is partly because the wreck was an early one, and therefore had not the opportunity to become "set" on wax for many years.

Here are two of the many versions of "The Wreck on the C & O," or "Engine 143."

Along came the F.F.V., the swiftest on the line,
Runnin' along that C and O road, just twenty minutes
   behind;
Runnin' into Suville, headquarters on the line,
Receiving their strict orders from the station just behind.

43

Georgie's mother came to him with a bucket on her arm;
She said: "My darling son, be careful how you run;
There's many a man has lost his life in tryin' to make
    lost time,
But if you run your engine right, you'll get there just on
    time."

Up the track she darted, into a rock she crashed;
Upside-down the engine turned, and Georgie's breast is
    smashed;
His head lay against the fire-box door, the flames were
    rollin' high;
"I'm bound to be born an engineer, on the C & O road to
    die."

The doctor said to Georgie, "My darling boy be still;
Your life may yet be saved, if it be God's blessed will."
"Oh, no," cried George, "this will not do; I'd rather die so
    free;
I want to die for the engine I love: One Hundred and
    Forty-Three."

And the doctor said to Georgie, "Your life cannot be
    saved."
Murdered upon the railway, and laid in the lonesome
    grave.
His face was covered up with blood, his eyes they could
    not see;
And the very last words poor Georgie cried were "Nearer,
    My God, To Thee."

"Suville" is a mishearing of Sewell, West Virginia.

Another version of the song, similar but longer,
collected by Charles Carpenter of Hinton, is sung to
the same tune.

'Long come the F.F.V., the fastest on the line,
Running on the C. & O. Road, thirty minutes behind
    time;
She run into Sewell, quartered on the line;
There received strict orders; Hinton behind time.

Chorus
Many a man's been murdered by the railroad,
    By the railroad, by the railroad;
Many a man's been murdered by the railroad,
    And laid in his lonesome grave.

When she got to Hinton the engineer was there.
George Alley was his name, with curly golden hair;
His fireman, Jack Dickinson, was standing by his side,
Ready to receive his orders, and in his cab to ride.

George's mother come to him, with a bucket on her arm.
Saying, "George, my darling boy, be careful how you run;
Many a man has lost his life making up lost time;
If you run your engine right you'll get there just in time."

"Mother, I know your advice is good; to it I'll take heed;
But my engine is all right and I know she will make
    speed;
It's over the road I mean to fly with speed unknown to
    all;
When I blow for Stock Yard Gate, you'll surely hear my
    call."

George said to his fireman: "A rock ahead I see;
I tell you death is there to snatch both you and me;
From the cab you now must fly, your darling life to save;
I want you to be an engineer while I'm sleeping in my
    grave."

"No, no, George, that cannot be, I want to die with you."
"No, no, Jack, that will not do, I'll die for me and you."
From his cab poor Jack did fly; New River it was high;
He kissed his hand to George, while Number 4 flew by.

Up the road she darted; upon the rock, she crashed;
Upside down the engine turned, and upon his breast it
    smashed;
His head upon the firebox door, the burning flames rolled
    o'er;
Saying, "I'm glad I was born an engineer to die on the C.
    & O. Road."

George's mother came to him: "My son, what have you
    done?"
"Too late, too late, my doom is almost run."
The doctor said to George, "My son, you must lie still,
Your life may yet be saved, if it be God's holy will."

"Oh, no, doctor, oh, no, I want to die so free;
I want to die with my engine, old 143."
His last words were, "Nearer my God to Thee,
Nearer my God to Thee, nearer to Thee."

As with so many other songs, the words were proba-bly gathered by word of mouth, and the song's lyrics added to and taken from at the will of the performer. There are many discrepancies in the various ver-sions. For example, the song is often sung under the title "Engine 143," when in fact the engine was No. 134. Many versions name Jack Dickinson as the fireman, a few "Jack Dixon" and one "Jack of Dixie." My theory is that he may have substituted on the run sometimes. We know that this was Lewis With-row's first day back on the job after a "lay-out" of several weeks, so it might have been assumed by whoever wrote the song that a substitute was still doing the run. Norm Cohen, answering my query, believes the same thing. Certain versions of the song relate how "Georgie's mother came to him with a bucket on her arm," but George Alley's mother had been dead seventeen years when the wreck occurred that killed her son. (That he had a stepmother hardly seems relevant.) Some versions top George off with golden curly hair, in keeping with American folk-convention in the description of heroes. But George Washington Alley, from his portrait, had a different sort of glamour: straight black hair, a drooping heavy moustache, and dark soulful eyes. In certain ver-sions of the song the New River is incorrectly given as the locale; the wreck occurred on the Greenbrier. Tom Dixon notes that "Stockyard Gate" refers to the C & O's stock pens located at Stockyard, West Vir-ginia, now called Pence Springs.

The erroneous name "George Allen" which ap-pears in many versions of the song may have its source in a later wreck. On May 3, 1933, Southern Train No. 52 wrecked near Danville, Virginia, kill-ing its engineer, one George Allen (pp. 177–81). On the other hand, Allen is just a more common name than Alley; one hearing "Alley" might quite easily assume it was "Allen."

In a 1929 letter to Alfred V. Frankenstein from L. F. Alley, George's brother, quoted by Cohen, there

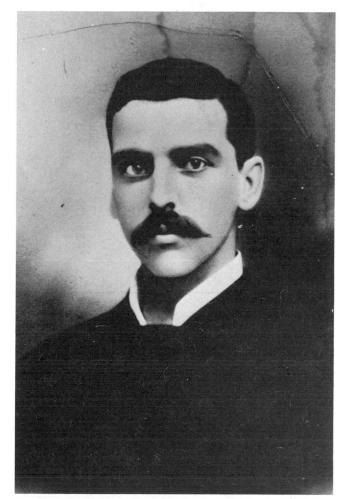

George Alley, from a charcoal drawing made near the time of his death. *Courtesy Ron Lane.*

Jennie Lyle studies the inscription on the side of George Alley's tombstone. *Photo by Royster Lyle.*

is an odd note: *"Mrs. Alley,"* he avers, *"was at the opposite end of the run when the accident happened, so there is nothing to the dinner pail story."* In every version I have seen, it is George's mother who brings the bucket to him, and she was long dead when the wreck occurred. Mr. L. F. Alley further comments, "I have never been impressed with the song, it being so far from the actual facts."

George Alley's gravestone in Alderson, West Virginia, bears the following touching inscription: "George W. Alley, B. of L. E., died from injuries received on C & O Ry. October 23, 1890. Aged 30 y's, 3 m's, & 13 d's. Rest sweetly Dear in thy lone grave

sleeping. While we are weeping thy soul has flown to God's white throne." And on the side of the stone a touching phrase reads: "Dear George: our home is sad and lonely without thee."

In September 1926, two years after Vernon Dalhart's popular recording of "The Wreck of the Old 97," Roy Harvey recorded a song (Columbia 15174-D) entitled "The Brave Engineer." It is an interesting combination of the two popular songs "The Wreck on the C & O" and "Old 97." About George Alley apparently, it is sung to a tune almost identical to that of "The Ship That Never Return'd," which was always "Old 97"'s tune.

The Brave Engineer

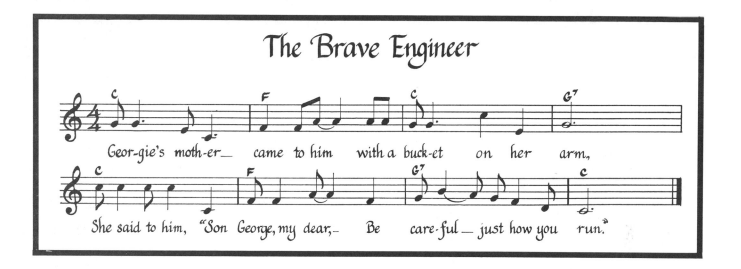

Geor-gie's moth-er— came to him with a buck-et on her arm, She said to him, "Son George, my dear,— Be care-ful— just how you run."

THE BRAVE ENGINEER

Georgie's mother came to him
With a bucket on her arm,
She said to him, "son George my dear,
Be careful just how you run,

"For many poor man has lost life
Trying to make lost time,
If you run your engine right,
You will get there just on the time."

"Mother, I know you're a mite too good;
To the letter I'll be keen,"
"Honey, you'll drive old No. 4,
The swiftest ever was seen."

Georgie to his captain said,
The throttle he did pull,
"Old No. four leaps out this morning,
Like a fire-eating big angry bull."

Georgie said to his fireman Jack,
"Shovel in a little more coal,
When we blow for the Big Bend Tunnel;
They will surely hear our sad call."

Georgie said to his fireman Jack,
"Big rock ahead I see,
I know that death is awaiting there,
To trap both you and me."

Up the road they rambled,
At that big rock they crashed,
Upside down that engine turned,
On Georgie's breast did smash.

His head was upon the firebox door,
Outrunning flames did roar,
Grabbed upon an engineer
To die on Old No. 4.

Fatal Run

Frank-ie's moth - er came to him with his din-ner un-der her arm,

Say-ing "Frank-ie Lee, my dar-ling boy, be care-ful how you run;

There's a man-y poor man has lost his life, mak-ing up for lost

time." If you will run that en-gine right, You'll nev-er be be-hind

time, De yo-del lay-hee- o lay-hee o - de-lay-de lay-hee.

And finally, Cohen has collected a version "written" by Cliff Carlisle around 1930, interesting largely because it shows the folk influence on a "modern" composer.

THE FATAL RUN

Frankie's mother came to him, with his dinner under her
    arm,
Saying, "Frankie Lee, my darling boy, be careful how you
    run;
There's a many poor man has lost his life, making up for
    lost time,
If you will run that engine right, you'll never be behind
    time."
Yodel:

Frankie said to his mother, a sad look on his face,
"Mother dear, my father's dead, I have to take his place."
"That is true, my darling boy, be careful and don't be late,
Your father didn't run his engine right, that's how he met
    his fate."

Climbing into his engine cab, and waving his mother
    goodbye,
Pulling the throttle wide open, to watch that engine fly;
He was headed round Dead Man's Curve, he looked into
    Forty-nine's face,
He thought of his mother and the folks back home; he'd
    run his final race.

Frankie's mother got the message, the tears streamed
    down her face,
To think that her only boy had run his final race;
Mister engineer, take warning from the fate of that boy of
    mine,
There's a many poor man has lost his life by making up
    lost time.

NOTES

Ron Lane became interested in the Alley family around 1960 while doing avocational research on C & O folkmusic. His subsequent letter-writing and visits over five years produced a geneology of the family, from which I borrowed much information. In addition to books referred to, sources used were Paul Shue; an article by Charles Carpenter in an undated Beckley, W. Va., newspaper; the Covington *Virginian*, 26 Oct. 1925, the Monroe *Watch*

man, Union, W. Va., 30 Oct. 1890; the Clifton Forge and Iron Gate *Review*, 24 Oct. 1890 and 31 Oct. 1890; the Hinton *Daily News*, 11 Oct. 1966; the Beckley *Post-Herald*, 4 Dec. 1968.

When I went on a fact-finding expedition to West Virginia in May 1982, I took my friend and neighbor Maureen Worth along. One of the things I was determined to find was George Alley's grave, which I thought was in Hinton. Everyone we met was a bit baffled but eager to help: we were directed to a cemetery in many sections that covered a large and extremely steep mountain. In 100 degrees and high humidity, we divided up the graveyards, and spent several hours looking in family plots thick with poison ivy and fenced-in cemeteries overrun with wild roses, only to give up in the face of an old-fashioned thunder-and-lightning-frog-strangling storm. Later that night Fred Long of Hinton assured me that Alley was not buried in his town at all, but "on row 18, to the left of the church, in the Greenbrier Baptist Church Cemetery in Alderson." We found the grave the next day precisely where he told us, the top of the obelisk broken off and lying beside it. Alley rests alone. Wherever his loving wife and children are buried, they are not anywhere near him. The marble monument is old and weathered, the dirt at the base of the obelisk without grass or weeds. An inquiry to Ron Lane brought prompt answers: Mrs. Alley remarried several years later and moved to Baltimore and had three more children. Alley was buried in Alderson because, until his marriage, he lived there, not fifty feet from the railroad right-of-way, in his father's house.

I have tried in vain to discover who Jack Dickinson, or Dixon, was. Shirley Donnelly, in the Beckley *Post–Herald* of 4 Dec. 1968, implies that he was a C & O fireman: "Jack Dickinson is named as fireman, but he was not on the engine the day the wreck took place."

Pick Temple in a letter to me commented that "these black engine-wipers were some guys, apparently all of them composers at heart, if we are to believe the folklore."

This seems as appropriate a spot as any to explain the three- or four-number designation of locomotives, for those who are as ignorant of the matter as I was only a few months ago. George Alley's engine, or locomotive, was a 4-6-0, for example, which means four "pony" wheels in the front which helped guide it on the rails, six "drivers," or driving wheels, which transmitted the motive power to the rail, and no "trailers" or trailing wheels to support the firebox and cab which were situated behind the driver.

In June 1982, while Maureen and I were interviewing West Virginia singer and songwriter Buddy Starcher, he expressed interest in seeing the portrait of George Alley that Ron Lane had just sent me. Staring at it, he shook his head. "In my song, he's got blond curly hair," he commented. "I reckon George Alley probably got aholt of some of that there Clair-oil."

The N&W Cannonball Wreck

**I mean to break the record for speeding up the line,
Make Petersburg at 6:15, and Richmond right on time.**

The Norfolk and Western "Cannonball" was a crack passenger train that ran two popular daily round trips between Norfolk and Richmond, Virginia, using N & W crews and locomotives over both the Atlantic Coast Line and N & W tracks. Trains Nos. 19 and 20 left Norfolk every morning

and returned at night, while trains Nos. 21 and 22 departed Richmond in the mornings and Norfolk in the afternoons.

On Saturday, June 27, 1903, the early Cannonball left Byrd Street Station in Richmond at nine o'clock for Norfolk. Thirty minutes later, traveling at speed through the interlocking plant at the junction at Dunlop, Virginia, about three miles north of Petersburg, the Cannonball, headed by N & W N-class 4-4-0 engine No. 29, plowed headlong into a stand-

An early example of a 4-4-0 engine, No. 6, a left side view with the engineman oiling around and the fireman in the cab. *Courtesy Norfolk and Western.*

ing northbound Atlantic Coast Line freight locomotive. The ACL freight was powered by a Copperhead 4-6-0 engine, No. 335. It had just picked up a car and, in doing so, fouled the interlocking mechanism. Thus the operator at Dunlop was unable to line the switch for the intended route of the Cannonball down the main line and into Petersburg. This should have been automatically indicated in the signals to the approaching train. But the Cannonball never slowed down.

At the moment of collision the freight train was standing on the side track to let her by, and the passenger train was diverted at full speed onto the sidetrack and into the resting freight. Engineer Harry Covington, forty-five, of the Cannonball, saw what was coming in time to apply his airbrakes, but not in time to avoid collision. At the last instant he jumped free of the cab, landing on his head on a tie. It was at first assumed that he died instantly.

There were many observers. They declared that

Courtesy C. C. Meeks.

the impact was terrific, reporting "a heavy crash, the stillness of death, and then the terrible cries of the wounded." The Cannonball's engine was totally demolished. The front of the mail car by the coal tender was "stove in." Engineer Covington's fireman, Robert Covington, his brother Thomas's son, was caught in the wreckage and killed instantly. He was entirely dismembered in the collision so that, according to the Petersburg *Daily Appeal* of June 28, "legs, arms, and head were gathered up in an undertaker's basket."

The Petersburg newspaper account seems to imply that there was an "understanding" between the young Mr. Covington and his landlady's daughter, a Miss Broadnax, and quotes her as saying that he had told her yesterday morning that he would be home to see her that evening.

Mr. Morton Riddle, a passenger on the train, reported that "I felt the train slacken slightly, as if a light application of airbrakes was made . . ." and then the crash.

A local judge, W. H. Mann, testified later, "I felt

the train go off on the curve . . . in a second the shock came, and a moment afterwards, the train moved forward, showing that whatever the train struck gave way, moving about five feet, I estimate." Later he "saw under the car on the right side of the track the body of Mr. Covington, dead as I then supposed. I went to see about the fireman but could not see him. It later transpired that Mr. Covington (the engineer) was breathing but unconscious . . . and died perhaps a half hour later."

Seriously injured in the accident was Captain Robert S. Eckles, the conductor of the Cannonball. Both of his arms were broken, and he sustained chest injuries and many cuts and bruises in his head and legs. A passenger on the Cannonball, Dr. George E. Font of Richmond, set the limbs of Captain Eckles at the scene of the wreck. Most of the twenty-five passengers on the Cannonball were slightly injured, including the well-known Judge Mann and a popular Methodist minister, Rev. Henry E. Johnson. The engineer of the ACL freight, a Mr. Bradshaw, jumped from his cab in time and was not injured.

A subsequent investigation had difficulty clarifying whether the block signals had been working. That the interlocking plant was fouled does not explain why Harry Covington ran through the southbound home signal which should have been automatically interlocked to indicate the *stop* position. The Richmond *Times-Dispatch* of June 30, 1903, reported that the coroner's jury investigating the crash eventually decided it was negligence on the part of the Atlantic Coast Line officials in not using diligence in having the line clear, and not Engineer Covington's fault. Mr. Ben Knight, however, with the background of a half-century of railroading, concludes otherwise: assuming that the signal system and interlocking plant were standard, and were fouled, Harry Covington went through a *stop* signal that should have given him time to stop, and therefore he must have been going too fast, since under ordinary circumstances he could have halted the train in time.

Mr. Cleburne Meeks was told the story of this wreck some years afterward by Mr. W. C. (Billy) Cousins, who had been a flagman on the Cannonball. Meeks wrote the lyrics of the song, and years after that gave the following letter to Paul Shue.

VERNON DALHART
120 WEST 45TH STREET
NEW YORK CITY

March, 13th, 1928.

Mr. Cleburne C. Meeks,
Route 3, box 104a,
Petersburg, Va.

Dear Sir:

In re: of two sets of lyrics received from you to-day, "WRECK OF THE N&W CANNON BALL" and the "LOVER'S SONG" beg to say that I will accept the first one and if agreeable to you will keep the latter for future reference; it may be that Robison can make up a little tune for this one that will go back to back with the wreck song, however I dont want to commit myself as having accepted the "LOVER'S SONG" at this time, but in the event we do something with it you will of course hear from me as usual, and I am inclined to think that we will use it as a tie-up.

I am enclosing herewith the usual contract for the "Cannon Ball" song.

Best wishes from Robby and myself

Very respectfully yours,

Vernon Dalhart

VD/R.

Courtesy Paul Shue.

The Wreck of the N & W Cannonball

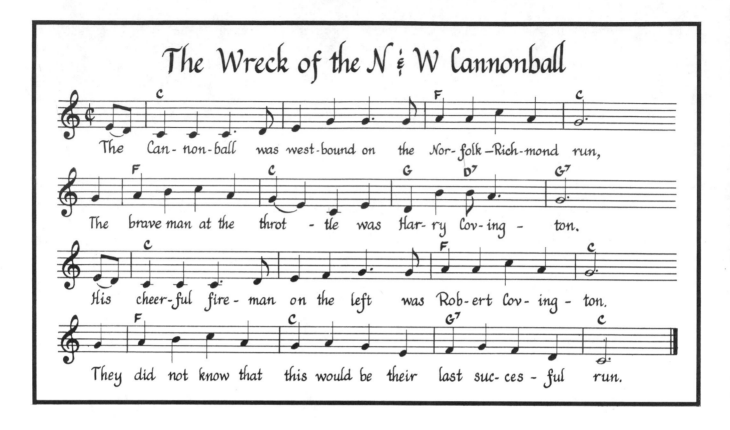

The Cannonball was west-bound on the Nor-folk—Rich-mond run,
The brave man at the throt-tle was Har-ry Cov-ing-ton.
His cheer-ful fire-man on the left was Rob-ert Cov-ing-ton.
They did not know that this would be their last suc-ces-ful run.

The song, which follows, has the usual cheery be-ginning, brave engineer, foreshadowing remarks; i.e., "I mean to break the record . . ." implying, per-haps erroneously, that speed was a component in the wreck. The conversation between the two men was a hallmark of Meeks's songs. Also typical of his songs is the accuracy of his facts.

WRECK OF THE N&W CANNONBALL

The Cannonball was westbound on the Norfolk-
  Richmond run,
The brave man at the throttle was Harry Covington.
His cheerful fireman on the left, was Robert Covington,
They did not know that this would be their last
  successful run.

There's nothing like railroading Bob, when once you pull
  the mail
I mean to run this Cannonball the fastest ever sailed.
I mean to break the record for speeding up the line,
Make Petersburg at 6:15, and Richmond right on time.

She pulled right into Petersburg, running right on time.
Switched over on the ACL for Richmond on the line.
Brave Harry at the throttle of engine twenty nine.
Sped right on into Richmond with the Cannonball on
  time.

Next morning the Cannonball left Richmond right on
  time
Brave Harry at the throttle of good old twenty nine.
Sped right on into Richmond with the Cannonball on
  time.

Paul Shue and Cleburne Meeks reminisce, July 9, 1982. *Photo by Katie Lyle.*

Next morning the Cannonball left Richmond right on time
Brave Harry at the throttle of good old twenty nine,
His cheerful fireman on the left, did shovel in more coal
When Harry looked in the fire box door, his burning blaze did roll.

A freight train on the ACL at Dunlop on the line,
Was backed in on the siding for the Cannonball on time,

The brave crew on the Cannonball never knew the switch was wrong,
And crashed into the freight train on the ACL that morn.
Poor Bob and Harry Covington died when the engine crashed
Threw Bob against the boiler head, as the tender body smashed,
Threw Harry from his seat box, by the boiler he did fall,
He died a daring engineer, running on the Cannonball.

NOTES

On July 9, 1982, Paul Shue and I paid Mr. and Mrs. Meeks a visit at their home in Colonial Heights, Virginia. Mr. Meeks, who has known Paul for many years, recalled writing the song, though he, born in 1902, of course could not remember the wreck. Mr. and Mrs. Meeks treated us graciously, and Mr. Meeks recalled his years of songwriting with us. He seemed amused at my question, "How did you decide what wrecks to write about?": "I just got an idea, and wrote it up." For fifty years he was a hostler for the N & W, someone who prepares the incoming engines for their next trips. He wrote the N & W Cannonball song after moving to Petersburg in 1927 and hearing about the wreck. The trip was very important to me, as I have sung Mr. Meeks's songs all my life. His stepdaughter, Eliza C. Myrick, told me in advance that he had severe arteriosclerosis. When his wife reminded him of a religious parody he had written, called "Mary Had a Little Boy" (His soul was white as snow), he shook his head, unable to recall it. "I always thought it was a lamb," he told us. He gave me some poems he had written but never got around to setting to music. It seems appropriate to print one of them here.

ONE MORE TIME

An old time engineer came to the round house
And he looked as if he had a worried mind.
With trembling voice he said "I am retiring"
You will only have to call me one more time.

Tell the round house clerk to have the caller call me.
Tell him he will find me in room No. 9

Tell him I would like a little time for coffee.
And I want to sign the call book one more time.

Tell the round house foreman I want my old engine.
She's the old five hundred, best one on the line.
Whether it be slow run, time freight or a special.
I want to pull the throttle one more time.

Tell the hostler when he checks my engine over.
To be sure that everything is working fine,
Set my driver brakes to standard piston travel
For I want a perfect engine one more time.

Check the space between my engine and the tender
Oil the friction wedge and set it back in line.
Check the friction block and bolt wedge to the tail bar
For I want to ride in comfort one more time.

Check my whistle bell, and line it to the sound plate.
Straighten whistle rod and set it back in line.
When I make my final run tomorrow morning
You will hear a lonesome whistle one more time.
(The whistle bell is a very important part of a steam whistle and
   has nothing to do with the engine bell.)

C. C. MEEKS
Colonial Heights
Life member BLF&E

Other sources were the Petersburg *Daily Index-Appeal*, 28–30 June 1903; Richmond *Times-Dispatch*, 28, 30 June 1903.

The New Market Wreck

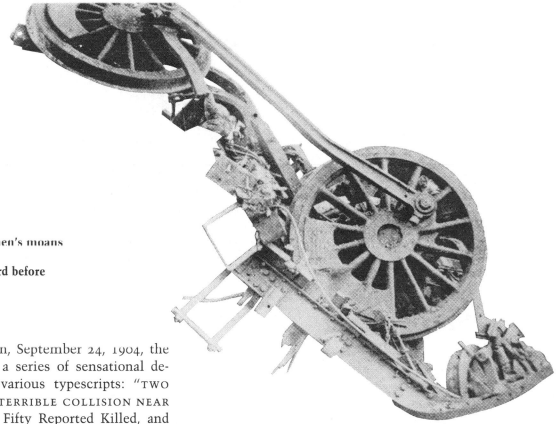

And oh, the men and women's moans
Did echo through the air;
Such cries were never heard before
From humans in despair.

On Saturday afternoon, September 24, 1904, the Knoxville *Sentinel* ran a series of sensational descending headlines in various typescripts: "TWO PASSENGER TRAINS IN TERRIBLE COLLISION NEAR NEW MARKET TODAY / Fifty Reported Killed, and 125 Injured / Every Coach of East Bound Train, Save Sleepers, Said To Have Been Demolished / Engineers Parrott and Kane Lost Their Lives / Failure to Observe Orders Assigned As Cause."

In Richmond the next day, September 25, the headlines suggested a more mysterious story: "Fifty-Four Lose Lives In Awful Crash of Trains / Over One Hundred Others Injured, Several of Whom May Die. / Engineer Failed to Obey Orders / Possible That Death Had Already Palsied the Hand at the Throttle / Accident on Southern's Tennessee Division / Both Engineers Were Killed and Real Cause of Tragedy Can Never Be Known—Major Portions of Trains Demolished—Story of Eye-Witnesses." Only after these introductions did the news story begin.

KNOXVILLE SENTINEL.

12 PAGES TODAY · **4 O'CLOCK Edition.**

VOL. XVIII. NO. 230   KNOXVILLE, TENN., MONDAY AFTERNOON, SEPTEMBER 26, 1904.   TWO CENTS.

64 IN DEATH-LIST--INJURED NUMBER 141
KNOXVILLE, IN SORROW, BURIES ITS DEAD

MORGUE AND HOSPITAL TASKS NOT COMPLETED

Nine Funeral Were Held Here Today.

Bodies of Dead Being Shipped to Homes at a Distance. Scene of Wreck Been Cleared. M Injured Remains in City Hospital. Officials Investigating.

THIS AFTERNOON AT 3 O'CLOCK THE LIST OF CASUALTIES ON ACCOUNT OF THE NEW MARKET WRECK OF LAST SATURDAY SHOWS 64 DEATHS AND 141 INJURED. IT IS NOW STATED THAT NONE OF THOSE WHO SURVIVE WILL DIE.

SUPERINTENDENT GEORGE R. LOYALL. OF THE SOUTHERN RAILWAY, PLACES THE NUMBER OF DEAD AT 53 AND THE NUMBER OF INJURED AT 162.

NINE FUNERALS WERE HELD IN THIS CITY TODAY, AND OTHERS WILL OCCUR TOMORROW. THE SHIPPING OF REMAINS TO OTHER POINTS CONTINUES. MANY GOING OUT TODAY AND OTHERS WILL FOLLOW TONIGHT AND TOMORROW.

A BODY AT E. B. MANN & CO'S MORGUE WAS THIS AFTERNOON IDENTIFIED AS THAT OF DAVID S. FOX, OF BIRMINGHAM, ALA., AND THAT WHICH WAS SHIPPED TO BIRMINGHAM YESTERDAY FOR FOX IS NOW SAID TO BE J. M. DALEY, OF DETROIT.

THE BODY WHICH WAS SAID TO BE GEORGE LEE, OF CARROLLTON, KY., WAS THIS AFTERNOON IDENTIFIED AS K. S. KONRAD, OF CINCINNATI.

CONDUCTOR CALDWELL FORGOT HIS ORDERS
—SAYS FELLOW - RAILROADER.

"Conductor W. B. Caldwell, who was running train No. 15 that collided with take a chance to make a run from New Market to Hodges, hoping to get to the

LOCOMOTIVE AND COMBINATION MAIL AND EXPRESS CAR OF EAST BOUND TRAIN.

Machinery of locomotive of east bound train piled upon machinery and trucks and trucks of locomotive of west bound. Engineer G. M. Parrott's body was pinioned under the wreckage of these locomotives. He was probably instantly killed.

thereto. Hundreds of people called at the institution to make inquiries as to injured relatives or friends, but few were admitted. The large corps of nurses that had been brought into service had all they could do.

Many instances are related of the sufferings of those injured and the manner in which they met death. No greater interest is felt as to any bereavement than which has come to the home of W. A. Galbraith who with Mrs. Galbraith was killed outright. The remains of both father and mother have been taken to the home on Henley street. The bodies were not found until after several hours, though they were not as badly mutilated as was anticipated. For this reason the identification was more easily accomplished than expected and the bodies were easily recognized when they were reached. The funeral over the decedents has not yet been determined upon and may not be until the last of the week. William Galbraith, an ensign in the navy, is at San Francisco, but he has wired that he will be here by Thursday at the very latest, and for this reason the remains are being held so long. The interment will be in Gray cemetery in the Galbraith

"Wrecks Too Frequent," Says Pall Mall Gazett

LONDON, Sept. 26.—The recent railroad accidents in the United States are attracting no little comment in England. The Pall-Mall Gazette says:

"They are far too common in America, especially of late. The fact that it is a large country, with plenty of room for them to happen in, is not sufficient to explain them. Probably the fundamental cause is the hasty and imperfect construction of the lines, the makeshift arrangements for saving time and the general rush of strenuous national life."

ALL AT CITY HOSPITAL EXPECTED TO RECOVER

Reports this afternoon at ... N. C. that homes. It is reported that

ROSTER OF THE DEAD

The following are known to be dead:

MONROE ASHMORE aged 19 of Knoxville.
JOHN BLACK of White Pine, Tenn.
JAMES P. BIRD of Jefferson City, Tenn.
K. S. CONRAD of Cincinnati.
JOHN CARNER foreman of roundhouse Knoxville
MRS. JOHN CARNER, Knoxville
IRA CRAWFORD Bardstown Ky
MRS J. H. CAMPBELL Mohawk
WILLIAM CUNNINGHAM, fireman of train No. 17.
MISS ... CLEPP of Knoxville
CHAS. ... colored, Telford
B DEGROAT Jefferson City Tenn.
J. M. DALY of Detroit
S. DAVIS of Knoxville
J. J. DANIEL Tedloy s Mill
W T. ELLIS Greensboro, N C
J S EARNEST Johnson City, Tenn.
W. F. GANTT Shelby N. C.
ROCHELLE HILL of Gaffney S. C.
REV. ISAAC EMERY of Knoxville
D S FOX Birmingham, Ala
W A GALBRAITH Knoxville
MRS W. A. GALBRAITH Knoxville
MRS. J. R. GASS Dandridge
JOHN GLENN Morristown
ARTHUR GASS colored, Greeneville
R P GIDDENS of Jefferson City
MRS R S GREEN Sylvia, N C
MARY GARDNER of Knoxville
CLAYTON M. HEISKELL of Memphis
MR W D HADDOX of Knoxville, daughter of Mrs J H Gass
E S HORNER Morristown
MRS. LAURA HILL, Gaffney, S. C.

RUTH HILL seven year old daughter of Mrs. Laura Hill.
W B HILL of Gaffney S C
WILLIAM JONES of James Jones of South Knoxville
JOSEPH KING of Newport
BONNIE KING of Newport
WILLIAM KANE of Knoxville, engineer of the east bound train
MRS K D KINZELL of Knoxville
... KNIGHT of Dandridge
MRS J A LAMON Knoxville
RALPH MOUNT ASTLE of Knoxville
JAMES MILLS colored of New Market
MRS ANNIE MALAY of Birmingham
MRS M J M EWEN of Knoxville
MR ALBERT M MAHAN of Newport
JOHN MOLYNEUX, of Glen Mary, Tenn.
ROY M MAHAN of Newport
NEP MILLER son of Greeneville
J B PLUMMER of Chapel Hill, N C
G M PARROTT of Knoxville, engineer of the east bound train
MRS ... A RUSSELL and two children aged 5 and 7 years of Knoxville.
J R RHEA of Whitesburg
MRS NANCY J RUMLY of Watville
W A STEPHENS of Washington
MRS R B WEST of Jefferson City
TWO WHITE MEN unidentified.
UNKNOWN NEGRO.
Unknown man, initial G B wore Masonic pin, wore No 16 collar, No. 11 cuff No 7 shoes and 14 glove.
Unknown man, whose watch is number 19,40, works of A. Kolbach.

THESE WERE INJURED

A
J. E. Arthur, of Union, S. C.
J. M. Anderson, of Morristown, bruised
Joseph T. Alderson, of Rogersville.
L. E. Altme, Lowell, Tenn., not serious.

B
Mrs. L. C. Blankenship, of South Knoxville, both limbs broken.
Miss Mary Bryan, of Hendersonville, N. C., bruised.
Mrs. George Braughton, of Jackson, Ill.
George Brodger, of Talbott, Tenn., serious.
h. D. Blackham, Jefferson county, Tenn., not serious.
Rev. W. B. Brady, Asheville, N. C., slight.
L S Baker, Asheville, N. C., leg and hip injured.
J N Ballou, Mohawk, Tenn., not serious.
Three colored women named Barry H D Bassington, or H. D Brassington, Detroit, not serious
J A Brady, Witts Foundry, Tenn.
W J Bell, Pullman porter, Johnson City, Tenn, not serious.
Richard Brown, White Pine Tenn. not serious.
Mrs George Brogter, Jackson, Ill. of serious.
John Belshew, no address not serious
John Beech, scalp wounds

H
J S Helms, of Knoxville.
J Hare of New Market.
Mrs Lu y Harbin, of Morristown, N C
Mr. and Mrs. He , of Burlington, N C
E H Haylou, Birmingham, Ala. leg broken
Paul Henry, Asheville, N C (or Knoxville), badly hurt
Ivan Harrison, Dandridge, slight.
M. J Harrison, slight
W M Hickey, attorney Southern railway Morristown, not serious
Jim Hartsell, colored, Washington College Tenn, not serious
Mrs W M Houston, of Charlotte, N not serious (She is the mother-inlaw of J W Provost, Southern Express agent of Knoxville.)
L S Horah, Pullman porter, arms and legs hurt.
Samuel F Harder of Baltimore Md.

J
J A Jones of Knoxville face bruised, not serious
Mrs J Jones, of Union S C
Mrs Will Jones, of South Knoxville, slightly bruised
Miss Pearl Jones, of South Knoxville, slightly bruised
Robert Jackson, Johnson City not serious
Minnie Jane, Greeneville serious

K
William Kennedy, Johnson City, not

September 24, 1904, was a fair warm morning in Tennessee—sixty-six degrees at ten o'clock. The roadbed was in good repair, the rails in "a high condition of maintenance" on the East Tennessee Division of the Southern Railway, and the crews were "old and trusted employees." The event took place "in broad daylight."

Two trains sped towards a regular meeting at Hodges Station in the northeastern part of the state, between Knoxville and Bristol. No. 12 was a heavy eastbound freight on its way from Knoxville to Salisbury, North Carolina, pulled by Southern locomotive No. 1051, a 4-6-0 Baldwin built in 1897. This tenwheeler was a "class 21 × 28 10 WP." (This means, according to Tom Dixon, that the engine had twenty-one-inch diameter cylinders with twenty-eight-inch stroke; the 10 WP means ten-wheel passenger type engine.) At the throttle was Engineer E. M. "Dick" Parrott of Knoxville. A Conductor Murphy was in charge of the train. No. 15 was a westbound local passenger train pulled by a lighter engine, Southern's No. 1838, an "18 × 24 8 WP" built in 1887. It was coming from Bristol, due into Knoxville at 11:00. In its cab were engineer William Kane, black fireman Jim Mills, and in charge of the train was Conductor Bill Caldwell. Orders had been given to both trains to meet at the New Market, Tennessee, station, a regular meeting place. The Knoxville *Sentinel* reported two days later that it was "customary for trains 12 and 15 to meet at Hodges if on time, but in this case #15 was running late and orders were issued at Morristown for the trains to pass at New Market. So in the habit of meeting #12 at Hodges were the crew of #15 that the changes was forgotten."

Engineer Kane and Conductor Caldwell of No. 15, apparently disregarding orders or forgetting them, rushed by New Market instead of stopping, and a few moments later, at 10:18, on a curve just a mile east of Hodges, crashed into the eastbound train that was making for New Market in compliance with instructions. The two trains met with such an impact that both boilers exploded, demolishing both engines, along with several of the coaches of the eastbound train. Both engineers were killed instantly, as were over sixty people in the eastbound train, mainly in the forward coaches. The sleeping cars were spared serious damage.

John Brown, a Rogersville, Tennessee, newspaper editor, was in a rear coach of the westbound train when it crashed. He related that all the seats in the car in which he was riding were torn loose by the force of the impact, and that passengers and seats were hurled together to the front end of the coach. After a moment of silence, he began to hear the screams and groans of the injured and dying in every direction. "I left the car as soon as I could, and walked up to the main part of the wreck. It was the most horrible sight I ever witnessed. I saw a woman pinioned by a piece of split timber which had gone completely through her body. A little child, quivering in death's agony, lay beneath the woman. I saw the child die, and within a few feet of her lay a woman's head, while the decapitated body was several feet away. . . ." He continues for some space the gory catalogue.

64 IN DEATH·LIST

1

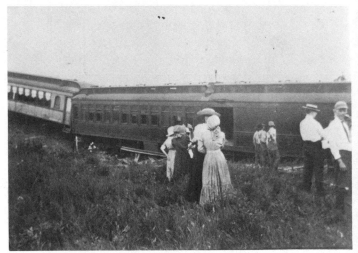

2

The New Market Wreck, on September 24, 1904, was one of the worst in the history of railroading. In the first picture, mail sacks are being removed from the wreckage. The second and third pictures show some of the jammed-together cars in which "half a hundred forms silent in the last sleep" died, and scores were injured. The fourth picture was taken inside one of the mailcars. The fifth picture shows the splintered remains of a boxcar from the freight train, and a tank car jack-knifed across the tracks. *All photos from the J. W. Reams collection of the McClung Historical Collection. Courtesy Lawson-McGhee Library, Knoxville, Tennessee.*

3

4

5

The twisted and torn locomotives. The driving wheels are from No. 1838, and Engine 1061 is underneath.
Courtesy Shelby F. Lowe.

The engine on train No. 15 was telescoped by the heavier locomotive that had been pulling No. 12, and lay a battered and dramatic mass of metal twenty-five feet east of the other engine, both of them derailed on the outside part of the curve, the southern side. Engineer Parrott's body was thrown thirty feet from his engine cab.

A Tennessee senator injured in the collision Henry R. Gibson, glanced around him after recovering from the shock, and saw "a mass of human be-

The combination coach-baggage car crushed into the tender of 1838. The locomotive's driving wheels can be seen up in the air. Engine 1061 was wrecked totally beneath Engine 1838. *Courtesy Shelby F. Lowe.*

ings, backs of car seats, grips, baskets, and wearing apparel of all sorts—and not a sign of life."

Relief trains were dispatched from Knoxville within an hour, and the *Sentinel* the next day reported that the first train from the wreck had arrived back in Knoxville at four-thirty that afternoon carrying seventy of the injured, six of whom died on the way. By midafternoon, thousands of people had arrived at the crash scene. Some came, of course, to try to help identify the victims, but many were vandals, opportunists, and a ghoulish public. The day was warm and cloudless, and the scene took on the aspect of a fair or a circus.

On the freight train had been a car of chickens that had burst open, and the birds roamed the scene freely as "Angels of mercy" did all they could to aid the injured and dying. As day faded and the evening grew chilly, fires were lit and many of the hapless chickens were killed and fried. Concessions sprang up. At around six that evening a second train left for Knoxville from the wreck, carrying the bodies of forty-three victims.

Around midnight, Engineer Will Kane's body was extricated from the wreckage, and on it was found his copy of the meet order. In a Knoxville hospital, fireman Jim Mills died of his injuries about the same time. By three o'clock the next morning the tracks were cleared.

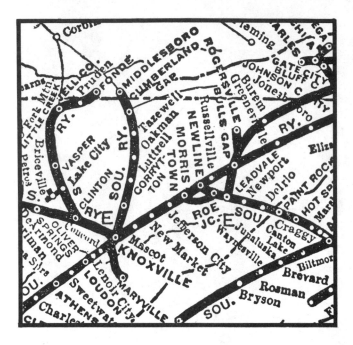

The accident occurred under such puzzling circumstances that there was at first speculation that the engineer of No. 15, William Kane, might have suffered a fatal heart attack or an apoplexy prior to the concussion, or at the very least somehow fallen asleep. The Richmond *Times-Dispatch* reported that both trains were on time, and so concluded that there was no question of failure to stop in an effort to make up lost time.

Then Conductor Caldwell of Train No. 15 stepped forward to take the blame upon himself, stating to the *Sentinel*, "I forgot to stop at New Market. It was all my fault." An unnamed Southern Railway spokesman corroborates this, saying, "Bill Caldwell did not take any chances. He simply forgot his orders to stop at New Market." The final death count varies—56, 62, 72. Fifty-six can hardly be right, as fifty-five were known dead the night of the wreck and several others of the injured were reported to have died on subsequent days and even weeks later.

An interesting detail is that two friends, Post Office Inspector B. B. Webb and mail clerk Jennings J. Dunlap, had passed each other in trains on September 27, 1903, when Dunlap was clerking aboard Old 97 while Webb, a regular on Old 97 who happened to be on No. 36 that day, waited on a siding at Chatham, Virginia. Only a few minutes later, Dunlap was in the wreck of the Old 97, one of several mail clerks lucky enough to come out alive. Now, one year later, both friends were in the New Market wreck, this time on the same train, No. 15, and both survived.

Webb reported to the Richmond *Times-Dispatch* in 1933: "I jumped for the safety rod at the top of the car and the other two clerks did the same. At that instant the two trains collided, and the tender . . . telescoped into our car. A two-by-four timber with a point on it like a javelin whistled by my stomach, and nearly tore my trousers off, but it didn't scratch me.

"Of course all three of us would have been killed if we hadn't jumped for the safety rod just before the smash. Sixty-nine people were killed on our train, most of them being horribly mangled when the cars in which they were seated were telescoped. Many of them were returning from the St. Louis World's Fair, and were on the way to their homes."

One especially devastating story made the newspapers: a man named Lee Hill had been killed two days before the New Market wreck, in a powder mill explosion in Jellico, Tennessee. His father, his wife, his four children, and a sister had gone to claim his body and were returning to Gaffney, South Carolina, for his burial. All seven were killed in the wreck. All eight were buried together in Gaffney.

This wreck inspired at least two songs. Soon afterwards, a frankly commercial song appeared. "The New Market Wreck" lyrics seem evidence enough of the depths to which early twentieth century American folk poetry could fall. It is easily the poorest

The New Market Wreck

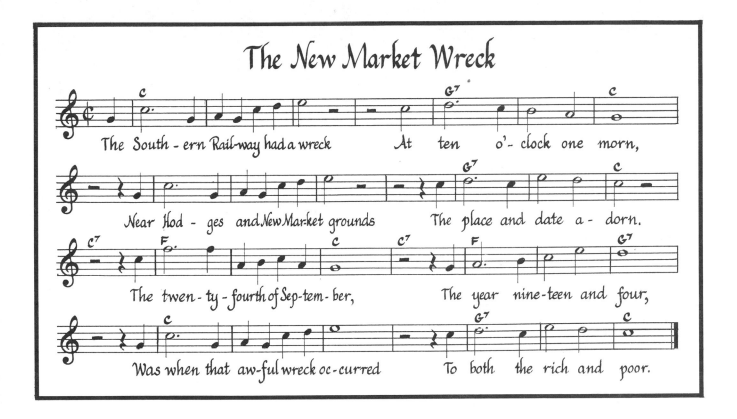

The South-ern Rail-way had a wreck   At ten o'-clock one morn,

Near Hod-ges and New Market grounds   The place and date a-dorn.

The twen-ty-fourth of Sep-tem-ber,   The year nine-teen and four,

Was when that aw-ful wreck oc-curred   To both the rich and poor.

quality wreck song of them all, hastily and carelessly penned. The song apparently began as a broadside, for it adjures the reader, "You'll see a picture of the wreck / Just over on the back." (This sort of authorial intrusion is, of course, a deviation from acceptable ballad form.) The song accurately damns the conductor of the westbound train as the villain of the day, but is poorly composed, with little further regard for fact. It claims, for example, that the engineer on the eastbound train had time to write a note directing that his body be taken home for burial, though in truth he was killed instantly. The rhymes are forced, obvious, and jarring, and in at least one case, meaningless: "the place and date adorn." It also adds a farewell scene between the engineer of No. 15 and his wife, though nothing suggests that such a scene had any basis in truth. The lines were composed by a poet of leaden ear, whose name may have been Joshia Adams.

The tune is pleasant, somewhat reminiscent of hymn tunes. If the ballad enjoyed popularity, it is probably attributable to public interest in the wreck, which was among the worst in the history of railroading, and to the attractive melody of the song. The version which follows is similar to others I have seen.

THE NEW MARKET WRECK

1. The Southern Railway had a wreck,
   At ten o'clock one morn,
   Near Hodges and New Market grounds,
   The place and date adorn—
   The twenty-fourth of September,
   The year nineteen and four,

When that awful wreck occurred,
To both rich and poor.

Chorus
The people were in sadness then,
For they were all in fear;
As there were many on the trains,
That seemed so dear.

2. The trains were going east and west,
And speeding on their way.
They ran together on a curve,
And what a wreck that day.
The cars were burst, torn, and split,
And spread across the track.
You'll see a picture of the wreck
Just over on the back.

3. Conductor on the west bound train,
Did make a grand mistake.
He never read his orders right,
And caused the awful fate.
He hurt one hundred and a half,
And there were seventy dead.
I hope he's got forgiveness now
And lives without dread.

4. The engineer on the east bound train,
He kissed his darling wife,
Before he got on board his train,
Then he had to give his life.
I trust he was pure in heart,
And now is with the blest,
And that his wife may meet him there,
Then be with him at last.

5. They found a note he wrote,
And this is what it said,
"Please take me home and bury me."
They found his body cold in death.
And then they sent it home,
To bury him with long-gone friends,
With whom he used to roam.

6. And oh, the men and women mourns [men and
women's moans?]
Did echo through the air;
Such cries were never heard before
From humans in despair.

The little children cried aloud
For mercy to their God,
But now they all are dead and gone,
And under earthly sod.

(*Collected in Washington County, Tenn.,
by Geneva Anderson, 1932*)

A second song, collected by Emory L. Hamilton, of Wise, Virginia, is from the James Taylor Adams folklore collection, housed at Clinch Valley College, Virginia, and Ferrum College's Blue Ridge Institute at Ferrum, Virginia. It appears to have been written by an eyewitness, and is printed without a tune. Mr. Hamilton learned it from Miss Linda Ramey of Clinch Valley, Virginia. It ends with the obligatory moral tag.

NEW MARKET WRECK

One autumn morn in Tennessee,
    An awful wreck was heard,
East of Knoxville and near New Market,
    Was where the crash occurred.
The east and west bound passenger trains,
    Were running at high speed,
They struck each other on a curve,
    'Twas a terrible sight indeed.
The engine crew on the westbound train,
    Their orders had misread,
About one hundred and fifty were hurt,
    And near seventy are dead.
The passengers were riding along,
    And chatting the time away,
Reading and smoking, and laughing and talking,
    And all seemed bright and gay.

Chorus
The people were excited,
    They wept aloud and said:
My God there's a wreck on the railroad,
    And many we hear are dead.
Of how much of sadness,
    Of how many pains,
Many sad hearts are aching,
    For friends on the ill fated trains.

But in a moment the scene was changed,

To one of sad despair,
For shrieks of dying men and women
    And children filled the air.
The track was strewn with dead and dying,
    'Twas an awful sight that day,
The engine crews were buried alive,
    Without even time to pray.
A little girl with her head mashed,
    Called 'Mamma' each dying breath,
Her parents lay not far away,
    But they were still in death.
One lady, a sharp piece of wood,
    Her body had pierced through,
Her little babe lay in her arms,
    But death soon claimed it too.

A headless woman's body lay there,
    Her head was lying near.
One dying woman prayed to live,
    Just for her children dear,
Nurses and doctors soon arrived,
    From Knoxville on a train,
And they all labored very hard,
    To save life and ease pain.
People in Knoxville rushed to the depot,
    More news to ascertain,
Little could they learn till four o'clock,
    A train pulled in that day,
With seventy-one who were badly hurt,
    Six dying on the way.

Excitement was not over then,
    For people were filled with dread,
Till eight o'clock a train pulled in,
    Bearing forty-two dead.
And many who kissed their friends farewell,
    Before they went away,
Soon were brought back to them in death,
    With lips as cold as clay.
The next day was the Sabbath day,
    And many were laid to rest,
We trust they were on the Lords side,
    And now are with the blest.
And when we board a railroad train,
    Its little do we know,
That we may meet the same sad fate,
    And into eternity go.

NOTES

Information is from the Knoxville *Sentinel*, 24 Sept. 1904 and the two weeks following, and the Richmond *Times-Dispatch*, 25 Sept. 1904 and 21 Mar. 1933. Jeffrey Lanigan of the Knoxville Public Library was most helpful to me in obtaining photographs.

Billy Richardson's Last Ride

The C & O's legendary engineer Billy Richardson in his white coveralls and hat poses with his new American engine No. 70 at Huntington, after a run from Hinton in 1891 with the FFV "Vestibule Limited." Between the cab and tender a man stands on the gangway, and behind his head can be seen the poker with which clinkers were raked from the fire. The fireman leans out of the cab. *Courtesy C & O Historical Society, Alderson, W. Va.*

The fireman then said, "Billy, you know you're old and gray;
Your name is on the pension list—you should retire some day."
But Billy said: "Dear fireman, the truth I'm telling you—
I must die right in my engine cab, and nothing else will do."

William S. Richardson deserves a place in railroad wreck songs, even though his story does not actually involve a train wreck. "Uncle Billy," as he was called, is probably the most colorful character to appear in any railroad disaster song. Popular all along the C & O, he waved and whistled to everyone. He was known among his contemporaries as "a fast runner," a hogger especially good at making up lost time. He earned the nickname "Wild Bill" among his fellow railroaders by his frequent "hooking her up," which means, according to Ron Lane, "setting the reverse bar up close to the center of the quadrant after the train had been started to give the valves a short, quick steam cut off. This increased the speed of the engine."

Everyone along his run knew him. Richardson's trademark was a "foot-long beard that flew back over his shoulder in the wind as he swept past," although some writers, and two of his grand-daughters, say its length was vastly exaggerated. A photograph of him as a young man shows it considerably shorter than a foot, but still a long beard. Several recollections mention his piercing blue eyes. Cleburne Meeks, who wrote the song about his death, recalls that he "was not a tall man"; his daughters, however, say he was six feet tall or more.

Apparently he usually carried with him a copper or brass oilcan that he spent a lot of time shining up, for he is remembered by some as carrying a "gen-yew-ine gold" oiling can. Generally an oilcan was the utilitarian item it still is, soot-and-grease-grimed. All engines of the period, according to B. P. Knight, carried tall cans of oil which were kept in a rack on the tender. At the beginning of each run engineers would fill the oil reservoirs that would drip onto the piston rods and keep them lubricated for the journey, and oil the ball bearings of the driving wheels, lest they "dry out" and turn blue-hot from friction. And if the run was a particularly hard one, sometimes an engineer would even stop enroute and give a good oiling to the high driving wheels—a squirt or two on every ball bearing. Tom Dixon comments that "it was common for engineers to 'oil around' their engine at *any* extended station stops until modern engines appeared with automatic lubrication." Richardson polished up the brass on his engine also, placing high value on a fine appearance. After all, he engineered the FFV trains, the C & O's best.

It was said that on occasion, when Richardson was stepping into his cab at the beginning of a run and was feeling out of sorts, he would turn up his long-spout oiling can and drink a generous draught of the black engine oil, because, as he put it, he figured he "needed it" and knew it "would do him good."

Tales were told of Billy Richardson's fearlessness and disregard of the dangers that constantly confronted an engineer. In 1880 a heavy freight loco-

Hinton, West Virginia, passenger station, top. Behind it is the Railroad YMCA where many trainmen lived. In the far right rear of the picture is the New River Highway Bridge. The picture below is of the Hinton freight station. *Courtesy C & O Historical Society, Alderson, W. Va.*

motive was hauling thirty-five cars of merchandise across Guyandotte Bridge. Young Richardson was the engineer. He had just crossed the bridge, and the engine and one car were on solid track, when the bridge went down behind him. Letting his engine back until the one car behind was halfway over, he threw the throttle wide open and, snapping the car in two, rushed ahead to safety, leaving ten freight cars in the river.

Once, on a bad night when water poured off the mountainsides, thus increasing the danger of landslides, a fellow railroad man cautioned him about running too fast. He responded that he "had to make the time," and added that "a railroad man never knows when his end will come, and that risk is a part of the job." It was in all likelihood Engineer Billy Richardson who brought the FFV train from

At Huntington, about 1908, train No. 3 at rest. On the left is William F. Freutel, the engineer opposite Billy Richardson on the run. Richardson is readily identified by his lanky frame and white beard. The mustachioed man standing closest to the camera is Andrew Southworth, and the man on the far right is Marco Curry, signal operator. It is possible that one of the others is Cecil Lively, Billy's fireman. *Courtesy C & O Historical Society, Alderson, W. Va.*

Huntington to Hinton through the New River Gorge in the early morning of October 23, 1890, and from whom George Alley took over as engineer the morning he died. That was Richardson's regular run.

Uncle Billy was lucky. On one occasion an axle of the engine broke as he pulled No. 3 into Huntington. Had the accident occurred moments earlier with the train running at full speed, tragedy would have been inevitable.

Once, in 1908, Billy's engine plowed into a freight train at Handley, West Virginia, and overturned.

"Onlookers," according to Tom Dixon, "were astonished to see the hogger and his fireman crawl out from under the wreckage with only minor scratches. A yard goat hauled the coaches, undamaged, away from the shattered freight cars and Billy calmly continued his run, arriving at Huntington on schedule."

Several writers have noted that even after Uncle Billy had grown to be an old man "and taken on the look of a Scandinavian god," he was still allowed to handle the most important runs on the C & O, which proves the confidence his superiors had in him, and points to his expert handling of his train. There was until recently no mandatory retirement age for engineers, their ability being the only criterion for staying on the job. B. P. Knight recalls that some engineers kept at it into their eighties, even if they had to be "hoisted into the cab to drive it."

The railroads fostered a stern kind of morality. A tale is told in Lexington of a cadet at the Virginia Military Institute who was the son of the president of one of the big railroads. The cadet in his final year was accused of hazing, and the superintendent of VMI felt inclined to enforce a state law that had just been passed and have the boy tried in a civil court for the misbehavior. The boy's father happened to come to speak to the superintendent on the day after one passenger train on his line had run into the back of another. After the father explained who he was, the superintendent said, "I guess you'll really have to do something serious about that engineer, to see he never drives a train again." The railroad president said, "No, sir, he'll be back on his engine as soon as he can. He's had a clean record for 35 years, and if I can't respect that and make my judgment accordingly, what's the point of a man having a clean record?"

The VMI superintendent thought a moment and decided, this being the boy's first fall from grace in four years, to drop the charges.

Billy Richardson was born in Hanover County, Virginia, on April 29, 1848, and went to work at fourteen as a waterboy on the Virginia Central Railroad, a predecessor of the C & O. In 1878, he became a C & O engineer. Long a bachelor, at thirty-five he was wed to a widow with four daughters. He proved a devoted stepfather. One of his step-daughters recalled that he always brought them candy from Hinton, and on payday he would take the odd change left over from his pay and hand it around evenly among the girls. He also fathered three children of his own. The first was a son, George. Evidently he

The Hinton roundhouse turntable around 1875. Hostlers brought engines to and from the station. When an engine was on the turntable it was rotated until it connected with the track leading to a stall, and once in the stall the engine was worked on by machinists and pipefitters to prepare it for another run. *Courtesy C & O Historical Society, Alderson, W. Va.*

wanted more sons, for when his second and third children, both daughters, made their appearance, they were named Frank and Will! An article in the Huntington *Advertiser*, December 24, 1910, states, "His friends observed a marked change in his conduct after he became a Christian. He came out firm and strong on the Lord's side, and never wavered from his position till the day of his death."

His great friendliness was the trait that accounted for his enormous popularity along his run. There is the story of a young girl along his way who took ill and could no longer get out and wave to Uncle Billy on his daily runs. When he learned of this, Richardson made a trip to see her. It is said she recovered after that, and attributed her miraculous cure to his visit! Another story says that once, while he was attending the First Presbyterian Church in Huntington, a young girl approached and asked where he had been. He explained that he'd hurt his elbow three weeks before, at which the pretty fifteen-year-old burst into tears, saying she'd listened for his whistle ever since she was a baby. Such was his magnetism, at least with the fair sex. Ben Knight recalls that engineers and firemen in his time frequently waved at pretty women along their ways. The long-distance flirtations were harmless, and added a little spice to normally uneventful days. The trainsmen developed a side-to-side handwave that was distinctively different from the ordinary American forward-to-back-to-forward wave. This was so that, in the event that some jealous sweetheart or husband should happen to observe the signal and challenge the engineer, he would say, "Oh, I wasn't waving at your wife; I was just shaking the cinders out of my gauntlet!"

For most of his railroading life Billy Richardson pulled the FFV's, the pride of the C & O road. His regular run was westbound on No. 3 from Hinton to Huntington; his return trip was on eastbound No. 4, back into Hinton. "He was an engineer with an enviable reputation for his ability to handle the big iron horse," Paul Shue says. He was considered to be "unexcelled in the arts of easy starting, smooth stopping and handling emergency situations with wisdom and with skill," and for twenty-seven years he pulled his trains through the West Virginia mountains. It is said that people set their watches by Uncle Billy's trains; he never liked being behind schedule.

He had a habit of leaning far out of his cab window, waving and whistling to all his friends along his way. He was repeatedly warned about the danger of hanging out of his cab like that, but he claimed he liked to keep an eye on the rails ahead. With his fireman on his left, the engineer rode on the right side of the cab, handling the throttle with his left hand, thus freeing the right hand for the brake. But in winter and summer alike, Billy Richardson leaned his head out of the right side of his engine, craning his neck to see, pushing his right shoulder against

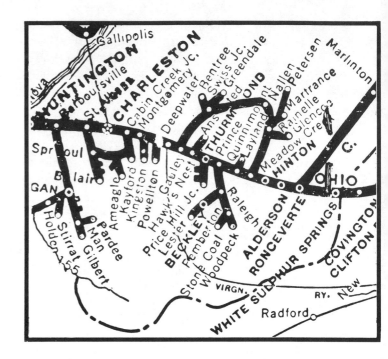

the door. It was observed that this habit wore his clothing through so that he was always threadbare on the right shoulder.

As in many good stories, it is remembered that there was an early incident that apparently foreshadowed the manner of his death. Charles Conner, writing in the Hinton *Daily Mail*, relates that Uncle Billy wore a watch fob that he valued highly and claimed saved his life. New engines were constantly being built that were more powerful, heavier, and wider than the old ones. In numerous cases, the railroads were slow to make the necessary renovations to accommodate the new locomotives. For example, the mail cranes had not been moved back to make passing them in an engine safe, especially for an engineer who loved to lean out of his cab window. In the early incident, a mail crane hit Billy's elbow and a piece of the metal snapped off, then flew inside the cab, but instead of hitting him, it deflected off his watch fob.

Billy Richardson with his family. Frank, still alive in 1982, is seated at her father's right. *Courtesy C & O Historical Society, Alderson, W. Va.*

On December 14, 1910, he was at the throttle of locomotive No. 161, an F-15 Pacific (4-6-2) built by Alco in Richmond in 1907, pulling Train No. 3, The Fast Flying Virginian. Billy Richardson had picked up No. 3 at 9:20 A.M. in Hinton. The train was headed west through the rugged New River Gorge with Uncle Billy leaning out of his cab window as usual. It was around one in the afternoon. Billy had just waved to some friends at Scary, West Virginia, a small flag stop station near St. Albans. He blew his whistle to warn some people walking on the tracks ahead. One man raised his hand to acknowledge the warning. According to Billy Richardson's daughter, Mrs. Will Woodward, her father looked down to see if either oil or water was draining as it should, and then he raised his head. At that instant, the Scary mailcrane hit Billy, crushing his left temple.

Cecil Lively, his fireman, glanced up from his work "a few moments later" and saw the engineer slumped over the cab window. At once he realized what had happened, and took over the train. He stopped long enough to carry Engineer Richardson back to the baggage car, and brought the train safely to Huntington, where an ambulance already waited, information of the accident having been telegraphed along the line from Scary. Billy's wife, visiting her family in Richmond, left at once for Hinton upon being notified of her husband's accident. Uncle Billy never regained consciousness, and died only a few minutes after reaching the C & O Hospital, about three o'clock.

There was a consensus among his friends that it was how the old man would have chosen to die. Word of his death brought "shock and heartache up

Billy Richardson's Last Ride

Through the West Vir-gin-ia moun - tains came the ear-ly morn-ing mail; Old
Num-ber 3 was west-bound, the fast-est on the rail. She
pulled right in - to Hin-ton, a junc-tion on the line, — With a
Bald-win Moun-tain en - gine, they made the run on time.

and down the tracks of the C & O," and made the front page of all the state papers the next day. His obituary in the December 15, 1910, Hinton *Independent Herald Weekly* says he was survived by six children.

Cleburne Meeks was a child of eight when Billy died; years later he wrote this song.

BILLY RICHARDSON'S LAST RIDE

Through the West Virginia mountains came the early morning mail;
Old Number 3 was westbound, the fastest on the rail.
She pulled right into Hinton, a junction on the line,
With a Baldwin Mountain engine, they made the run on time.

Billy Richardson at Hinton was called to take the run,
To pull the fastest mail train from there to Huntington.
His fireman he reported for duty on the line,
Then reading their train orders, left Hinton right on time.

Then Billy told his fireman that he would happy be
If he could die while pulling a train like Number 3.
"I want to die on duty, right in my cab," said he,
"While pulling eastbound Number 4, or westbound Number 3."

The fireman then said, "Billy, you know you're old and gray;
Your name is on the pension list—you should retire some day."
But Billy said: "Dear fireman, the truth I'm telling you—
I must die right in my engine cab, and nothing else will do."

Then pulling down New River came westbound Number 3,
By Thurmond, then by Cotton Hill, no danger could he see.
His head then struck a mail crane, while pulling down the line.
He'll never pull his train again to Huntington on time.

He's pulled the fastest freight trains, he's pulled the
U.S. mail,
He's pulled the fast excursions to the music of the rail.
He lost his life on duty, in his engine cab so free;
He'll never pull his train again on westbound Number 3.

Now, ladies, if your husband is a railroad engineer,
You know he is in danger, and death is ever near;
You know he loves you dearly when he is by your side;
Remember well that his next run may be his farewell
ride.

Oddly, in this, the only song that names the man-
ufacturer of the engine, the story has got it wrong,
though Baldwin was a good guess, as that company
made many engines for the C & O. "The early
morning mail" was a nickname for the FFV trains;
though primarily passenger trains, they carried several working mail cars, according to Ben Knight, and
three or four sealed mail cars with mail directed to
Cincinnati or west of it. Tom Dixon agrees that they
definitely did not have a "Mountain"-type engine, as
the Mountain was not developed until 1911.

The song follows Meeks's usual formula: best engineer, fastest train, foreshadowing conversation,
Billy's imagined words, "Dear fireman, the truth
I'm telling you— / I must die right in my engine cab,
and nothing else will do." It ends with the usual
warning to the effect that "in the midst of life we
find death."

When the facts of Billy Richardson's life are
known, the song contains a satisfying element of ret-
ribution. It was, of course, his refusal to heed warnings that led to his death. Thus, despite his enormous popularity as an engineer, his death restores a
balance.

NOTES

My grandfather, Captain Greenlee Davidson Letcher (1867–
1954), might have known Billy Richardson. Certainly he knew
about him, and from my early childhood I heard what a "fine gentleman" he had been, and how he died the way he would have
chosen. I was delighted, therefore, to renew acquaintance with
Billy Richardson through Ron Lane's "Billy Richardson's Last
Ride," in the *C & O Historical Society Newsletter* of July 1970.
Other sources were the Hinton *Daily News and Leader*, 14 Dec.
1910; Hinton *Independent Herald Weekly*, 15 Dec. 1910, 24 Dec.
1910, and 15 Jan. 1913 (article on the Guyandotte Bridge Disaster
which relates the earlier story of the bridge involving Richardson); the Huntington *Advertiser*, 24 Dec. 1910; Meeks's letter
from Paul Shue's private collection; and original work done by
Thomas W. Dixon, Jr., of Alderson, W. Va. James P. Austin offered
information.

I visited the home of Frank Richardson Alderson (born in 1887)
in Alderson, July 24, 1982, and spoke with her briefly, and two of
her daughters, Frances Alderson Swope and Alice Todd Alderson,
at more length. Mrs. Alderson, 95, was swathed in pink night-
clothes and pink bedclothes. She is physically helpless, as frail as
a butterfly, her long delicate bones nearly visible through her
parchment skin, but her facial structure is unmistakably like her
father's. Her daughters told me that although she might be inca-
pable of speaking clearly, her mind was sharp. "I am writing a
book about train wreck songs and I'm doing a chapter on your
father," I said. "That wasn't a wreck," she said, hardly able to get
the words out. She understood everything I said, and wanted to
know what Lyles I was kin to, and laughed easily. She was very
sad and very impressive.

Her daughters answered many questions for me. The "S" in Mr. Richardson's name didn't stand for anything. It was their grand*mother*, already the mother of four girls, who wanted sons and named their daughters Frank and Will. Their grandfather, they said, was *delighted* to have more girls. He had blue eyes and brown hair, they said. They did not know if "Uncle Billy" died at home or in the hospital. He served the C & O for 33 years, 9 months, and 13 days.

Tom Dixon, of the C & O Historical Society, explains how the mail cranes worked: "Mail cranes were, of necessity, set close to the track. When the local postal personnel attached a special mail sack with letters in it for a train which did not stop at that station, its arms were set outward . . . only a foot or two from the train as it passed by. . . . One of the clerks in the Railway Post Office car would be watching for the crane through a small windshield located at one of the RPO doors . . . and at the proper moment he raised a "catcher arm" which snared the mail bag and he could bring it then into the car. . . . At the same time he would throw or kick a bag of mail off to the waiting postal person on the ground. . . . It was quite an operation to see.

"Only when the crane was set with mail was its arms dangerously close to the train, otherwise when the mail was 'caught' the arms dropped and the main body of the crane was well back."

Information about railroad technicalities, from oil cans to mail cars, is from Ben P. Knight of Buena Vista.

In a charming article by L. T. Anderson, entitled "The Man Who Was Billy Richardson's Fireman," clipped from an unknown paper, unknown date, which Mr. Meeks gave me on July 9, 1982, Cecil Lively is described: ". . . a gentle, smallish, soft-spoken man with red hair and a ready wit. He . . . chided neighbors for any household improvement work, expressing the mock fear that his wife Maggie would be inspired to have him do the same thing." L. T. Anderson, by the way, is, according to C. C. Meeks, the son of W. H. "Sky Jack" Anderson, who was killed in 1953 when the boiler of his engine, 1642, exploded (see page 167).

The Hamlet Wreck

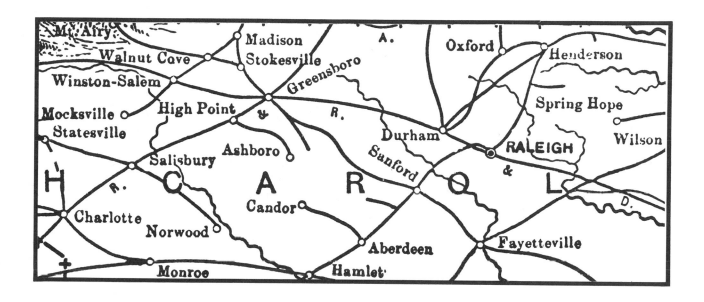

Isn't it sad? Isn't it sad?
So many have lost their lives.

On the clear hot morning of Thursday, July 27, 1911, a Seaboard Air Lines dispatcher sent an order advising an eastbound freight train that all overdue passenger trains had arrived in Hamlet, North Carolina. Because there was a steep grade on a long curve there, the freight was relieved from stopping to check the train register in Hamlet, sixty miles east of Charlotte. But the dispatcher had forgotten that there was coming through that morning a special train, Second No. 33, carrying 912 black passengers from Durham to Charlotte for a day's excursion. The occasion was the annual outing of the St. Joseph's African Methodist Episcopal Sunday School. Many of the travelers had never before been so far from home. They had left Durham at 7:15. At 10:40 A.M., this special train crashed headlong into the slowly-moving freight in the Hamlet yards, right in front of the roundhouse.

After the first crash, the screams and groans of the injured began to rise. The two engines were, according to the Charlotte *Daily Observer* of July 28, "beside the track locked fast to each other in a grasp of death." Henry Fetner, ninety-one, of Hamlet, was the baggage-master and flagman on the excursion train. He recalled, in August 1982, "I had gone through the train from head to rear just a few min-

The two engines "beside the track locked fast to each other in a grasp of death." So great was the impact that the telescoping of the engines did not stop until the pistons were resting against each other. *Courtesy F. N. Brubaker and the National Railroad Museum and Hall of Fame.*

utes before. There was seven wooden coaches, jam-crowded. The coaches were built to hold fifty people, would maybe hold 100 if a lot stood up." These seven coaches held 912 human beings. Mr. Fetner continued, "The train stopped suddenly. I was standing on the rear platform. Suddenly, black people began to get off the train, going around me. I told them to 'hold on, we'll pull down [pull out] in a minute.' And they said, 'No white folks on this train. They's a mess down front. Won't be no pulling down.' So I stepped down, the train was on a curve, and I could see the two engines head-on, jammed tight. I went to try to find the conductor—he's in charge of the train—some people were standing around. I said, 'What happened to the fireman?' and they said, 'He jumped and took off running.'

"Then I came down the right side of the train and back on the left. I'd just been talking to four black preachers. I looked down and there was one of those preacher's heads on the ground. Ten killed in all, nearly 100 injured. When I found the conductor, he was in the washroom, you know, cleaning up a cut. Not a bad injury, he didn't have to go to the hospital, you know."

Fetner confirms that only one man was decapitated, though another local source assured me that six or seven were, that they'd all been riding "with their heads out the window." Fetner further remembered that the fireman on the freight train was killed in a later accident, along with the engineer, "over at Lilesville."

A hackman, Will Malone, of Durham, was seated in the fourth or fifth car talking to two women when he heard a crash. "It seemed like the cars were coming down"; the next thing he knew he was pinned tight by a beam and his two female companions

Injured passengers rest in the shade of a small shed following the Hamlet Wreck, the men in their Sunday-go-to-meeting suits, the women in their white summer dresses.

Courtesy Carolina Archives and the Durham County Public Library.

were dead. Tim Waldon, in much the same plight, worried that the car might catch fire before he could be rescued. Both were freed after about a half hour.

The crash called the whole town to the scene, where they witnessed "great carnage in the fourth and fifth cars. . . . Samuel Miller was asleep with his head in the window. The telescoping wall clipped off his head and it rolled clear of the wreck." Where the fourth and fifth cars jammed together, people were packed four deep, "the lifeblood of those on top dripping upon the wounded below." Hats, shoes, and torn bloody garments were scattered on the ground.

Rescuers cut away the sides of the cars to free those still alive, who were then laid on the ground under the repair shed, where doctors and nurses from nearby Rockingham, Laurinburg, and Aberdeen ministered to them. Sixty people were seriously injured, eight had been killed outright, and both engineers and firemen were seriously injured. Six of the

seven coaches of the excursion train "crumpled like pasteboard," and the engines "looked like one and the same mass of iron."

It was the second such wreck; almost exactly five years before, on July 22, less than a mile away, there was another head-on collision on the SAL, and for exactly the same reason: the dispatcher in that case forgot to give any orders about an approaching excursion train. That time, in 1906, 26 passengers, all of them black, died.

After the second wreck, the Raleigh *News & Observer* of July 29, 1911, noted a "soberness among railroad men not natural to that lighthearted class." One prominent engineer, his name unmentioned, commented that "the whole world is going too fast." Another railroad employee opined that the frail construction of the cars was to blame. "The public and management want too much speed," the account declared. The Seaboard sent representatives at once to settle with survivors of the dead and the injured. The Raleigh *News & Observer* "understood" that the amounts ranged from a dollar to a thousand. In the next days, two more died.

North Carolina folklorist Frank C. Brown collected this version of the lyrics.

THE HAMLET WRECK

1. See the women and children going to the train.
   Fare-you-well, my husband, if I never see you again.
   The engineer turned his head
   When he saw so many were dead.
   So many have lost their lives.

   Chorus
   Isn't it sad, isn't it sad?
   Excursion left Durham, going to Charlotte, North
     Carolina.
   Isn't it sad, isn't it sad?
   So many have lost their lives.

2. Some of us have mothers standing at the train.
   'Farewell-well-well, my daughter, I may never see you
     again.'
   And the train began to fly,
   And some didn't come back alive.
   So many have lost their lives.

3. The fireman said to the engineer, 'We are something
     late;
   We don't want to meet up with the local freight.'
   The local was on the line,
   And they could not get there on time.
   So many have lost their lives.

4. When the news got to Durham, some said it was a lie,
   But some was in the hospital almost ready to die.
   And their poor old mothers, you know,
   They were running from door to door.

The Hamlet Wreck

This tune is from the sound track of "Folk Music of the Rails," a slide show made in Hamlet, North Carolina. The song, according to the script, "seems to have originated in the Durham tobacco factories."

WHOLE WORLD'S GOING TOO FAST

An Engineer's Expression
Directed at Fatal Wreck
at Hamlet Thursday

TWO MORE VICTIMS DEAD

Wrecking Crew at Hamlet Cleared Up
Debris Yesterday—Railroad Men
Say Public Demands Too Great
Speed—Force of Collision Crushed
Both Boiler-Heads of Locomotive—
Oscar Ford and Joe Warren Died,
Making Total Number of Fatalities

So many have lost their lives.

5. Now, colored people, I will tell you to your face,
   The train that left Durham was loaded with our race,
   And some did not think of dying
   When they rode on down the line.
   So many have lost their lives.

6. They put the dead in their coffins and sent them back
       to town,
   And then they were taken to the burying ground.
   You could hear the coffin sound
   When they let those bodies down
   So many have lost their lives.

Although one would not wish to make too much
of this, this particular song is unlike most other
wreck songs in several ways. First, it incorporates in-
cremental repetition (of the last line of each stanza),
a characteristic of Afro-American music. Second, it
has a chorus, which most wreck songs do not have
but most spirituals do. Third, the imagery is typical of black poetry: it is visual, almost palpable:
"You could hear the coffin sound . . . ," "And their
poor old mothers . . . were running from door to
door. . . ." In short, "The Hamlet Wreck" is more
like black American music than white, and the only
"black" wreck song we have.

NOTES

The Raleigh *News & Observer*, 28 July through 2 Aug. 1911;
Richmond *Times Dispatch*, 28 July 1911; Charlotte *Daily Observer*, 29 July 1911. My thanks to Louis Rubin for ferreting out
information on this wreck, to Anne Berkeley of the Durham Public Library, to Eliza Ford and Lin Carrington for help in obtaining
pictures, to Harry Fetner for his story, and to Dan Bennett of the
Hamlet National Railroad Museum and Hall of Fame, for sending
a picture.

The Guyandotte Bridge Disaster

The 1885 wreck at the Guyandotte Bridge, showing one car upside down and another plunged sideways off the trestle. *Courtesy C & O Historical Society, Alderson, W. Va.*

Ed sat in his cab window so peaceful and so fair;
He did not know that on the bridge that death awaited
  him there.
Fireman Cook walked across the bridge and stopped on
  the other side;
He did not know that Webber was taking his last ride.

Robert Reed, in *Train Wreck*, writes that bridge collapses were all too common on the railroads. In 1887 alone there were twenty-one. The railroads, he explains, were more devoted to economy than safety.

The Guyandotte Bridge in West Virginia did not have a particularly sterling record. In 1880 a train had wrecked on the east span of the bridge. In 1889

an engine had gone through the bridge, carrying its engineer, Chesley Freeman, to his death. As early as September 1, 1909, the Hinton *Independent-Herald* announced that the C & O would reconstruct the Guyandotte Railroad Bridge at the east end of Huntington. The piers, which showed signs of deterioration, would be taken down to a point below the defect and replaced with concrete. The abutments also were to be remodelled, and a modern double bridge built to take the place of the then-existing triple-span structure. In 1910 the C & O had taken over the CC & L, giving the C & O a line from Cincinnati to Chicago; and the Kanawha and Michigan &

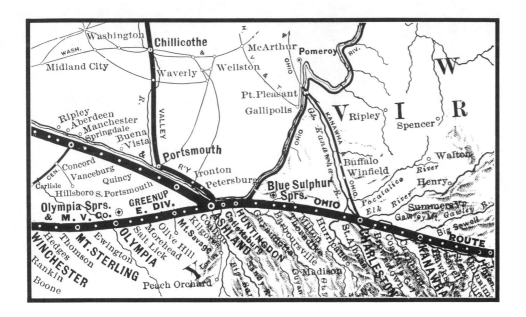

Hocking Valley lines, which gave the C & O direct access through Toledo to the Great Lakes trade. All this meant that increasingly heavy burdens were placed on the C & O.

On January 1, 1913, the Guyandotte River, also locally called the Guyan, was swollen from heavy rains, and the current was swift. "Guyandotte" is an Indian name, meaning "narrow bottom," according to William Anderson. In fact, there had been extremely mild weather and high water all winter, leading up to the famous 1913 flood that would inundate towns all along the Ohio and all through West Virginia that spring. That New Year's Day, the Guyandotte Bridge was taxed beyond its strength, and collapsed.

It was being double-tracked at the time of the disaster. In previous years the coal business from the Logan and Coal River fields had boomed, and C & O traffic had increased to such an extent that this bridge was an annoying bottleneck, since the main line on either side of the bridge was already double-tracked. Furthermore, the new K-1 Mikado (2-8-2) engines and the huge H-2 Mallets (2-6-6-2) were much heavier than the older G-7 and G-9 Consolidations (2-8-0), providing yet another reason to refurbish an old bridge which had been built for the lighter locomotives. Finally, Mikados had all their weight concentrated on fewer axles than Mallets, which made them "heavier."

Overnight the river had risen considerably, and

Courtesy Robert Chapman.

Rufus H. Meadows, the C & O bridge foreman, had already that day voiced his opinion that the bridge was not strong enough for Mallets and Mikes. Some workers were hesitant to go to work on the bridge that morning. But fifteen trains had already crossed the bridge since daylight, allaying their fears. False-work had been placed under the bridge while the repairs were being made, and those in charge believed the bridge was safe for trains.

At about 10:30 the second section of train No. 99 arrived at the bridge, and stopped short of it. The crew was notified of the overnight rise in the water and the possible danger. Engineer C. B. "Shorty" Webber checked, then decided the bridge was safe for his large Mikado engine, No. 820. Built in Rich-

mond in June, 1912, the largest 2-8-2 then in service on any U.S. railroad, it weighed nearly half a million pounds. His fireman and brakeman disagreed, and refused to ride the big engine across, walking ahead while engineer and train waited for a truckload of lumber to be unloaded. Some of the thirty or so iron-workers on the bridge, aware of the weakness, left their posts to let the freight go by, but others, according to the Huntington *Observer,* "laughed at the possible dangers and were carried down with the wreckage when the bridge collapsed under the weight of the train." Brad M. Parent, an electrician, said later that he warned Shorty Webber of the danger. When the engineer insisted on crossing the bridge, so certain was Parent of the potential for disaster that he went to a place where "I could watch the train crash."

Guyandotte Bridge was 152 feet long, each span roughly fifty feet. It was fifty-two to fifty-five feet above water level. At 10:40, Webber took his engine, No. 820, onto the bridge. He was quoted later as having said, "I'll ride this baby across anyway." We can imagine the workmen milling nearby, or watching, tense but ambivalent. They knew trains had been crossing all morning; the chances were good that this one would make it, too, even though she was heavier by several thousand pounds than any other train that had passed over that day.

Just as the locomotive reached the center span, the bridge gave way without warning. The engine went down backward and the tender buckled over it. Engineer Webber was pinned between engine and tender. According to the Hinton *Daily News* of that day, "Men were caught like rats in a trap and hurled into the turbulent stream." The big Mikado dropped fifty-five feet and all but disappeared beneath the murky water, amid falling timbers and bodies and distorted metal, carrying with it a gondola and a boxcar.

Several men reappeared and struggled to safety on land, clinging to timbers, calling for help, and receiving it from bystanders, some of whom went into the water to save their fellow workers. But eight men, including Engineer Webber, never surfaced.

Two thousand people were on the bank within an hour. By the next day the engine had sunk entirely below the surface. Foreman Meadows and Foreman Brightwell, who had between them nearly forty men on the bridge, were reported as "prostrated by the loss." "The bridge," Meadows mourned, "had been known for *weeks* as dangerous."

The story made the front page of local and state papers every day for almost two weeks, as rescue workers tried vainly to recover bodies.

Rail traffic was tied up for ten days. Professional divers came all the way from New York, Norfolk, and Cincinnati when local divers failed to recover any of the bodies. C & O President George W. Stevens visited the disaster site. So did an estimated seventy-five thousand others, undismayed by constant rain and freezing dismal weather. Rumors spread that the bridge was cursed, a "hoodoo" bridge, which brought the curious public in droves.

A C & O work train on the Guyandotte Bridge at Huntington soon after the collapse of the middle span. *From the Edgar Billups collection. Courtesy C & O Historical Society, Alderson, W. Va.*

A few of the estimated 75,000 people who visited the scene of Ed Webber's fatal plunge into the Guyan River. *Courtesy Robert Chapman.*

Divers search the murky waters for bodies, while onlookers line both shores. Freezing rain did not deter visitors during the days after the third collapse of the "hoodoo" bridge, causing the deaths of seven men. *Courtesy Aldine Womack.*

Engine Crashing Through Bridge

On January 4, the C & O saw the prudence of issuing a local news release to the effect that, on its Clifton Forge Division, 207 miles long, not a passenger had been killed since 1891—twenty-two years! Its irrelevance probably didn't allay many anxieties, since the Guyandotte Bridge was on the Huntington Division.

On January 6, at noon, the body of Webber was finally brought out of the murky water, nearly cut in half but in a state of good preservation. The Hinton newspaper reported that as the body lay in the morgue of the Johnston Undertaking Company, hundreds passed by, and gazed at the face, which had a smile on the lips. There were two "light cuts" above the right eye, but the visage was otherwise unmarred. Webber's left arm was broken above the wrist, which had been frozen on the throttle. The tragedy was heightened by the fact that he left behind a widow and eight children. (One account says nine.) Only a couple of the other bodies were ever recovered, with one possible exception. On January 10, a floating body was recovered from the Ohio River at Cattlettsburg, Kentucky, fifty miles to the west. It was thought to be one of the lost crewmen, but by the time someone from Guyandotte arrived to claim it, it was too disintegrated for positive identification, and was generally believed to have been in the water longer than the elapsed ten days.

Even though one hundred men were put to work night and day to repair the trestle, the downed bridge affected power in the entire Ohio Valley for the rest of the winter. The B & O handled passengers from Guyandotte to Huntington, but the bottleneck caused by the collapsed bridge was so severe that Island Creek Coal Company notified its customers as

SEVEN BODIES ARE IN GUYAN RIVER

While Hundred Men Toil Day and Night to Clear Away Wreckage

DIVERS FAIL TO FIND MEN WHO WERE KILLED

Curious Watchers Gather Around Bonfires Near the "Hoodoo" Bridge.

far away as Cincinnati to "use coal stingily" as it would be short for many months.

It was weeks before the 820 was pulled from the river. Another fireman, J. A. Coulter, recalls seeing it at the shops afterwards. "'She was a sorry sight, nothing left but the boiler on wheels and mud all over.' She was later rebuilt and used for many years." The engine subsequently saw many years of service as No. 1120, and was scrapped around 1950.

The poem below may have had music, for it appears in several folksong collections (though each time without music). Combs mentions that it is

Carries Seven Men to Death;

THINK HIGH WATER WEAKENED PIERS CAUSING BREAK

New Year's Day of 1913 Brings Sudden Tragedy to Huntington

DUPLICATES WRECK OF TWENTY YEARS AGO

Fast Freight Plunged Into Guyan River, Killing Seven, Injuring Others

THREE DIVERS TO HELP IN SEARCH OF GUYAN RIVER

Work of Recovering Bodies is Hampered by Muddy Water

HUNDRED MEN LABOR TO RESTORE BRIDGE

Divers Declare Engine Is Buried Deep In Mud Under River

At 3:30 o'clock this morning it was reported from the scene that three of the bodies had been located by the divers. The bodies have not been identified.

similar in tune to the song about George Alley. Since they sometimes share a title, "The Wreck on the C & O," there may have been some confusion. Gardner and Chickering, Michigan collectors, call it "The Seno Wreck"—and refer to the Seno Bridge, a likely mistake to someone from outside the area. Although it is firmly in the same tradition as the others, this song seems somehow more consciously artistic, and therefore perhaps more awkward. It seems likely, though, that it was written on the spot, or soon thereafter, by someone intimate with the details of the tragedy. Though Meadow's name is misspelled, the other details are essentially accurate. It is interesting that even though the disaster was multiple, the focus is on the single death of the engineer.

THE GUYANDOTTE BRIDGE DISASTER

It was New Year's morning, Nineteen hundred and
  thirteen,
Engine eight-hundred and twenty went down with fire
  and steam.
It was on this sad morning at about eleven o'clock,
The C. & O. bridge at Guyandotte began to tremble and
  rock.

When the train reached Guyandotte the engineer was
  there,
Ed Webber was his name; he had dark and wavy hair.
  He pulled his engine to the bridge, but the flagman he
  was there.

He held out the red as if to say, "You may cross here if
  you dare."

Ed sat in his cab window so peaceful and so fair;
He did not know that on the bridge that death awaited
  him there.
  Fireman Cook walked across the bridge and stopped on
  the other side;
He did not know that Webber was taking his last ride.

Rufe Medders was the bridge foreman, a kind, good-
  hearted man.
He stood there giving orders and signals with his hands.
  His crew was working on the bridge, but this I think
  you know;
A-working for their families and for the C. & O.

Brakeman Williams gave the signal and the engine
  started on,
But when she hit the trestle, he knew that Webber was
  gone.
  The bridge rocked for a moment, and then went
  tumbling down;

A temporary track was constructed alongside the river to get Engine 820 out. The engine handling the cranes can be seen on the left. It took three cranes to pull the heavy Mike out of the Guyan. *Library of Congress.*

They heard the engine crash below with a sad and
  mournful sound.

Conductor Love looked across the bridge, then turned
  and bowed his head;
He knew that faithful Webber was numbered with the
  dead.
  Thirteen men were on the bridge, and when the bridge
  went down,
Six of them were rescued, while seven of them were
  drowned.

Ed Webber was the engineer, a brave and faithful man;
He went down with his engine, with the throttle in his
hand.
His body was recovered and placed beneath the sod;
We trust that he is resting with our Savior and our God.

Ed Webber left a loving wife and eight little children
dear;
May God protect and comfort them while they remain
down here.
Were those men religious? This I do not know;
But when our Savior calls us, we surely have to go.

God bless their families, their dear old mothers, too;
God bless their brothers and sisters, as they journey
onward through.
Now all of us that see this song, be good and be true,
For God has said in his own words, that death will visit
you.

NOTES

Information for this chapter came mainly from the following sources: *Hinton Daily News*, 1–15 Jan. 1913; Richmond *Times-Dispatch*, 1, 2, 10 Jan. 1913; Huntington *Advertiser*, 1–10 Jan. 1913; "Folkmusic of the C & O—Part 2," *C & O Historical Society Newsletter*, Dec. 1969, by Ron Lane; J. A. Coulter, *C & O Historical Society Newsletter*, Sept. 1969. Also I spoke with Ben P. Knight, of Buena Vista, Virginia, retired C & O official. Corollary works were *Native American Balladry* by Laws; *From Mine to Market* by Joseph Lambie; *Train Wrecks* by Robert Reed. Tom Dixon of the C & O Historical Society provided vital information about the engines. My thanks also to Aldine Womack and Robert Worrell, who sent photos.

On July 9, 1982, Robert Chapman of Huntington took Maureen Worth and me to photograph the bridge as it is today. It seemed surprisingly small, dwarfed by the trees that now crowd the banks, thirty or forty feet tall. The slow green river beneath us seemed hardly more than a creek that hot midsummer afternoon. It is difficult to find a spot on either side of the river from which to photograph the bridge. The metal end posts are dated 1912, presumably the beginning of the reconstruction. The bridge is old now and the timbered floor of it blackened. A C & O freight train crossed as we watched, the stringers yielding under the weight of every car. When we later walked across the bridge on the timbers between the double tracks, we came upon some contemporary prophet's two warnings, scrawled in yellow chalk: "crack," one of them said, and "loose knee brace," said the other, with an accusing arrow showing where.

Still in service on the C & O, the Guyandotte Bridge remains under periodic observation in order to avert another disaster such as that of 1913, as evidenced by the yellow chalk markings on the ironwork reading "crack" and "loose knee brace." *Photo by Katie Lyle.*

Mrs. Ada Anderson and her son William R. Anderson, of Huntington, also sent me information in October 1982. Mrs. Anderson, then Ada Legge, was not quite eleven when the collapse occurred. Her parents ran a rooming house near the bridge, and she had gone to the bridge to carry lunch to her father, Tom Legge, who ran the water tower, when the collapse came. She recalls that the bridge "slowly went down, just like it melted." She sang me the song, to a tune very similar to that of the "Titanic," which may have been popular at the time, the Titanic having sunk only a year prior to the bridge collapse. Possibly, too, both songs derived from a common source.

The Wreck of C & O No. 5

Engine 137, built in 1919 to U.S. Railway Administration standards. The *U.S.* on the side dates from the nationalization of the railroads during World War I. *Courtesy the Smithsonian Institution.*

Until the brakes are set on time, life's throttle valve shut
down,
Some day he'll pilot in the crew that wears the Master's
crown,
With a clear block in to Heaven's gate he'll pull his
mighty train,
And there in God's own roundhouse he will register his
name.

Engine 137 was the pride of the C & O, considered virtually indestructible. But no locomotive can survive a broken rail at high speed. She was a USRA class J-2, a 4-8-2 Mountain-type engine built by Bald-

win in June 1919. She pulled a passenger train westward, running from Washington to Cincinnati.

The train left Washington on time on October 5, 1920. She came south to Charlottesville, then turned west through the Blue Ridge Tunnel at Afton, Virginia, and through the Shenandoah Valley and into Staunton, then on southwest to Clifton Forge.

Engineer R. D. "Dolly" Womack and his fireman, Charles T. Poteet, were called to run Engine No. 183 at Hinton, West Virginia, at three o'clock that day. Engine 183 pulled express train No. 5 eastward to Clifton Forge, arriving there around 6:15

P.M. Womack and Poteet were relieved then until nine o'clock when they were called for westbound train No. 5. According to the official register they left Hinton on schedule, and arrived at the next stop, White Sulphur Springs, on time. There they were ordered over onto the eastbound track, to run against the current of traffic to Ronceverte. A freight on the westbound line near Whitcomb, West Virginia, had a derailed car, and so a Ronceverte tool car and work force had been called out that night at ten to put the car back on the tracks. It was this minor incident that cost the lives of Engineer Womack and a railway postal clerk, Charles H. Gulley, who was working on the train.

The switchover to the eastbound track cost them several minutes, and Dolly Womack, checking his watch as they rolled out of White Sulphur Springs at 10:27, was heard to say, "We are four minutes late." The train carried some two hundred passengers into the night, bound for Charleston, Huntington, and points farther west. It was under the care of one of the C & O's most esteemed engineers. He had been in its service twenty-five years.

The 1920 timetable scheduled No. 5 into Ronceverte at 10:35 and Hinton at midnight. The wreck occurred three miles west of White Sulphur Springs and 2.3 miles before Ronceverte, but the train was running some minutes late, so the time of the wreck was never precisely determined. Perhaps she was running fast, though the estimated speed at the time of the accident was thirty miles per hour. Close to the switchpoint, there was a broken rail on the eastbound track. No. 5 hit it, bumped a short distance along the track, then the engine hurtled off the tracks into a shallow ravine and buried itself in dirt and foliage up to the boiler. The railway post office car carrying Charlie Gulley struck the cab and back frame of the engine and tender broadside, and its steel structure was broken at the center of the car. A combination car and two daycoaches left the tracks

THE GREAT JERRYS RUN FILL IN THE ALLEGHANIES.

Courtesy Thomas W. Dixon, Jr.

Engine No. 137 being rerailed after the wreck of the C & O No. 5, 3.1 miles west of White Sulphur Springs, West Virginia, on October 5, 1920, in which engineer Dolly Womack and mail clerk Charlie Gulley lost their lives. *From E. M. Whanger photo collection. Courtesy Paul Shue.*

but remained upright. The fireman, Charlie Poteet, jumped out of the engine and saved his life.

Dolly Womack, like the good engineer that he was, stuck to his post. On the impact the coal tender telescoped into the engine cab and filled it with tons of coal, trapping the fifty-two-year-old engineer by the legs so he had no way to escape when a steam pipe broke. Rescue workers found him hanging out of the cab with scalding steam pouring over him from a broken boiler gauge pipe. Rescuers threw sacks of mail into the cab to protect Womack from the boiling water and steam, but it was too late. The Hinton *Daily News* of October 6, 1920, reported that even though fatally wounded, Engineer Womack attempted to talk but was largely unintelligible. They thought he said, "My feet are caught." Those who rushed to him were powerless in their efforts and he died in about twenty minutes. "Charlie Gulley was

caught just at the point where the mail car was broken, and mortally wounded." He also was conscious and directed rescue efforts, but "death soon ended his suffering." Charlie Poteet, the fireman, had only a small scratch on the back of one hand. Most of the two hundred passengers aboard were in the five sleeping cars. The sleepers remained on the track and were not damaged. No one else was seriously hurt, though thirteen passengers and crew members were treated for minor injuries. According to the news story, the track was torn up for fifty yards, but there was only a four-hour delay in the run.

In 1948, Tom Bryan, the foreman of the tool train that went to the rescue, recalled some of the details of the wreck for Pick Temple, who was taking a sentimental journey on the C & O from Washington, D.C., to Austin, Texas. Womack had been an Elk and a Mason. It happened that, at the time of the acci-

The railway mail car in which Charles T. Gulley of Staunton, Virginia, died. He was unfortunate enough to be caught at the very point where the car buckled. *From the E. M. Whanger photo collection. Courtesy Paul Shue.*

dent, the Hinton Elks were convening at the White Sulphur Springs Hotel. When they heard about the wreck, they all went by car in an effort to help. It was Elks who lifted the body of their lodge brother from the wreckage when the tons of coal had been cleared away. For his funeral, a special train brought Elks and Masons to Hinton from all over, and both groups sent special wreaths to the funeral.

Womack's obituary in the Hinton *Independent Herald Weekly* ended: "He went about life's duties in a quiet pleasant way that won him the respect of people, and his sad death was a great blow. He left a wife, 2 sons, Robert and George, and 5 daughters, two married and 3 unmarried."

Charlie Gulley was taken back to Staunton for burial. Engine No. 137 was refurbished and later (1924) renumbered 547.

Paul Shue treasures a letter he owns, given him by C. C. Meeks. The letter is dated February 23, 1927: "Dear Mr. Meeks," it begins, "Robby informs me that he sent you contract last night on C & O. We have two wreck songs ahead of yours, so it will not be worked on immediately altho it is booked for Columbia for next week. Robby has put a nice tune to it, and I like it very much, as I think of it. I wish you'd make a point of getting this Poteet to give you permission to use his name, and send it along to us. As I understand it, *he is very much alive,* and that permission is necessary. . . ."

The letter goes on to discuss another song, "The Three Drowned Sisters," and ends: "If the above is consistent with your idea please advise us. Very respy Yours, Vernon Dalhart." "Robby" is Carson Robison. The song follows.

From Washington to Charlottesville, then Staunton on
the line,
Came the old *Midwestern Limited*, train Number Five on
time.
She was a Cincinnati train, the fastest on the line,
Through the valley of Virginia into Clifton Forge on
time.

The engineer at Clifton Forge, Dolly Womack was his
name,
Was there to sign the register and pull the speeding train.
His fireman, Charley Poteet, was standing by his side,
And receiving their train orders they climbed in the cab
to ride.

Then Dolly to his fireman said, "Oh Charley, well you
know,
For years I've been an engineer to ride the C and O.
For many years I've had this run, just twenty-five in all,
And when I blow for Covington they will surely know
my call."

From Covington to Jerry's Run, old Number Five did roll,
Through the Allegheny Tunnel with a crew so brave and
bold.
Then westward to the mountain state, White Sulphur
Springs on time.
With orders to switch over there and take the east main
line.

"I know my engine is all right, she's the U.S. Mountain
kind,
One hundred thirty-seven she will put us there on time."
Said Dolly to his fireman, "We are running way behind,
But when I pull the Big Bend Tunnel I mean to be on
time."

Just four miles farther down the line he hit a broken rail,
No more to pull old Number Five, no more to pull the
mail.
The engine did not overturn but a steam pipe broke in
two,
Two hundred pounds of pressure killed poor Dolly brave
and true.

Until the brakes are set on time, life's throttle valve shut
down,
Some day he'll pilot in the crew that wears the Master's
crown.
With a clear block in to Heaven's gate he'll pull his
mighty train,
And there in God's own roundhouse he will register his
name.

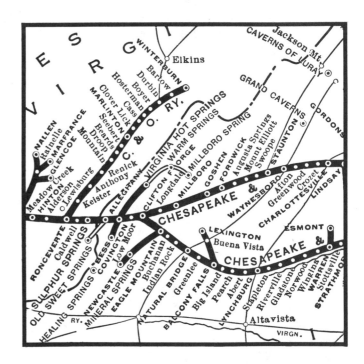

Engineer Womack Killed

The Wreck of the C&O No. 5

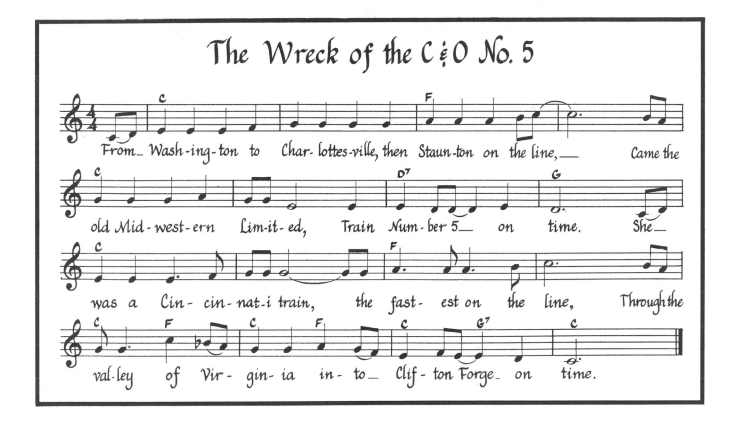

From Wash-ing-ton to Char-lottes-ville, then Staun-ton on the line,— Came the old Mid-west-ern Lim-it-ed, Train Num-ber 5 on time. She— was a Cin-cin-nat-i train, the fast-est on the line, Through the val-ley of Vir-gin-ia in-to— Clif-ton Forge— on time.

This is another account of a wreck occurring when an engineer tried to make up lost time, though in all probability Womack was not speeding, and the broken rail would have wrecked the train anyway. Gulley's death is not mentioned in the song. Laws comments that "the ballad with a single victim or hero has a much better chance of popularity than one in which many are killed. Mass tragedies can be looked upon with some detachment, but the death of an individual whose character has been delineated is far more moving and meaningful."

Why is this? The era of the twenties was full of single heroes like Lindbergh, conqueror of the skies; William Jennings Bryan, the King Arthur of the decade, fighting to preserve Christianity against the barbarians in the Scopes Trial; and Floyd Collins, a hill-

In White Sulphur Wreck

C. C. Meeks, in 1935, filling an engine's water tank, a part of his job as a hostler for the N & W. The head of the engine he is tending is out of the picture to the right. The engine on the left is waiting in line to be tended. *Courtesy C. C. Meeks.*

billy trapped in a cave and unable to be saved, whose situation commanded national attention for weeks, proving the concern of Americans for each other, but also showing man's helplessness against the greater forces of nature. John Henry, America's greatest indigenous folk hero, was raised to popularity at this time also, along with Casey Jones. The deaths of the men in the railroad disasters capture the imagination in much the same way. At this time, the American character was still forming: the American epiphany seems to have been the realization of our singular impotence and our combined strength.

Though Meeks's song is selective, it is fairly accurate. From Meeks's recollection to Shue (see notes), it is clear that he was interested in the truth. Of course, he was himself a trainman, a hostler on the N & W. Unfortunately, we have no record whether Poteet, the only occupant of the engine besides Womack, remembered Dolly's recalling his twenty-five years with the C & O, or if this detail was invented. Meeks, claiming to record his last words, ignored the reported fact that Dolly directed his own rescue effort. Note that the lyrics of the "N & W Cannonball Wreck" and "Billy Richardson's Last Ride" are cut out of the same pattern, and even have some similar phrases.

Robert D. "Dolly" Womack and his wife standing on the right side of the porch of their boarding house in Hinton, 1891, right by the post. *From the E. M. Whanger photo collection. Courtesy Paul Shue.*

The final stanza may bear some explication: if the brakes are not *set* on time, the train does not stop. Only in Heaven are the brakes *always* set on time. The throttle controls the throttle valve, which, when opened, powers the locomotive. When the valve is shut down, the engine stops. Only in death would "life's throttle valve shut down." The engineer will, after death, pilot in the heavenly crew. A block is a section of track, usually five miles. A block signal conferred the right to pass from one block to the next, or made the train stop, or warned an engineer to be cautious. A clear block meant the assurance that the track was clear and safe. And so in this song the engineer is transformed to another plane, a heaven in which he will carry on his chosen profession in eternal bliss and perfect safety. The poetic imagery of that last stanza is striking.

NOTES

The October 6, 1920, Hinton *Daily News* carried the wreck story. The October 7, 1920, Hinton *Daily News* states that No. 5 wrecked "last night," and C. C. Meeks gave the wreck date as October 6. But the C & O Press Relations Division in a letter to Paul Shue dated July 18, 1952, averred that the wreck "was based in fact and occurred October 5." Further information on the wreck came from the Staunton *Newsleader*, 1 Apr. 1970; "A

Folksinger Rides the C & O," Part 3, 1-2 May 1975, by Pick Temple and Ron Lane; The Washington *Post*, 6 Feb. 1925; and a letter from Cleburne Meeks to Paul Shue, undated. Charlie Poteet continued working for the C & O. He committed suicide years later. Norm Cohen mentions a recollection of an old railroad song called "The Death of Billy Waumack." In the absence of a text, I would guess it is a version of this wreck song.

A curious note on the final stanza of this song comes from my good proofreader Pick Temple: he heard from his friend Ben Botkin, the famous folklorist and formerly the curator of the Library of Congress Archive of American Folk Song, that the wording of this stanza appears almost verbatim on a tombstone in a cemetery in or near Richmond, Virginia, and predates the song by some years. This might well explain why this stanza exceeds the others in grace and imagery. Pick Temple called my attention to the discrepancy between the previous verses and the final one. To quote Pick, "As Thomas Gray said, perhaps 'some mute inglorious Milton' wrote it!" In an interview with Mr. Meeks on July 9, 1982, I inquired about whether he might have found that verse elsewhere. He said it was his own original composition. Later, leafing through Lance Phillips' *Yonder Comes the Train*, I came upon a photograph, and the caption: "In old Hollywood Cemetery, Richmond, Virginia, this shaft was erected to the memory of 32-year-old James E. Valentine, who died at the throttle of his 4-4-0 wood-burner on December 20, 1874, in a wreck on the New Orleans, St. Louis & Chicago (long since a part of Illinois Central). Exposed to the elements for [a century], parts of the inscription are just barely legible:

> Until the brakes are turned on time,
>   Life's throttle valve shut down,
> He wakes to pilot in the crew
>   That wears the martyr's crown.
> On schedule time on upper grade
>   Along the homeward section,
> He lands his train at God's roundhouse
>   The morn of resurrection.
> His time all full, no wages docked,
>   His name on God's payroll,
> And transportation through to Heaven
>   A free pass for his soul."

Valentine's obituary in the Richmond *Dispatch*, Dec. 1874, confirms the above, except that it names the Mississippi Central railroad.

"The Wreck of the C & O No. 5" mentions the most famous of all C & O tunnels, The Big Bend. I was puzzled to find engraved over the old arch of Big Bend "Great Bend Tunnel." I asked Ron Lane about this. His reply, as always, was thorough: an 1872 C & O map, an 1886 C & O map, and a 1912 USGS map, all call it Big Bend. "Thus," in Ron Lane's words, "the question is . . . not why the songs didn't refer to Great Bend, but why the C & O *named* it Great Bend."

Tom Dixon, of the C & O Historical Society, adds two interesting notes to this chapter: "The Allegheny subdivision, one of the busiest on the C & O, began to be double tracked about 1900, and by about 1910 was double tracked the entire 80 miles between Hinton and Clifton Forge. At convenient intervals crossovers allowed trains to cross from one track to another as might be needed. In the early days there was indeed a 'current of traffic' in that eastbound trains ran on one track and westbounds on the other normally, but quite often in order to make meets and get trains around each other the dispatcher would issue an order to cross the train over and run on the opposite of its normal opera-

tion; this was called in slang 'wrong railing.' As signal systems became more sophisticated on the C & O in the 1930s and 1940s, the current of traffic became less important. With the advent of Central Traffic Control—electronic routing of trains from a central location by signal indication only—operators and train orders were eliminated."

About the final stanza of Meeks's song, Tom has this to say: "*My* interpretation of this stanza is that the brakes are set on TIME . . . that is, time itself is stopped, and likewise when the throttle valve is shut, that ends the life of the engine by discontinuing its supply of steam. So the writer is saying when time is finished and life is stopped, the resurrected engineer will run his train for the Master."

Photos by Royster Lyle.

The Wreck of the 1256

Engine 1256 back in Clifton Forge after being hauled out of the river, 1925. *Courtesy Ron Lane.*

Railroad men, you should all take warning,
From the fate that befell this young man;
Don't forget that the step is a short one,
From this earth to that sweet Promised Land.

Though in a head-on collision the engineer and fireman were always the most vulnerable, the consensus of such writers as Robert Reed, Norm Cohen, and Freeman Hubbard is that the riskiest job on the rails was that of brakeman. Although Harry Lyle was "only a brakeman," his death on the cold night of January 3, 1925, inspired one of the loveliest of all of the rail disaster songs.

There were many popular songs at the time that praised simple people, including several titled "Only a Brakeman." In America alone is a man supposed to be judged not by "who his people were" but by

Harry Lyle, 1919. *Courtesy Ron Lane.*

what character he develops, and what actions he performs. Americans seem to be especially fond of stories in which a man is placed under stress, and shows unimpeachable character. Yet apparently so unimportant was Harry Lyle that I could find no mention of the incident that caused his death in the Richmond *Times-Dispatch* for any date during the several days following the accident. Miss Mary E. Davis of Clifton Forge, who was engaged to be married to Harry Lyle on January 28, 1925, wrote of him, "He was a very fine gentleman, religious and cared for by everyone, with no bad habits."

Just as it says in the song, it was a bitter winter night when Engineer Sam M. Anderson, fireman Sidney G. Dillard, and head brakeman Harry F. Lyle headed out of Clifton Forge, Virginia, on the James River Line of the C & O. They were headed for Gladstone, Virginia, 125 miles away, in the cab of a freight train hauled by engine 1256, a huge, almost-new K-3 Mikado, or "Mike," built in the Richmond works of the American Locomotive Company in 1924. The 2-8-2's were named in honor of the Emperor of Nippon because the first one was constructed by Baldwin for a Japanese railroad in 1897. It was six years before an American railroad requested one.

Snow had fallen, and the ground was frozen hard. No. 1256 was a freight train, and therefore when it met passenger train No. 9 from Richmond on the single-track line, a mile east of Clifton Forge at Iron Gate, No. 1256 was the one that had to take the siding. No. 9 was due to pass Iron Gate at 7:23 P.M.; following the meet, locomotive 1256 resumed its journey.

As the train rolled along on the level tracks that followed the banks of the James River, Sidney Dillard recalled years later, a slide of dirt, shale, and rock made brittle by the water expansion caused by freezing had fallen down the mountain to cover the rails. As there were no automatic signalling devices on the James River Line of the C & O at the time, there was no warning to the crew of three men, comrades talking and joking to keep each other awake during the lonely night. This night they very likely were joking about Harry Lyle's coming marriage, for it was his last run before his marriage leave.

The slide was hidden around a curve as 1256 approached Alum Rock Bluff, just west of Glen Wilton, Virginia. By the time the train headlights had picked up the obstruction, Dillard remembered, it was too late: according to Mrs. Dillard, her husband recalled that at the final moment Harry Lyle turned to him and laughingly said, "Sid, do you love me?" Quicker than any of them could react, the engine hit the slide, and fell on her left side half into the James River, the head of the engine resting in the water.

Harry Lyle was apparently killed instantly by a crushing blow to the head. In 1976, Mary Davis wrote to Ron Lane that "he was found in the engine under the fire box door, with a terrible hole in the top of his head, and his body badly steamed." Sam Anderson, the engineer, broke an arm and leg, but was thrown clear of the wreck. Sidney Dillard was stunned, his back sprained. Luckily for him, several "young fellows" were hoboing that night on 1256; they came into the water and pulled Dillard out, helping him onto the bank and building a fire to keep the two drenched crewmen from freezing to death. Only later did Dillard and Anderson learn that one of the cars they were hauling was a gasoline tanker. Had the fire been too close to that car, a far worse tragedy might have ensued.

The wreck time has never been officially calculated; it occurred sometime between 8:30 and 9:00 P.M. at Alum Rock Bluff, seven miles from Clifton Forge. Harry F. Lyle was thirty-nine and the head brakeman. He died at once, according to the newspaper accounts. He left four brothers and a sister, as well as his fiancée, Miss Davis, who was never to marry.

At home in her house on a hill high above Clifton Forge, Sidney Dillard's widow recalled the evening fifty-seven years before from her point of view: two of her daughters were in bed, two still up. She heard the wreck whistle at the C & O yards, which blew three times for the mountain run and five times for the James River. After three she waited, and heard two more blasts. She knew her husband should be just about at Alum Rock Bluff, and she was sure, before they called to inform her, that her husband's train had wrecked. She could only wait for the news. When word did come, it was the message, "Come to

Engine 1256 before she wrecked. *Courtesy Ron Lane.*

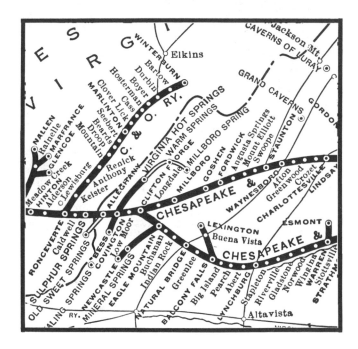

the wreck and bring dry clothes." Mrs. Dillard commented that Sid always dressed up for a run "like he was going to see Mrs. Astor." She didn't know whether she was taking clothes for his burial until she arrived and found him wet and cold but unharmed. He stayed off work thirteen months, then went back as an engineer.

Ben P. Knight recalled that special tracks were laid at the scene in order to get engine 1256 out of the river, and still it took nearly three months to get the 731,340-pound locomotive out of the river. The expense was estimated at $150,000.

The time it took to clear a wreck away was usually amazingly short. The James River line was open a day later after 1256 crashed. Knight, recalling how a crew worked, explained that, in the event of a wreck, both the Train Master and the Superinten-

This scene was photographed January 4, 1925, after Engine 1256 had wrecked at Alum Rock on the James River, twelve miles below Clifton Forge. The engine is near the bottom in the center, on its left side, just at the water's edge. *Courtesy C & O Historical Society, Alderson, W. Va.*

Three wrecking cranes and a boom for hoisting. The higher the boom, the more load it could lift. The booms were anchored to the track, but the question in raising an engine from a river was always, will the engine come up or will the crane go over? Special tracks were built down to the water's edge to hoist the engine onto, once it was out of the water. *Courtesy C & O Historical Society, Alderson, W. Va.*

dent of Track are called. They ascertain the magnitude of the wreck, determine what equipment is needed to retrack the line, and call the Wreck Master, who is in charge of tool cars, which have big steam (or, by the 60s, diesel) derricks. Of course if there were injuries or fatalities, they took priority along with the emergency transportation of passengers. After that, opening the line was the first priority, then removing the debris. The Wreck Master, along with the toolcar foreman, would also survey the damage to equipment and estimate what it would take to rebuild or replace a car. Some cars were rebuilt and some scrapped; but if the main frame of a locomotive or car was bent, it had to be scrapped. The railroads always tried to rebuild wrecked engines, if possible, as locomotives were very expensive.

Sidney Dillard went once more into the river, the second time as engineer. On February 6, 1951, Dillard was the engineer on 2767 when it hit another slide a few miles down the river from the site of the previous wreck. The big K-4 also did a roll into the James, with about seventy coal cars following "throwing coal all over the place." Again Dillard came out unscathed. The fireman, Mr. W. G. Johnson, according to Mrs. Dillard, held her husband's head out of the water until help came, or Sid would have drowned. This was the last trip as engineer for Dillard, who finished out his career as a motive power inspector for the C & O. Mrs. Dillard explained that he became what was called a "traveling fireman." Paul Shue recalls Dillard's philosophical remark while telling of his railroad career: "When you can't see what's around a curve, you got to have a lot of faith."

Ben Knight knew Sidney Dillard well, and tells how he raised four daughters, and how one of them married a yardmaster and thus perpetuated the family profession. Mr. Knight discussed the second accident Dillard was in: "Limestone will ravel, you

On February 6, 1951, Engine No. 2767, a K-4, eastbound out of Clifton Forge, hit a slide at Salt Petre Cave, twenty-five miles down the James River. Sid Dillard was the engineer. This aerial view shows the freight cars jammed together on the riverbank that snowy day. *Courtesy C & O Historical Society, Alderson, W. Va.*

know, starting at the bottom of the cliff, and eventually a slide will drop out. The ravel goes higher and higher, and the overhang gets worse. It came down heavily that day and the K-4 hit it and went in the river. We had to fix that thing, and Division Engineer Hal Orr came up with the 'pincushion theory': you go up and drill holes through the strata and put iron rods down through it—maybe 10 feet long, inch-and-a-half diameter. Well, he tried it and they held—there've been no slides since, where they did it."

Literally dependent on each other for their lives, train crews developed close male bonding, hinted at in some of the songs. Sid Dillard told his wife that Harry Lyle's final words were, "Sid, do you love me?" We would be amiss in making too much of the comment, spoken as it was to a married man with four children by a man engaged to be married in a week. Yet the words indicate the sort of closeness that existed between crew members. The words would undoubtedly not have taken on significance had not the accident an instant later carved them into stone in Dillard's memory. Lyle may have been acutely aware, on his final "bachelor" run, of the sweetness of male comaraderie about to end.

Roy B. Anderson, in the C & O *Newsletter*, notes that it was interesting that another Harry Lyle, a distant cousin, was also later an engineer on the "Mountain Run" from Clifton Forge to Charlottesville, and he commented that he never pulled 1256 without recalling the tragedy.

Lillian Nordica, noted opera singer, who was only slightly bruised when train No. 9 wrecked.

The Wreck of the 1256

THE WRECK OF THE 1256

On that cold and dark cloudy evenin',
Just before the close of the day,
There came Harry Lyle and Dillard,
And with Anderson they rode away.

From Clifton Forge they started,
And their spirits were running high,
As they stopped at Iron Gate and waited,
Till old Number nine went by.

On the main line once more they started,
Down the James River so dark and drear;
And they gave no thought to the danger,
Or the death that was waiting so near.

They were gay and they joked with each other,
As they sped on their way side by side;
And the old engine rocked as she traveled,
Through the night on that last fatal ride.

In an instant the story was ended,
On her side in that cold river bed;
With poor Harry Lyle in the cabin,
With a deep fatal wound in his head.

Railroad men, you should all take warning,
From the fate that befell this young man;
Don't forget that the step is a short one,
From this earth to that sweet Promised Land.

There seems little that is arguable in the song about this wreck: the incident was minor, as wrecks go, and the wreck would take its place of anonymity among thousands of other such events were it not for the songwriter who saw how lucrative any such tragedy might be: Carson J. Robison, who copyrighted the words and music under the pseudonym of Carlos B. McAfee, July 27, 1925. Vernon Dalhart, also a pseudonym for Marion Trye Slaughter, had already recorded the song on June 22 of the same year, so scarcely six months passed between the wreck and the finished song.

Mr. Robison, in a 1925 article in *Collier's* magazine, explained how he composed his songs: "First I read all the newspaper stories of, say, a disaster. Then I get to work on the old typewriter. There's a formula, of course. You start by painting everything in gay colors—'the folks were all happy and gay'

stuff. That's sure fire. Then you ring in the tragedy—make it as morbid and gruesome as you can. Then you wind up with a moral. . . . These folks for whom we write and sing are finicky. They know the formula they like and they want no changes or improvements. . . . Take the story of The Wreck of the 1256, which has sold half a million and is still going strong. There's a simple story and a simple tune. There are only sixteen bars of music to the whole thing, repeated over and over."

Bill Malone reports that Mr. Robison was one of the most successful writers of hillbilly songs in the twenties.

Mr. Robison fabricated one of the most popular of all the train wreck songs out of, as they say, the whole cloth: "The Wreck of the Number 9" (also entitled "The Brave Engineer" and "On a Cold Winter Night") which follows:

The Wreck of Number Nine

On a cold win-ter night not a star was in sight, And the
north wind kept howl-ing down the line; With a sweet-heart so
dear stood a brave en-gi-neer, With his or-ders to
pull old Num-ber Nine. He__ kissed her good-bye with a
tear in her eye, For the joy in his heart he could not
hide; And the whole world seemed_ bright when she told him that
night, On to-mor-row she'd be his blush-ing bride.

1. On a cold winter night not a star was in sight,
   And the north wind kept howling down the line;
   With a sweetheart so dear stood a brave engineer,
   With his order to pull old Number Nine.

2. As she kissed him goodbye with tears in their eyes,
   And joy in their hearts they could not hide,
   For all the world seemed bright, when she told him
      that night,
   That tomorrow she would be his blushing bride.

3. Oh the wheels hummed a song as the train rolled
      along,
   And the black smoke came pouring from the stack;
   And the headlights agleam seemed to brighten his
      dream,
   Of tomorrow, when he would be coming back.

4. As he sped around the hill his brave heart stood still,
   For the headlights were gleaming in his face;
   And he whispered a prayer as he threw on the air,
   For he knew this would be his final race.

5. In the wreck he was found lying there on the ground,
   And he asked them to raise his weary head;
   As his breath slowly went this message he sent,
   To the poor maid who thought that she'd be wed:

6. "There's a little white home I had bought for our own,
   And I dreamed we'd be happy, you & I,
   And I will leave it to you for I know you'll be true,
   Til we meet at the golden gates, good bye."

Here the pattern is exactly the same: the song begins in happiness, and moves relentlessly towards tragedy and despair. It is a formula as old as Greek tragedy. Since this wreck is pure invention, no names, line, date, or landmarks are given, only the human situation.

Though No. 9 in "The Wreck of 1256" was, as has been mentioned, actually in this case a passenger train, the number '9,' an unlucky omen, appears in many railroad songs, especially fictional ones: "Lonesome Whistle" begins, "I was riding No. 9, heading south for Caroline. . . ." The narrator of the story mourns that "I'll rot here in this cell, Till my body's just a shell, and my hair turns whiter than snow. . . ." "Freight Train" enjoins the listener, "When I die, lawd, bury me / Down at the foot of Old Chestnut Street / So I can hear old No. 9 / As she rolls on down the line." There are many other examples. "Nine Hundred Miles Away From Home" is one of the most lonesome railroad songs extant. It was a No. 9 Hammer that killed John Henry, in some variants of that song.

These two songs prove that fact or fiction is equally good grist for the songwriter's mill. In addition to the themes consciously used, these songs share another motif, common to American popular song and poetry of the time: the theme of the young hero who is killed after having been engaged to be married. It is part of the folklore of Old 97 that one of the firemen killed, Albion G. Clapp, was engaged. It was true that Harry G. Lyle was engaged, though his relatively advanced age (thirty-nine) would seem to make that estate unlikely. Much later than his death, relatives of "Steve" Broady of Old 97 fame claimed for him the same condition.

It is difficult to know exactly what to make of this motif. First, it is surely romance-enhancing to have a young man's dying pointed up more poignantly by having him be in love, and it adds considerable interest to a young lady's life to have *been* engaged to someone who died.

Other sorts of disasters developed this motif, too. The well-known death of thirty-nine-year-old Floyd Collins in 1925 in a Kentucky cave is a case in point. Highly dramatized by the press, this case eventually "turned up" a fiancée for Collins, though in fact she hardly knew him and was baffled at her sudden rise to fame.

Norm Cohen, in *Long Steel Rail*, has collected half a dozen poems from railroad journals whose general sentiments are similar to "The Wreck of the

The True and Trembling Brakeman

Lis-ten now while I tell you ___ of a sto - ry you do not know of a true ___ and trem-bling brake-man ___ and to heav - en he did go. ___

1256": the hero was *only a brakeman*, but his death was of no less consequence than that of an engineer, or the president of the railroad.

"The True and Trembling Brakeman" is one such interesting song, apparently not about any particular wreck.

THE TRUE AND TREMBLING BRAKEMAN

Listen now while I tell you
of a story you do not know;
Of a true and trembling brakeman
And to heaven he did go.

Do you see that train a-coming,
Oh, it's [?through] old Ninety-nine;
Oh, she's puffing and a-blowing,
For you know she is behind.

See that true and trembling brakeman,
As he signals to the cab;
There is but one chance for him,
And that chance is to grab.

See that true and trembling brakeman,
As the cars go rushing by;
If he miss that yellow freight car,
He is almost sure to die.

See that true and trembling brakeman,
As he falls beneath the train;
He had not one moment's warning,
Before he fell beneath the train.

See that brave young engineerman,
At the age of twenty-one;
Stepping down from upon his engine,
Crying, "Now what have I done!

"Is it true I killed a brakeman,
Is it true that he is dying?
Lord, you know I tried to save him,
But I could not stop in time."

See the car wheels rolling o'er him,
O'er his mangled body'n'head;
See his sister bending o'er him,
Crying, "Brother, are you dead?"

Sighing, "Sister, yes, I'm dying,
Going to a better shore;
Oh, my body's on a pathway,
I can never see no more.

"Sister, when you see my brother,
These few words to him I send;
Tell him never to venture braking,
If he does, his life will end."

These few words were sadly spoken,
Folding his arms across his breast;
And his heart now ceased beating,
And his eyes were closed in death.

The Death of Jerry Damron

In the head of Marrow-bone Hol - ler, _____ where the crys-tal wat-ers flow, _____ Jer-ry Dam-ron met dis- as - ter _____ Up _____ there on the C and O. _____

In 1963, Dock Boggs recorded another ballad about the death of a C & O brakeman. I have been unable to discover who Jerry Damron was, or when he died, but his song is too charming to omit. It is the only wreck song I have come across in a minor key. The Blue Ridge Institute at Ferrum College has catalogued another ballad about the death of Cora Damron, by Wayne Camron, so perhaps this same "inglorious Milton" attempted to preserve in poetry the death of another relative.

THE DEATH OF JERRY DAMRON

1. In the head of Marrowbone Holler,
   Where the crystal waters flow,
   Jerry Damron met disaster
   Up there on the C. and O.

2. As he left the Coaldale junction
   On the head end of his train,
   Thinking not of unseen dangers,
   Frosty nights or drenchin' rain.

3. Perhaps his thoughts were of his sweetheart
   And on some earthly paradise,
   When his car gave indications
   That it was riding on the ties.

4. Then he got to safety,
   To make successful land,
   Then there comes that old, old story,
   One misstep or slip of hand.

5. Far from darkness came destruction,
   And the truth we'll never know,
   Of the feelin's of that train crew
   Up there on the C. and O.

6. Quick the angel cock was opened,
   But alas, it came too late,
   Jerry's soul had departed
   Through that far off golden gate,

7. Then we see the tool car passing
   With the boom a-swinging low
   As if it was mournin' for Jerry
   Up there on the C. and O.

8. Jerry, we miss you and we wonder
   If you see the C. and O.
   And your friends that are still
      mournin' for you
   Where the Marrowbone waters flow.

9. Jerry, we hope you're among the angels
   Way up there above the stars,
   Where there'll be no more worry,
   Ridin' heavy trains or cars.

10. Now you're sleeping, gently sleeping,
    Where the Big Sandy breezes blow,
    But your memory's still with us
    Up and down the C. and O.

11. And it's just another story,
    While friends sometimes must part,
    While your soul has gone to Glory,
    There remains a broken heart.

Marrowbone is on the Big Sandy division of the C & O, near Pikeville, Kentucky, in coalmining country. The song tells us that Jerry Damron when he died was riding "on the head end of his train," and that he "opened" the "angel cock" "too late." The "angel cock" is an "angle cock," a valve, or cock, on each end of each car that cuts the brake air supply system and brakes the train. Often an engine would get behind, and shove ten to fifty or so coal cars onto an empty supply track for loading. Rules required that a brakeman must ride at the head of the first car. His job was to watch out, and to stop the cars if any obstruction was on the track, or if anything happened such as the wheels leaving the track. The brakeman was supposed to find a safe place to sit or stand on the brake platform, and to use a safety device known as the backup-hose, or to operate the angle cock from his safe position. But it was easier to walk along ahead of the car and operate the angle-cock from the ground. As there was much debris along the tracks, mainly loose coal, a man might slip and fall beneath the wheels while trying to turn the angle cock. This dangerous practice was strictly forbidden, but Ben Knight recalls four or five fatal accidents of this type during his half-century with the C & O. Dock Boggs identifies Damron as "Mrs. Millard Gamble's brother," and reckons that the disaster occurred some time in the thirties. The song hints at the familiar theme of a sweetheart left behind.

NOTES

"The Wreck of the 1256" was perhaps my favorite song in my folksinging days; my husband to this day recalls that on the night we met in 1961 I turned to him and said, "Are you any kin to the Harry Lyle that lost his life in the 'Wreck of the 1256'? He says it is to this day near the top of his list of strange questions, as he was more used to hearing "What fraternity do you belong to?" At any rate, it got his attention, I am glad to say. We have not yet found this Harry F. Lyle, born around 1886, among our ancestors, illustrious and otherwise, though I must say that my husband's eyes are remarkably like Harry Lyle's. Information on the wreck is from B. P. Knight of Buena Vista, Virginia; "The Wreck of 1256" by Roy B. Anderson, *C & O Historical Society Newsletter*, July 1969; *Long Steel Rail* by Norm Cohen; "A Folksinger Rides the C & O" (1948) by Pick Temple in the *C & O Historical Society Newsletter* (Mar., Apr., May, and June 1975). Also I drew from an unpublished interview Paul Shue had with Sidney Dillard in 1970; an interview I had with Mrs. Sidney Dillard, July 9, 1982; and an article in the Hinton *Daily News*, 5 Jan. 1925. Tom W. Dixon, Jr., sent valuable information about this wreck, and C. E. Monroe offered information.

Pick Temple, pondering the pseudonym Carlos B. McAfee, offers the theory that Carson Robison, an intelligent and literary man, may have chosen to write some "terrible songs" that he knew would make money under a name that was a pun. Q: "Why did you write that awful song?" A: (in a Spanish accent, perhaps) "Carlos B. McAfee."

Paul Shue in his "Railroad Wrecks in Story and Song" asks, "What can account for the fact that the C & O has given us so many wreck songs?" He believes that the reason is twofold: the topography of the mountain region and an Anglo-Saxon tendency to turn tragedy into song. While it is true that a majority of the train wreck songs are from Appalachia, statistics show that Appalachia had, in fact, *fewer* train wrecks than the rest of the country! Robert Reed, in *Train Wrecks*, writes that from 1829 to 1853 there were probably no more than a dozen total fatalities. In 1853, however, 138 railroad wrecks occurred, killing a total of 234 people. The disasters escalated from then on. One illuminating fact: in the year 1890, 6,335 people were killed in railroad accidents in this country. Only one of these deaths, that of George Alley, was on the C & O. This is probably a fairer statistic than the songs, leading to the conclusion that the C & O did not have more wrecks, but only came to sing songs about the ones it did have more often than other railroads. Contrary to what our songs might lead us to believe, in fact, Pennsylvania, New York, New Jersey, and Massachusetts lead the other states with by far the greatest number of wrecks. An example, for the sake of contrast: thirty-five of Robert B. Shaw's "major wrecks" occurred in New Jersey, and only four in West Virginia. Furthermore, the C & O is exonerated by Shaw's study, appearing only once in his list of over three hundred "major disasters." That C & O wreck, by the way, as we might suspect, is not the subject of a song.

Tom Dixon, however, comments that "back in the early 1880's the C & O had many wrecks and killed people all the time, usually employees, though some passengers, too. The tale of "The C & O Curse" went about; . . . the newspapers in Virginia and West Virginia said it was God's wrath on the C & O for running trains and forcing people to work on Sunday. After the C & O stopped Sunday running briefly, the curse seemed to lift. Fewer accidents occurred even after seven-day-a-week operation started

again . . . and around the turn of the century the papers were talking about "C & O Luck" in that its wrecks seldom caused loss of life. . . ." Dixon adds this note: the C & O's K-class Mikados were all 2-8-2's, but were ordered at different times and had different dimensions. The C & O had K, K-1, K-2, K-3, and K-3a classes of locomotives.

Shelby F. Lowe, of Douglasville, Georgia, shared with me an article from the Atlanta *Journal and Constitution* magazine, 29 Dec. 1968, by Mrs. Jewell Alverson of Calhoun, said to be the "true" story behind "The Wreck of the Number 9." Engineer Ben F. Tracy appears larger than life. It was said that several years before his death, as he stopped his train at Sugar Valley Station, he noticed a girl trying to mount a skittish horse and said, "If that girl mounts that horse, she's my wife." She did, and he married her.

On Sunday, January 12, 1902, No. 9, mixed passenger and freight, left Atlanta. Ben Tracy, forty-five, said to his fireman, "I'll get to Chattanooga on time or go to hell." On a curve near Oostanaula, Ga., he wrecked. He leaped, but was caught between two freight cars and crushed. Among several injured passengers was Madame Lillian Nordica, a Metropolitan Opera singer who, though slightly bruised, reached Nashville in time for her concert.

After her husband's death, it is said that the beautiful Fanny Dobson Tracy bought a farm near Calhoun, and generously shared her "talking machine with a blue morning-glory horn" with all her neighbors. Much loved, until the day she died she wore a gold pin shaped like an engine, in memory of her beloved husband. According to Shelby F. Lowe, the song "The Wreck of the Number 9" was composed about this event.

The Church Hill
Tunnel Disaster

Remember the Church Hill Tunnel
   Near a mile under Richmond.
There's a story I want to tell you
   of a train that'll never be found . . .

By the time of the Civil War Richmond, Virginia, had become an important rail center, with four major railroads. However, the lines coming into the city did not connect with each other, but were separated by hills and ravines. Even before the War the situation caused logistical problems. After 1865, the increased rail traffic resulted in nightmarish confusion and interminable delays. The year after the War was over, a six-hundred-foot tunnel was excavated successfully under Gamble's Hill, connecting the Richmond and Petersburg Station to the Richmond, Fredericksburg, and Potomac Station. Nothing in the building of this tunnel foreshadowed the disastrous result that was to come from a longer tunnel years later.

The C & O—originally the Virginia Central—terminal was located over a mile from the James River Docks, resulting in grave inconvenience to shipping. In 1868 C & O President Collis P. Huntington presented the situation to the Richmond city council: "The lack of tracks to the docks at Richmond results in a charge for cartage, and extra handling accrues . . . on all freight destined for transshipment. . . . It is presumed that the citizens of Richmond are sensible of the importance of having this restriction upon its commerce speedily removed, and they will . . . propose to the Chesapeake and Ohio such rights of way and other facilities for extending its tracks to the water-line. . . ."

Thus it was that the Richmond City Council decided to try to insure the city's future as a deepwater port and rail center by building the Church Hill Tunnel, which was to run 3927 feet underneath residential Richmond from 19th to 29th Street. The Council in 1871 authorized a $300,000 bond issue to finance it.

Digging began on February 1, 1872, from both ends and from three shafts sunk at roughly equal intervals along the route. The construction was supposed to take a year. It was planned that, as the tunnel went farther into Church Hill, wooden arches would be moved in for support, and eventually brick ceilings and walls would be constructed.

From the very beginning the work went badly. The unstable nature of the earth under Church Hill began to be evident within weeks of the inception. The

This triple crossing in Richmond, photographed soon after the turn of the century, indicates the crowded conditions that prevailed on the railroads of the city and prompted the reopening of the Church Hill Tunnel. *Courtesy C & O Historical Society, Alderson, W. Va.*

layers of earth were composed of unconsolidated sediments, including a clay called blue marl. When dry, blue marl is hard and brittle; however, it absorbs moisture easily and melts to a slippery clay when saturated. Soon after the tunneling began, the marl began to slip and shift. On May 21, 1872, two workers were partially buried by an earth collapse in the middle shaft. On May 22, Peter Trendeman, an assistant engineer inspecting the archwork, was knocked unconscious by a falling chunk of clay. Two days later two more employees were hit by more falling marl in the first shaft, and on May 25 James Bolton, an assistant engineer inspecting Shaft 2, was crushed by a large piece of falling clay. He was brought out still alive, but died about five hours later.

Instead of giving up, the contractors redoubled their efforts to complete the permanent masonry vaulting before the timbers collapsed. By January of 1873, the yards of people living above the route had cracks and fissures appearing on the surface, and some gas lines broke. The escaping gas caught fire and blazed high for a night before the city could cut it off. Residents complained to the Richmond authorities. On January 13 a dangerous fissure appeared on 24th Street, and residents in the vicinity were evacuated. The next day a 120-foot length of the tunnel collapsed between 24th and 25th Streets with a noise "like musketry," carrying with it several houses newly vacated. This time, all the workmen in the tunnel escaped.

The C & O, according to an account by Walter S. Griggs, Jr., "made every effort to help those families, including the family of the rector of St. John's Church, left homeless by the cave-in, by giving them temporary shelter. The hole left by this cave-in became quite a popular place to visit and ladies from Richmond went in carriages to see it."

General Williams C. Wickham, C & O vice-president, Colonel H. D. Whitcomb, chief engineer, and the tunnel architects, went into the first shaft that very day, January 14, and, returning to the surface, optimistically reported to the curious crowds gathered to see the damage that only a small delay would occur, and that it was perfectly safe to resume construction.

The tunnel was scheduled to be completed on October 1, 1873. Indeed, the *Richmond Daily Dispatch* of that day prophesied, "Before the sun goes down the quiet shades of Chimborazo will reecho the snort of the iron horse as it seeks to reach Tidewater after its long journey from the banks of the Ohio." This buoyant prediction proved to be a bit premature, for there was another small cave-in just when the tunnel was almost completed, and the debris took a long time to clear because of a strike by C & O laborers. However, on Sunday, December 11, 1873, C & O locomotive No. 2, built in Richmond in 1849 and named the David Anderson, Jr., for a noted Petersburg educator, philanthropist, and board member of the Virginia Central Railroad, pulled one car through the tunnel.

The passage by the David Anderson, Jr., marked the completion of one of the longest tunnels in the country—through some of the most treacherous earth. The tunnel then became a part of the C & O's operations, and commerce began to move through it on the way to the docks on the James River. More than a decade passed without serious incident, though the old timers say that everyone worried some about the tunnel, and that minor accidents were common.

In 1886 a new tunnel was begun, to connect Byrd Street Station with Shockoe Bottom. On July 14, 1891, about fifty feet of it collapsed, thus halting work, and in 1894 City Council apparently finally faced the futility of further tunneling under Richmond. They revoked all of the railroad's franchises, and filled in the new uncompleted tunnel. Meanwhile Church Hill Tunnel continued in use until the James River viaduct was opened to traffic in

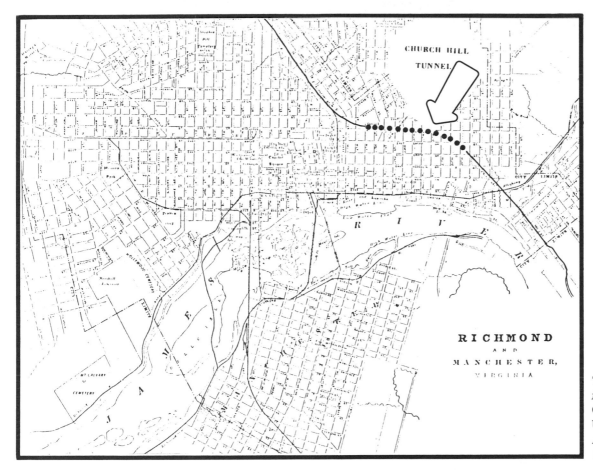

CHURCH HILL
TUNNEL

RICHMOND
AND
MANCHESTER,
VIRGINIA

*This map
is from
Cram's
Universal
Atlas,
1894.*

1901, connecting the James River Line directly with Fulton Yard and the C & O's Peninsula Subdivision. At that time Church Hill Tunnel was retired from active service.

In 1913, a concrete two-block extension was built at the tunnel's eastern end to keep the approach from eroding inward, as happens in the open cut parts of tunnels. But since the tunnel itself was still of questionable safety, the project went no further. In 1915 some of the masonry lining was replaced, but still the tunnel was not returned to use.

Time passed, and Richmond thrived. It is apparent that this tunnel, built at such cost, was always, even in its retirement, considered an option for future use. Finally, in 1925, seeing a need to relieve the congestion that prosperity had brought to Richmond, the C & O decided to overhaul Church Hill Tunnel and return it to service.

In January of that year, a water main over the tunnel broke, which should have indicated shifting and sliding of the earth. But the news story makes no mention of possible danger. Work began in September to drain accumulated water from the tunnel and to repair the track bed.

These workmen were hired to repair Church Hill Tunnel for re-use in 1925. Here they pause from their labors to stare somberly at the camera, possibly only days before the cave-in. The man at the right is probably a foreman. *Dementi-Foster Studios.*

Friday, October 2, 1925, was a cold rainy day. The water soaked into the ground above the tunnel. At two-thirty or so, Engineer Tom Mason opened the throttle of a 4-4-0 American-type passenger locomotive, No. 231, built in 1903 by Baldwin for the C & O, and pulled ten flatcars into the eastern portal of the tunnel to be loaded with dirt and brought out. He pulled the train nearly all the way to the other end, to within one hundred years of the western portal. There, Brakeman C. S. Kelso uncoupled the cars. Mason then prepared to guide the engine towards the western portal. Inside the tunnel were an estimated two hundred men, white and black, the engine, the tender, and the ten flatcars.

Just as Mason started the engine up again, a brick fell, then more bricks followed. The workmen must have startled, dropped their shovels, peered upwards, and caught each other's worried glances. There was a "crackling sound like electricity" along the roof. The lights in the tunnel dimmed, flickered. Instinctively, the men began to scramble for the exits.

Those who escaped later reported a sharp blast of

A scene in the tunnel after the cave-in. The cracks in the wall show here, and a partially dug-out flatcar. *Dementi-Foster Studios.*

air that nearly knocked some of them flat as the roof collapsed. The workers who realized what was happening headed for the eastern end, even though it was nearly a mile away. A few escaped through the choked western end, which was much nearer, but that exit was blocked within a few seconds. B. F. Mosby, the fireman on the locomotive, was heard to yell, "Watch out, Tom, she's a-coming in!"

The lights flickered again, then went out entirely. The darkness was absolute, full of the noises of collapsing earth, crashing timbers, and the cries and groans of frightened and injured men, as tons and tons of earth overhead crumbled down heavily into the tunnel space. As the roof fell, it crushed the loco-

Church Hill Tunnel, sealed up in 1926, is the grave of an undetermined number of workers. Vines and weeds work quickly to obscure history. *Dementi-Foster Studios.*

motive and broke the boiler gauge pipe, severely scalding Mosby. A small man, he was able with difficulty to extricate himself from the cab and find shelter beneath a flatcar. Finally he managed to crawl out of the tunnel into the rain. He called to bystanders to ask them to assure his wife and daughter of his safety, but his courage was not enough: he died that night in a Richmond hospital.

The burly engineer Tom Mason was pinned to the seat by the reverse lever, and could not move. It was postulated that, had he been a smaller man, he too might have wrested free and been able to save himself by sheltering under the engine or a flatcar. On October 6 the Richmond *Times-Dispatch* reported that Mason's son "had remained constantly in the vicinity . . . and insists he will stay near the workers until they locate the body of his father." The engi-

neer was still seated bolt upright in his engine cab when his decomposed body was dug out nine days after the cave-in.

Conductor G. C. McFadden and Brakeman Kelso were cut and injured, but managed to escape along with most of the work crew.

Immediately after the disaster, the C & O sought to learn how many men might still be buried in the cave-in. A day later they announced that only Engineer Mason and two black laborers, H. Smith and R. Lewis, were missing. But the workmen disagreed. They said a new construction gang had hired on that morning, whose names had not yet been listed on the company roster, and that still more black laborers had entered the western end of the tunnel to seek work just before the cave-in took place.

Rescue efforts continued for more than a week.

THE RICHMOND NEWS LEADER

1 DEAD, THREE MISSING, IN TUNNEL DISASTER HERE

that Mosby was buried from old St. John's Church and Mason from St. Patrick's Church, since both of these churches were located virtually on top of the tunnel."

Llewellyn Lewis, brakeman on the Southern Railroad, and Billy Pierce of Richmond composed and published a song about the disaster. I have been unable to find a tune or sheet music, and thus have only the words to report.

But new earth slides hindered digging, and after Engineer Mason's body had been retrieved for decent burial, all further work was halted as too expensive and probably futile—according to Paul Shue, the C & O estimated it would cost $38,000 to recover the buried locomotive. Church Hill tunnel, recognized at last as unsafe, was filled in with sand.

The buried locomotive and flatcars are still there today, possibly along with the bodies of an unknown number of tunnel workmen, which some estimates place as high as twenty-five.

It was later officially announced that the clay itself, the lack of longitudinal bracing in the tunnel, the disruption of replacing of foundations, and general water seepage had all weakened the masonry and cumulatively caused the collapse.

Mr. Griggs' account concludes, "The obituaries for Mason and Mosby were written in the hearts of Richmonders. Mosby was remembered for thinking of his wife before himself. It was also noted that Mosby was called for the fatal trip at the last moment to replace another fireman who could not make the trip. Mason was remembered as a brave and very popular engineer who left a wife and eight children to mourn him. Large contingents of railroad men carrying their gold Hamilton railroad watches attended both funerals, which were given extensive coverage in the news media of the day. It is ironic

THE TRAIN THAT WILL NEVER BE FOUND

Remember the Church Hill Tunnel
    Near a mile under Richmond.
There's a story I want to tell you
    of a train that'll never be found.

On a bleak afternoon in the autumn
    when the skies were overcast
A train and its crew were working
    In the tunnel performing their tasks.

None ever dreamed of danger,
    of a death that was hoverin' near—
They were happy while they were working
    For the loved ones home so dear.

When all of a sudden a tremble,
    A large gap in the slimy clay—
Then the earth claimed a few in its clutches,
    In the darkness the rest groped their way.

Many shovels and picks were diggin'
    For their pals in the buried train—
But the cold slimy clay held its victims.
    Soon their hopes were found in vain.

Many hours did they search for their comrades
    Who might live in the cold, cold cave,
But they never found one who was living
    Way down in their untimely grave.

Chorus
Brothers keep shovelin',
    Pickin' in the ground.
Brothers, keep listening
    For the train that's never been found.

This is an atypical train wreck song. It has much more in common with mining disaster songs, and with good reason, as the accident was much more like a mining accident than a train wreck. Mine disaster songs typically exhort the rescue workers to "keep digging" as this one does. The chorus functions as a work song, whose major use was to establish a rhythm for the hard labor which would result in more efficient rescue work.

Miners probably existed and functioned more as members of a group than trainmen did. As we know, engineers, brakemen, and others are always identified with their highly specialized jobs, in which they took great pride. So in train disaster songs, it seemed proper to identify victims by name and profession both. Not so with miners, if we are to look to the songs for clues. They are hardly ever individually named in songs about their disasters, possibly because both they themselves and the public viewed them as members of a group bound together by profession and a common fate rather than as individuals. And their disasters were, in fact, more impersonal.

Mining songs tend to begin with a singer's "Come-All-Ye." This song has a similar opening. Railroad wreck ballads do not, as a rule.

In all kinds of disaster stories, omens and fore-shadowings are common: in 1968, Mrs. Mason, widow of Tom Mason, reported to the Richmond *Times-Dispatch* that her husband "knew something was going to happen." She said he came back after leaving home that morning, and kissed her good-bye again.

NOTES

Material for this article came from "The Church Hill Tunnel Story" by Walter S. Griggs, Jr., a series in the *C & O Historical Society Newsletter* during 1972; "The Tunnels of Richmond" by Edward F. Heite, in *Virginia Cavalcade* Magazine, Winter 1964; "Collapse on Church Hill" by Suzanne Bower, in *Richmond Mercury Magazine*, 5 Mar. 1975; "Railway Tunnel's Collapse 24 years Ago Sealed in Engine and Crewmen" by Louis D. Rubin, Jr., in the Richmond *Times-Dispatch*, 8 May 1949; *Death in the Dark* by James Taylor Adams; the quotation by Collis P. Huntington to the Richmond City Council is from a mimeographed booklet *Chessie's Railroad* by George Selden Wallace, n.p., courtesy Mr. Ben P. Knight. Pick Temple adds an interesting note: the Collis P. Huntington, a Southern Pacific engine, was the first steam locomotive on the west coast, shipped around the horn of South America and up the coast to California. He also reminds us that another famous tunnel, "Great Bend," near Talcott, West Virginia, was being constructed by the C & O at the same time. This is, of course, the tunnel we associate with John Henry.

My thanks to Miss Robbie Quick of Dementi-Foster Studios, and to Susan Betts of the Richmond *Times-Dispatch*, for their help.

These ominous cracks in the ground above Church Hill Tunnel in 1925 alarmed residents of the area, and some were forced to abandon their homes temporarily. *Dementi-Foster Studios.*

The Freight Wreck at Altoona

From the air, the famous Horseshoe Curve on the Pennsylvania Railroad where Ed Scheline lost his airbrakes and ultimately his life on November 29, 1925. *Courtesy the Altoona Mirror.*

With all of the strength that God gave him,
He tightened the brakes with a prayer;
But the train kept right on down the mountain,
And her whistle was piercing the air.

The relatively minor incident of a runaway train on the Pennsylvania Railroad inspired a lovely and widely popular song.

On the Sunday morning of November 29, 1925, at 7:25, freight train No. 1262, a V-14 train hauling fifty-eight freight cars, was running east on Track A at Kittanning Point, Pennsylvania, a block station 3.3 miles from Altoona and the topmost spot on Pennsylvania's famous Horseshoe Curve, noted for its beautiful scenery.

Trains then had Westinghouse airbrakes and handbrakes both, the latter as a backup for the former. Trains customarily stopped in those days at the top of long grades to "turn up the retainers" before descending the grade. The Westinghouse system was better than the older handbrake system but still far from perfect, and the pumps could not restore air to the brake system fast enough for a long downhill run with many applications of the brakes, especially for a heavy freight with many loaded cars. So, just before starting down a long grade, the pressure had to be built up to seventy pounds, and valves on the tops of each car turned up or closed, by the brakeman walking along the tops of the cars, to retain this pressure to be used for the downhill braking. Once down the hill safely, the brakeman went once more along the tops of the cars, this time turning down the retainers, for on a normal grade the air pressure could be built up and maintained in between brakings.

It took about fifteen minutes to turn up the retainers and recharge the train's air system. Probably what happened to 1262 is that Engineer F. C. Scheline, forty-eight, of Sharpsburg, Pennsylvania, anxious to get on with his run, did not wait long enough, and started downhill with a partially depleted air-brake system.

Altoona, just down the mountain from Kittanning Point, is in the Pleasant Valley of Pennsylvania. The main shops for the Pennsylvania's steam engines run-

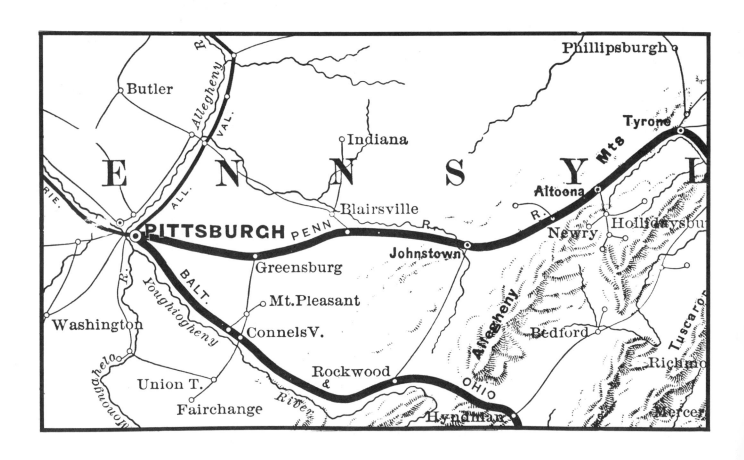

ning between Philadelphia, Harrisburg, and Pittsburgh were located there. Once down the mountain, the area is level, and the freight yards are on fairly flat ground.

At any rate, 1262, after what the Altoona *Mirror* called "a short stop," proceeded east, downhill all the way, when Engineer Scheline discovered that he had not enough differential to apply adequate braking power. From Kittanning Point to the city, the tracks followed a sharp descent that would not level out for nearly five miles. Scheline signaled for the brakes, a long sharp whistle, and at once Conductor W. E. Perry and Brakeman G. M. Pincuspy went out on the cars and tried to set the brakes by hand. But by then the train had too much momentum. Scheline signalled again, then began pulling the whistle cord continually in warning, while the locomotive, with the additional thrust of fifty-eight loaded freight cars behind it, picked up speed every second, dashing faster and faster down the mountainside and thundering into the railroad yards at Altoona, streams of sparks flying in its wake. Somewhere along the wild route, Perry and Pincuspy jumped off, or, in train lingo, "joined the bird gang." Pincuspy suffered a broken ankle and Perry was not hurt at all, though it was a near-miracle that either survived.

As the train hit the freight yards at Altoona, bystanders and people on the station platforms leaped to safety or ran, seeking places of shelter. Given Lotz, of Altoona, later recalled to Pick Temple how the yardman at the freight yard tower saved himself: when he saw the train coming, he scrambled down from the tower, ran across the tracks, and scaled a high fence. Seconds later the yard tower was shorn from its foundation and demolished.

Engineer Scheline and Fireman H. F. Taubler, who was twenty-seven, at some point made the decision not to jump, probably hoping against hope that the train could be brought safely to rest on the level ground. By the time the train reached the bottom of the mountain, it was estimated to be travelling at more than sixty miles an hour.

At the Seventeenth Street Bridge, the train encountered a series of switches and left the rails with a noise like thunder. The engine, when she "jumped," snapped clear of the trailing cars, ran seven-tenths of a mile along the roadbed, crashed through a fence, and fell over on her side. Half a mile behind her, the freight cars began to pile up into a shapeless mass of splintered wood.

The Altoona freight yards, about 1920. *Courtesy the Altoona* Mirror.

Ed Scheline's engine, exhausted finally, lies on her side at the end of her long flight down the mountain into Altoona. The long arm of the wrecking crane hovers over the spent engine. *Courtesy the Altoona Area Public Library.*

Westbound freight No. 266 was passing on a nearby track. When its engineer saw what was coming, he tried to get his train beyond the danger zone, but it was struck by zigzagging cars from 1262; his engine was knocked from one track onto another, and twelve of his cars derailed. Most were total losses, as were thirty-three of 1262's cars.

The damage, needless to say, was extensive. The Altoona *Mirror*, on November 30, told the graphic story of how the freight cars "buckled and splintered and piled on top of each other." Only a total of eight cars from both trains remained undamaged. All the tracks in the yard were blocked, and the switches torn up. Lumber, corn, stone, cement, slate, lamp black, and miscellaneous food supplies were scattered over a wide area.

Fireman Taubler was dead when rescuers reached him, and it was presumed he died instantly from the impact. Scheline was unconscious but alive; he died 2½ hours later of internal injuries. Given Lotz, who was then a young boy, told Pick Temple that he had been walking to church with his father when they heard first the frantic blasting, over and over, of the whistle. His father said, "There's trouble on the railroad!" and then they ran. As they did, they heard a tremendous roar, and a great many crashing sounds,

Hundreds of people crowd the area, swarming upon bill-boards and even the roofs of houses, to view the damage wrought by 1262 on her early morning flight. *Courtesy the Altoona Area Public Library.*

then a dreadful silence. They arrived just as it was all over. What impressed Lotz most was that a steel girder bridge had been twisted a foot off its foundation by the weight and motive power of the engine. By noon, according to the Altoona *Tribune*, five thousand people had gathered to watch, climbing telephone poles and covering the roofs of nearby houses! The bridge was out of commission for many days afterwards.

In the next few days, three switches were replaced and twenty repaired. Seven-tenths of a mile of track had to be straightened. Eventually it was determined that the engine's air pump was faulty, and did not deliver air to the brakes.

Norm Cohen's research uncovered the information that Carson Robison wrote the music to accompany a poem about this wreck by Fred Tait-Douglas. Whoever Tait-Douglas was, he knew the formula and got to his task at once, for less than two months elapsed before Vernon Dalhart recorded the song, on January 15, 1926. The song is quite accurate. Below is a version of the song collected by Cohen. The one I learned as a child was similar. I would guess it to have been one of Vernon Dalhart's since my grandfather was a great fan of his and collected his records. Sadly, some of them have disappeared in time, this one among them.

The Altoona Freight Wreck

They had just left the point at Kit-tan-ing,
Freight num-ber Twelve six-ty two; She
trav-eled right on down the moun-tain And
brave were the men in her crew.

THE WRECK AT ALTOONA

They had just left the point at Kittanning,
Freight number Twelve Sixty Two;
She traveled right on down the mountain,
And brave were the men in her crew.

The engineer pulled at the whistle,
For the brakes wouldn't work when applied;
And the brakeman climbed out on the car tops,
For he knew what the whistle had cried.

With all of the strength that God gave him,
He tightened the brakes with a prayer;
But the train kept right on down the mountain,
And her whistle was piercing the air.

And on down the grade she went racing,
She sped like a demon from Hell;
With the engineer blowing the whistle,
And the fireman was ringing the bell.

She traveled at sixty an hour,
Gaining speed every foot of the way;
And then with a crash it was over,
And there on the track the freight lay.

The engine was broken to pieces,
The frieght cars were thrown far and near;
And a mile up the track lay the wreckage,
The worst wreck in many a year.

It's not the amount of the damage,
Or the value of what it all cost;
It's the sad tale that came from the cabin,
Where the lives of two brave men were lost.

They were found at their posts in the wreckage,
They died when the engine had fell;
The engineer still held the whistle,
And the fireman still hung to the bell.

This story is told of a freight train,
And it should be a warning to all;
You should be prepared every minute,
For you cannot tell when He'll call.

I would attribute the comparative popularity of
this wreck song mainly to the tune, which Norm
Cohen calls "more engaging" than most. It seems an
impersonal touch that the engineer and fireman are
not named. This is really the only oddity in an otherwise conventional wreck song.

As is too common in songs of this type, a probably
careless engineer is transformed in song to a heroic
man choosing to die at his post. And the last stanza,
as usual, transforms the piece from song to ser-
mon. A version found in Tennessee by folklorist
C. P. Cambiaire, obviously a mishearing of the original, garbles the name Kittanning to "Chitamia"
and titles the song "The Wreck at Latona" instead
of Altoona.

NOTES

The information in this chapter is mainly from the Altoona
Mirror and the *Tribune* during the several days following the accident, and from Pick Temple's notes of Given Lotz's childhood
recollections. Timothy Doyle of the Altoona *Mirror* kindly sent
the zinc plate-prints of Horseshoe Curve and the Altoona freight
yards, and the Altoona Area Library sent photographs.

My friend Ben Knight initiated me into the mysteries of train
brakes, with great patience. I am grateful to Alberta Haught of the
Altoona Area Public Library for her help.

The Wreck of the Royal Palm

Engine 1456 on the left, and 1219 on the right, following the December 23, 1926, wreck at Rockmart, Georgia. *Courtesy Shelby F. Lowe.*

It was an awful sight
Amid the pouring rain,
The dead and dying lying there
Beneath that mighty train . . .

The evening of December 23, 1926, was a dark and stormy one in Rockmart, Georgia, a station on the Knoxville-Bristol line of the Southern Railroad. At 6:45, two "crack" passenger trains, filled to capacity, were due to pass each other momentarily at Rockmart. The southbound Royal Palm, train 101, stood waiting at Rockmart, in accordance with orders re-

ceived by A. M. Corrie, engineer of the luxury train. The northbound Ponce de Leon sped towards the meeting. Although outside the rain drove against the windows, inside the coaches and diners it was cozy and bright. It was dinner hour. The dining cars of both trains were "happy places full of people merrily chatting," traveling home or to visit relatives for the Christmas holidays.

Engineer Corrie was letting his train drift south at about six miles an hour towards the head of the new switch, when he saw the Ponce de Leon approaching through the blinding rain. He thought it was going to

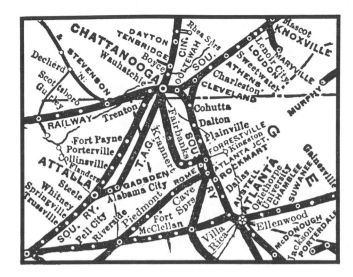

A.M. Corrie. *Courtesy Shelby F. Lowe.*

take the siding. Suddenly, to his horror, he saw that it was heading straight for his train.

Corrie thought fast. He set the emergency brake, instructed his fireman to jump, pulled hard on the whistle cord as a warning, and then jumped himself and ran clear, stumbling in the rain. He told ICC investigators that from twenty feet away in the driving torrent, he turned back and watched the Ponce de Leon coming fast, fifty miles an hour or even more. The *Atlanta Journal* of December 24, 1926, as quoted by Norm Cohen, says the engineer, as he rolled down the embankment, "heard the most awful noise I ever heard. It was the two trains coming together. I will never forget it. It sounded like the heavens had split open. I don't want to hear anything like it again." Engineer Corrie watched the diner run under the tender and push it right up into the air, and saw simultaneously the daycoach which was following telescope its way into the dining car, its fit "as even as a piece of paper fitting into an envelope."

Because of Corrie's quick thinking, no one on the Royal Palm Express was hurt, although most passengers were shaken up and bruised, and some were treated for minor injuries. But those aboard the fast-moving Ponce de Leon were not so fortunate. Two young Rome, Georgia, natives were traveling together that Thursday night and lived to describe the event. Thomas Warter, Jr., was coming home for the holidays from Oglethorpe College in Atlanta, while Walker Chidscy was returning to Rome from South Georgia College. They met on the train, and were riding in the daycoach behind the diner. Before the first crash came, Warter told the Rome *News-Tribune*, it sounded as if the engineer was trying to stop the train. They heard clearly the grinding of brakes. Then came the crash, and the two boys were

133

A coach of the Ponce de Leon sliced into the dining car, where many were killed as they were eating their dinners. *Courtesy Shelby F. Lowe.*

knocked from their seats to the floor as the lights went out. Everyone in the coach began to scramble to get out.

When the boys finally got up, dazed and shocked, it was to discover that their car had run through the diner, and portions of the dining car could be seen on either side of the coach. Then they began to hear the "moans of the dying and the wild screaming of those pinned underneath the wreckage."

The boys had to climb down out of the car, suspended as it was several feet in the air. Warter explained, "I could not possibly describe the scene that greeted me when I finally was safe on the ground. A person with the most vivid imagination could not

begin to tell how horrible it was. . . ." As far as Warter and Chidsey could tell, no one in their car was killed. All but one person in the dining car, however, were killed or severely injured.

On Christmas Day, the Associated Press reported that "Screams of women pinned beneath the wreckage were mingled with the hoarse shouts of men and prayers of a negro waiter when he was released, uninjured, from a hole in the side of the dining car. He had refused aid until the white passengers had been cared for."

Mrs. George Hardy, badly mangled, unable to move under a fallen beam, begged rescuers to help her seven-year-old son and her three-year-old daugh-

The dining car of the Ponce de Leon where death claimed all beneath the day coach. From the little hole in the side of the diner a two-hundred-pound black chef popped out, laughing and crying at the same time. It is said that he hit the ground running. *Courtesy Shelby F. Lowe.*

ter. Both were brought out dead. The mother died later in surgery, mumbling to the last about her children.

F. W. Swaen, of Boulder, Georgia, recalled, "I had gone to the dining car, and hadn't gotten the meal I ordered. I felt the train jar when the brakes went on and was thrown against a table across the aisle. It was awful in the car—no lights, women and children and men screaming and everybody fighting to get out, and nobody able to move."

A. R. Meyer, of Detroit, a rider in the coach, said, "I had just commented on the queer jolting we were getting when the crash came. The lights went out and I found myself thrown to the floor, through which the tracks seemed to have risen. It was terrible. Screams from all sides and the smell of escaping steam made some of them think that the car was on fire. It seemed hours that we were there, but I suppose it was not more than fifteen minutes. Too much time was wasted trying to break in the doors, which were jammed. Eventually we were all lifted out through the windows, which had been broken in the smash."

After the immediate shock of the crash wore off, uninjured people in many cases helped the injured. Others, however, wandered aimlessly about in the rain, unable to do anything. A special relief train bearing doctors and nurses was dispatched from

THE WEATHER
Body probably followed by rain and Friday; warmer in tonight; warmer Friday.

Local Quotations
Strict middling 12
Middling 11¾
Hens, 18c; Fryers, 45c; Stags, 18c; Eggs, 38c.

Rome News-Tribune

9, NO. 177.   N. E. A. Service, Inc.   ROME, GEORGIA, FRIDAY, DECEMBER   1926.   Member Associated Press   5c a Copy—15c Week by Carrier

INETEEN ARE KILLED WHEN FAST TRAINS CRASH

Rome to the scene of the accident. According to the Rome *News-Tribune*, "The scene . . . tested the strength of strong men. Bodies of victims crushed and mangled beyond description were . . . unreachable because of tons of weight on them. The roof of the diner was rolled up like paper. The body of one man was hanging from a window, his legs pinned beneath the heavy weight." It was speculated that he had tried to jump from the train. Rain and mud only added more horror to the scene. As the injured were brought out, they were put on a special train for Atlanta. Later on, the dead were removed.

In all, thirty people died in the wreck, including the Road Foreman of Engines, Robert M. Pierce, who had taken over a little before the crash from the regular engineer of the Ponce de Leon. There was nothing unusual about this procedure. Pierce lived several hours after the crash, had an arm and a leg amputated in an effort to save his life, but died of his massive injuries. Also dead was the fireman in the engine with him, H. R. Moss, killed instantly. His arm was torn from his body and later found in the cab. W. H. Brewer, the baggagemaster, died a few

hours later. Another thirty people suffered severe injuries. Counting minor injuries, the number of casualties eventually reached 123.

The official statement on the cause of the wreck, issued a day later, declared that it was due to the failure of the engineer of the Ponce de Leon to heed an order. It added that he had previously an unblemished record.

Actually the cause of the wreck is to this day not known. S. J. Keith, the regular engineer, had been directed by Pierce twelve miles down the track from the wreck to "go back into the train." According to Keith's later statement, Pierce was running behind time at a high rate of speed, "dropping down off the mountain below Rockmart." At the time of collision he was driving headlong into the blinding rain. Some speculated that Pierce was perhaps not familiar with a new switch head and ran past it. Others believed the block had been thrown but that for some reason the switch did not open. A third speculation was that in the driving rain Pierce mistook a freight engineer's signal from a siding further up the line as the Royal Palm's signal that all was clear. If this were so,

Engine 1219 after the wreck, with the coach behind telescoped into the dining car "as neatly as a letter fitting into an envelope." *Courtesy Shelby F. Lowe.*

it would have explained why he kept going: he thought he had an open track ahead. In all, the third possibility is the likeliest. Pierce's record was absolutely clear, and he had gone through the ranks to become Road Foreman of Engines. The ICC analysis concluded that the wreck occurred because the Road Foreman of Engines Pierce who had relieved Engineman Keith either failed to have a thorough understanding with the engineman as to the contents of train order No. 92 or else forgot it. A Rome doctor named Shaw, who cared for the dying Pierce, reported that Pierce made the cryptic statement before

he died that "there was no excuse for the occurrence of the accident."

The song that follows was written by a blind local songwriter, the Rev. Andy Jenkins of Atlanta, within three weeks of the accident. It was recorded, according to Norm Cohen, on January 14, 1926, by Vernon Dalhart; thirty-six thousand copies of it were sold.

The focus of this wreck song is somewhat different from the usual. No mention is made of the engineer's death—all attention is upon the passengers. A preacher who was not a railroadman must be forgiven for "seeing" the wreck through his lay-

The Rockmart wreck on the night of Dec. 23, the Ponce de Leon and the Royal Palm met 1926, was one of Georgia's worst. Twenty were killed and 50 injured when head-on. Most of the casualties were passengers hurrying home for the holidays.

man's eyes. An oddity is the title of the song. One would expect it to be called "The Wreck of the Ponce de Leon," as all the serious casualties and fatalities were aboard that train, and not the Royal Palm. It seems likely that the good reverend composed it so hastily that he got mixed up about which train was which. For he has the Royal Palm "making time" when it was waiting, barely drifting; he also has a later reference to the dead having been on the Royal Palm, which is inaccurate.

The Wreck of the Royal Palm

THE WRECK OF THE ROYAL PALM

1. On a dark and stormy night
   The rain was falling fast.
   Two crack trains on the Southern road,
   With a screaming whistle blast,
   Were speeding down the line
   For home and Christmas Day.
   On the Royal Palm and the Ponce de Leon
   Was laughter bright and gay.

2. Then coming around the curve
   At forty miles an hour,
   The Royal Palm was making time
   Amid the drenching shower.
   There came a mighty crash—
   The two great engines met,
   And in the minds of those who live
   Is a feeling they can't forget.

3. It was an awful sight
   Amid the pouring rain,
   The dead and dying lying there
   Beneath that mighty train.
   No tongues can ever tell,
   No pen can ever write,
   No one will know but those who saw
   The horrors of that night.

4. On board the two great trains
   The folks were bright and gay.
   When like a flash the Master called
   They had no time to pray.
   Then in a moment's time
   The awful work was done,
   And many souls that fatal night
   Had made their final run.

5. There's many a saddened home
   Since that sad Christmas Day,
   Whose loved ones never will return
   To drive the gloom away.
   They were on the Royal Palm
   As she sped across the state;
   Without a single warning cry
   They went to meet their fate.

6. We're on the road of life
   And like the railroad man,
   We ought to do our best to make
   The station if we can.
   Then let us all take care
   And keep our orders straight;
   For if we get our orders mixed,
   We sure will be too late.

The last stanza once more recalls the many "road-of-life" poems popular at the time, and especially the widely-sung "Life's Railway To Heaven," beginning:

Life is like a mountain railroad,
With an engineer that's brave,
You must make the run successful,
From the cradle to the grave;
Watch the curves, the fills, the tunnels;
Never falter, never quail;
Keep your hand upon the throttle,
And your eye upon the rail.

NOTES

My roommate at Hollins College in 1955–56, Susan Gilbert Harvey of Rome, Georgia, whose grandfather, Dr. Harbin, went to the wreck to help the wounded, kindly provided me with copies of the original stories on the wreck and semi-centennial articles: The Rome *News-Tribune*, 24 Dec. 1926; and the Rockmart *Journal*, 24 Aug. 1972. As usual Norm Cohen's *Long Steel Rail* provided me with a good background for my chapter. I also used information from the A.P. story in the Richmond *Times-Dispatch*, 25 Dec. 1926. In *Trapped!*, Murray and Brucker relate an incident in which Polk C. Brockman, a talent scout and record producer, approached Andy Jenkins about writing a song on Floyd Collins. If the tale is accurate, Jenkins sat at the piano and wrote the song in an hour. This may be an indication of the amount of "research" that went into his compositions.

Shelby F. Lowe of Douglasville, Georgia, kindly sent information on this wreck, and both he and Howard Gregory lent me photographs from their personal collections. According to Lowe, the "only blame put on 'Stony' Keith was that after reading the meet orders he should have turned them over to Pierce instead of putting them back in his pocket." Pierce, however, as determined in the investigation, understood that he was to meet the Royal Palm and take the siding, which he failed to do. "So Keith," Lowe writes, "was blamed for holding the orders."

The Wreck of the Virginian Train No. 3

It was a bright spring morning on the twenty-fourth of
  May,
The train crew was at Roanoke, they were feeling fine
  and gay;
Train No. 3 had left Roanoke en route for Huntington,
These poor men did not know that they were making
  their last run.

The Virginian was something of an anomaly
among railroads. It was built from Sewalls Point,
near Norfolk, Virginia, to Deepwater, West Virginia,
by wealthy financier Henry Huttleston Rogers.

Upon its opening in 1909, the Norfolk *Ledger-Dispatch* reported that it was "different from any
other railway in the world." Most railroads were
built to join population centers; they followed water
grades and snaked around mountains, tunneling
through only if the way around was absolutely impractical. Not so the Virginian. Ben Knight, retired
from the C & O, says it was "built as if the Virginia
landscape weren't there." The railroad went straight
through mountains and across rivers and trestled its
way over valleys, paying no heed to the natural con-
tours of the land, consequently costing so much that

A coal train with four electric motors hauling it. *Courtesy Norfolk and Western.*

it came to be known, at least among rival railroads, as "Rogers' Folly." Much of its mountain trackage west of Roanoke was electrified. But Rogers was rightly convinced that it would pay back enormously in the end, according to Lloyd D. Lewis of the C & O, who is currently writing a history of the Virginian to enhance Reid's famous work of twenty years ago. It was built with one purpose: to get coal out of West Virginia and to the Atlantic Ocean. Ninety-five percent of the tonnage on its rails was coal.

According to the *Book of Rules*, based on the Standard Code of the American Association of Railroads, passenger trains were first class—after all, they had schedules to keep. Freight trains were third or fourth class, normally taking the siding to let the passenger trains by. But the Virginian's primary reason for existence was the movement of coal, not passengers. Thus it was one of the few railways in the country that consistently gave over the right of way to freight and coal trains instead of passenger trains. It was almost entirely single-track.

In May 1927, E. George "Dad" Aldrich of Roanoke had been with the railroad twenty-one years. At seventy-five he was the oldest engineer on the Virginian and had a total of forty-four years as an engineer behind him. He could have retired years earlier, but, according to his old friend Bernice "Si" Coleman, he "loved his engine." He was extremely popular with his fellow railroaders, and knew many folks along his run. John Boyd Weeks of Princeton, West Virginia, remembers him as a hearty, heavyset fellow who liked to talk and make people laugh. "I was still in school. I'd go down to talk to Aldrich in the summer when the train stopped at Princeton—everyone liked him. He never met a stranger, and he didn't feel he was better than anyone else. He was fixing to retire. He was on his last run. . . ."

The building of the Virginian Railway, 1907. This photo shows a typical timbered trestle, of which there were dozens across little valleys. The Virginian was built as straight as possible through the rugged and mountainous Virginia and West Virginia terrain. *Cook collection, Valentine Museum.*

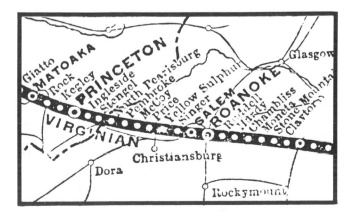

Aldrich's fireman that day was Frank M. O'Neal, about twenty, of Page, West Virginia, and he was engaged to be married shortly to Miss Katherine Kelly, also of Page.

Westbound train No. 3, running from Roanoke to Charleston on Thursday, May 24, 1927, was pulled by steam locomotive No. 212, a Pacific 4-6-2 engine. Conductor Hamilton was in charge of the train, and brakeman Agee completed the crew.

As has been said, a passenger train had automatic right-of-way over any freight train. The crew that was running No. 3 wouldn't have had to look out for another train unless they got a meet order. But in this case, as frequently happened on the Virginian, the standing rule was impractical: No. 3 hauled only five passenger cars westbound, and the train that was coming east on the same piece of track, extra No. 103, hauled ninety laden coal cars behind two electric-powered locomotives. Sensibly, the crew of No. 3, due at Ingleside, West Virginia, at 11:51, had orders to take the siding to let the long coal train continue with its momentum. But the meet order was given twenty-five miles before the meeting, and all the crew somehow forgot or overlooked it.

At 11:52 A.M. on Thursday, May 24, 1927, as it emerged from a tunnel just west of Ingleside, No. 3 collided with extra train No. 103.

The accident was spectacular. "Like some monster alive," the Hinton, West Virginia, *Daily News* reported the next day, the steam locomotive drove right up on top of the big electric motor and hung there, "the pilot reared to the sky; the tender,

crushed and wrecked, hung under the weight of the engine from which huge volumes of steam still escaped an hour after the crash." It was as if the smaller passenger engine tried to go right up and over the larger one, determined not to be bested by a mere coal train!

Aldrich and O'Neal both died, scalded to death by the steam from their ruptured steam pipes. J. L. Weaver, the engineer of the electric train, was badly injured but survived. About thirty passengers were knocked about; doctors and nurses from a Princeton hospital, five miles away, left at once to minister to the injured.

The newspapers theorized that the crash might have been much worse if No. 3 had not been just leaving Ingleside and the other moving slowly towards the meeting. In fact, no cars derailed on either train, though there was a considerable concussion.

John Boyd Weeks, a student then, was going by train to Deepwater that day from Kellysville. Just

"The engine climbed up on the motor, but she did not overturn. . . ." E. G. "Dad" Aldrich and Frank M. O'Neal died when they overlooked their orders and their engine, No. 212, collided with eastbound freight 102. The catenary, or overhead wire system of the electric train, shows above the cars. *Courtesy Edgar Shew and Bernice B. Coleman.*

out of the Ingleside tunnel he felt a sudden lurch, and the train started moving backwards. Immediately, he recalls, a large black woman leaped up and began to pray loudly, asking the Lord to save her husband, who sat in his seat looking embarrassed, without a scratch. Weeks wanted to get out and find out what had happened, but the hysterical woman, "as big as all outdoors," wouldn't let him by, so he "walked over the backs of the seats to the end of the car. The door was jammed." Finally he was able to open the door and jump out into a ditch by the track. He landed nearly to his knees in hot water from the exploded boiler. When he walked up to the front of the train, he saw his old friend Aldrich "scalded like boiled chicken."

Bernice "Si" Coleman was a station agent for the Virginian at the time of the wreck. He remembers that Aldrich's wife wouldn't let them take him out of the cab until she'd seen him. He recalls the wreck all too well, and how afterwards the Virginian was careful to deliver train orders as reminders. Mr. Coleman explained that when the crew of any train received orders of any kind, they were read and repeated back to each other by each crew member, then hung on a hook before their faces so they were in sight at all times. He thinks that the crew that day "undoubtedly had previous orders to meet other eastbound trains before Ingleside," and that the confusion may have arisen from so many meet orders. He says that only one passenger was "seriously" injured, claiming a fractured neck. The Virginian, Coleman recalls, paid him thirty thousand dollars; the man received the money and took off his "horse collar" soon afterwards.

The ICC investigation of the accident concludes that the crew of No. 3 was to blame. The ICC count of injured was twenty-nine, and this report also comments that it would have been worse had the train built up to full speed.

Three different songs were composed about this wreck. It occurred at what may have been the very apex of the popularity of railroad disaster songs. The first ones that we know of were composed in the mid-nineteenth century, but the first to achieve wide popularity probably dates from some time in the 1890s: the song about the wreck on the C & O that killed George Alley late in 1890. By 1927, the idea and the formula of railroad disaster songs was common; it is therefore not too surprising that three people, Roy Harvey, John McGhee, and Alfred Reed, in learning of this wreck, leaped upon the bandwagon of the day to write and profit from musical accounts. All three songs were recorded before the year was out.

So firmly rooted was the tradition of railroad disaster songs by then that each song has Aldrich and O'Neal happy, and each ends with a philosophical observation about life, yet clearly they are independent compositions. Only one of the poets, Roy Harvey, chose to mention the overlooking of the meet order, and he does not, in the song, editorialize, but merely reports the fact. John McGhee's version is the most "poetic," perhaps because he was a clergyman, accustomed to the clerical idiom. His song lyrics strike me as "cinematic," in today's terminology. Set against a lush and sensual landscape, a train moves closer and closer to its inexorable doom. Little railroad detail is offered. At the end of the first three, descriptive, stanzas, there is a cut from the brilliant May morning to a lonely midnight watch. Then comes a closeup of the two doomed men, loyal, unsuspecting, devoted to duty. The climax is not seen, underplayed in the extreme. It is as if we watch the train enter the tunnel, perhaps hear the crash, but, as in Greek drama, the tragedy occurs offstage. And finally there is the cosmic statement. I find this song in many ways the best, the most effective, of all the wreck songs. It is dramatic yet subtle, and quite original.

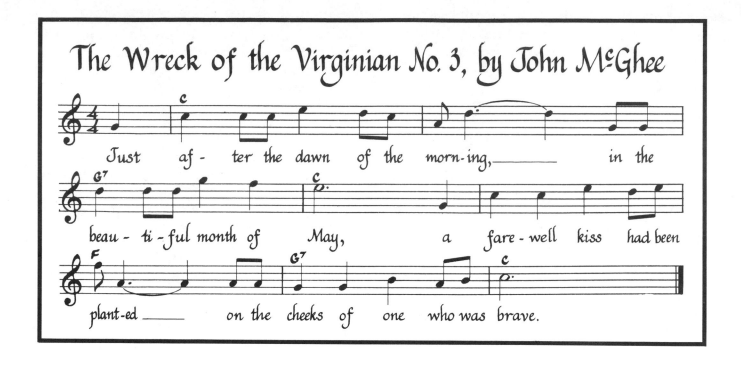

The Wreck of the Virginian No. 3, by John McGhee

Just af - ter the dawn of the morn-ing,_____ in the beau - ti - ful month of May, a fare - well kiss had been plant-ed _____ on the cheeks of one who was brave.

THE WRECK OF THE VIRGINIAN NO. 3

Just after the dawn of the morning, in the beautiful
     month of May,
A farewell kiss had been planted on the cheeks of one
     who was brave.

The morning was fresh in its glory, the sunlight was
     piercing the leaves,
As they plunged their way through the mountains with
     Virginian Train Number Three.

The soft winds were laden with perfume, which swept
     o'er the green valley wide;
And onward they rushed toward the peril which awaits
     them at Ingleside.

Some time at the dead hour of midnight, some prayers
     may be whispered at home;
For someone far out in the darkness may be crushed and
     dying alone.

"Dad" Aldrich was proud of his engine, and fireman
     O'Neal of his run;
For little they thought of approaching their final and last
     setting sun.

Together they wended the mountains, together they
     watched for the slides;
Together they looked for obstructions, together they
     perished and died.

It's ever the same with the trainmen, their lives are in
     danger, we know;
Through rain and through sleet and through darkness,
     wherever they're called they must go.

Blind Alfred Reed recorded his song, according to
Norm Cohen, on July 28, 1927. Lyrically, it is better
than some, though quite conventional in form: the

146

The Wreck of the Virginian No. 3, by Alfred Reed

Come all you brave, bold rail-road men and lis-ten while I tell, The fate of E. G. Al-drich, a good man we all loved well; This man was run-ning on a road known as Vir-gin-ian line, He was a faith-ful en-gin-eer and pulled his train on time.

moral, the happy crew, the come-all-ye beginning, are all the familiar appurtenances of folk songs.

Come all you brave, bold railroad men and listen while I tell,
The fate of E. G. Aldrich, a good man we all loved well;
This man was running on a road known as Virginian line,
He was a faithful engineer and pulled his train on time.

He was the oldest on the road, we always called him Dad,
He loved his engine very much, he was the best we've had;
Frank O'Neal was his fireman, he was faithful, true, and brave,
He stayed with Dad, he died with Dad, and filled a new-made grave.

It was a bright spring morning on the twenty-fourth of May,

The train crew was at Roanoke, they were feeling fine and gay;
Train No. Three had left Roanoke en route for Huntington,
These poor men did not know that they were making their last run.

Dad pulled his train, a pleasing smile on his bright face did beam,
He did not have to grumble, Frank sure kept him lots of steam;
At eleven-fifty-two that day they'd just left Ingleside,
An eastbound freight crushed into them, they took their farewell ride.

It seems that all good engineers to duty always sticks,
Dad entered into service in the year nineteen and six;
He did not have to work to live, they begged him to retire,

But Dad would not give his consent, to run was his desire.

Dear ladies, if your husband runs an engine on the line,
You may expect a message of his death most any time;
All railroad men should live for God and always faithful be,
Like Dad and Frank, they soon may pass into eternity.

Roy Harvey wrote and recorded the third version, also in July, with the North Carolina Ramblers: this one is the most factual of the three, but also the most awkward lyrically. It is interesting that the Virginian Railway asked Victor to remove the song from its catalogue soon after the record was issued, according to Norm Cohen. Victor complied. One wonders if this was because the Virginian felt the song to be inaccurate, or merely because the song embarrassed the railway. Lloyd Lewis of the C & O corrects "Northcross" to "Norcross," where a Norfolk & Western branch line crossed the main line of the Virginian, thus Nor-cross.

Roy Harvey, with his guitar, wrote and recorded one of three songs about the wreck of Virginian Train No. 3. Charley Poole is seated with banjo, and Posey Rorrer holds his fiddle and bow. *Courtesy Kinney Rorrer.*

On one Thursday morning, in the latter part of May,
Old Number three left Roanoke station, it was on their fatal day.

The engineer's name was Aldrich, happy he always did feel,
There with his young, cheerful fireman, his name was Frank O'Neal.

Up through the Valley of Virginia, over Allegheny Mountains so high;
But little did the men ever think of that day in the cab they would die.

Dad Aldrich said to his fireman, who was riding by his side,
"For twenty long years I've pulled this run, with Two Hundred and Twelve, my pride."

At Northcross they received their orders, eight-thirty-one it had to be;
For they were to take a siding, and meet eastbound Hundred and Three.

But they overlooked this order, at the station called Ingleside;
For they failed to take a siding, side by side in the cab they both died.

The engine climbed up on the motor, but she did not overturn;
With all of the steam pipes broken, two hundred pounds, they did burn.

Now railroad men, take this warning: heed your orders well,
For how soon the Lord may call you, no human tongue can tell.

The Wreck of the Virginian No. 3, by Roy Harvey

On one Thurs-day morn-ing, in the lat-ter part of May, Old

Num-ber 3 left Roa-noke Sta - tion; it was on their fa-tal day.

NOTES

Information is from the Roanoke *Times*, 25 May 1927; the Hinton *Daily News*, 25 May 1927; E. A. Lilly of Princeton, W. Va., sent me an article from the Roanoke *Times*, 6 Dec. 1959. Lloyd Lewis of the C & O provided me with two sources: "The Winding Gulf Coalfields," from Sam R. Pennington's Feature Stories Magazine (Apr. 1934) and *The Virginian Railway* by H. Reid.

On August 2, 1982, Paul Shue and I went to Princeton, West Virginia, where we talked to Bernice B. "Si" Coleman. He said he would play his fiddle for us, but that he didn't sing anymore: "I lost my voice trying to get my wife out of bed." Play he did, a regular concert, a medley of songs ranging from "The Wreck of the Sportsman" to "Soldier's Joy." He recalled vividly the Virginian wreck and "Dad" Aldrich. Born in 1898, Coleman got his nickname when he was a Virginian telegraph operator; they all had one- or two-letter signatures to save time, and his was "Si."

Others who helped with this wreck were Roy B. Atwell, Michelle and Boyd Weeks, E. R. Belcher, and D. R. Dunn. Charles "Chuck" Crawford of Charleston sent pictures. Also my thanks to Kinney Rorrer who provided me with Roy Harvey's tune, and, as always, to Norm Cohen. Tom Dixon comments that the "electric motors" mentioned in the newspaper account refer to the fact that they were not "engines" since they didn't create their own power; they simply transformed it from the electrical current in the overhead lines to mechanical energy which was applied to the rails and made the train move.

Three in Kentucky

Now you brave railroad men all take warning,
Make your peace now with God, don't delay.
Let Him strengthen your hand on the throttle,
For it may be your last run today.

When you live by the railroad, you live by its sounds. You come to know the right sounds, and to be alerted to the wrong ones. In your bones you know when the noon freight whistle is going to blow, and you set your watch by the mail train. Even in your sleep you incorporate the railroad into yourself, and its rhythms become part of the rhythms of life.

Early one foggy July morning in 1918, Samuel Tur-man, farmer, folksinger, and sometime legal aid, sat down to breakfast with his house guest, professor John Harrison Cox, of the University of West Virginia, who had come to visit and collect the songs that Mr. Turman knew.

"What time is it?" Mr. Cox asked.

"Must be six o'clock," Mr. Turman answered. "I hear the motor cars coming."

Within seconds, the two men heard three big smacks. Puzzled and alarmed, they went to see what the noises had been.

A few minutes later, on the same day, July 15, 1918, Mr. Turman's daughter Bessie was riding C & O train No. 36 home from Cattlettsburg where she had been visiting her aunt. Her family's house

Bess Turman in 1918, age twenty. *Courtesy Mrs. B. G. Lockwood.*

Buchanan, and that they were headed north for Hampton City, aboard gasoline-powered maintenance motor cars, to lay rail. The empty or "light" engine with her fiancé on it would be coming back southward to Paintsville.

She watched the familiar countryside slide by, and knew it was about time for her young nephew to be riding the family horse to pasture. She was wondering if she would see him when No. 36 stopped suddenly, right at the crossing, right in front of her house. Looking out of the window she saw their horse running across the field, riderless, and immediately she was afraid that the train had hit her nephew and killed him.

She scrambled out of the coach and ran to the front of the train. There she could not believe the horror that met her eyes: the empty, southbound locomotive had hit and nearly demolished three motor cars, and men were lying on both sides of the track. The motor cars were open flatcars with low rails, offering no protection if hit.

A hand car, predecessor of and similar to the motor cars in the 1918 wreck. Note the unprotected construction. *Dementi-Foster Studios.*

was right by a curve in the railroad track between Burnaugh and Buchanan, a big frame house with a wide front porch. She had to ride past her house to Buchanan to get off the train. She was twenty years old, and engaged to be married to Bernard Garred "Ben" Lockwood, a C & O brakeman.

Bessie knew that Ben had gone with his crew from Paintsville up to Ashland the night before to deliver a Mallet engine for repair. She knew also that a crew of twelve men had started out that morning northbound from Chapman, picked up a second crew of twelve at Louisa and a third crew of twelve at

And her mind absorbed another shock: Ben Lockwood was on that light engine!

She was paralyzed with fear. In the surreal fog of the morning, a man encased in a ball of fire ran wildly across their pasture and collapsed there, dead. One man, Paul Diamond, was cut into pieces. A third man kneeled at the pasture gate, his arms in the air, praying aloud, "Oh, dear God, help me!" He died there. Other voices cried out. Everywhere injured men lay groaning and screaming. Where was Ben?

There was nothing to do but to run on home across the road and begin helping her parents and Dr. Cox to minister to the injured. Passengers alit from the train; she and others helped to carry the injured men up onto their porch. The engineer of the light locomotive, Jay Thompson, and his fireman, Doc Compton, had not been injured. Thompson ran the engine to Buchanan, about a mile away, to get Dr. Alan Prichard, and brought the engine back with Dr. Prichard on it. Of the thirty-six men on the motor cars, only one escaped unscathed. Nowhere could Bessie see Ben, though she was assured that no one in the light engine was hurt. Eventually a member of the crew told her he had laid off that morning in Ashland.

After the injured men had all been brought up onto the porch of the big house, Mrs. Lockwood re-

calls that her mother set the broken leg of one, Ira Tabor. Her father, who kept whiskey for medication though he himself was not a drinking man, gave whiskey to the wounded to ease their pain, pouring it down their throats as they lay there. Mrs. Lockwood recalls that her father picked up the last dead man, Paul Diamond, in nine pieces, placed the remains in one of her mother's bedsheets, and tied it into a bloody bundle. They finally loaded all the injured men and all the remains of the dead onto the baggage car taken off the passenger train, and took them to Louisa, where there was a hospital.

The dispatcher at Ashland had forgotten about the motor cars, and given the light engine clearance to Louisa. It had been going sixty or seventy miles an hour when it hit the open steel motor cars, says Mrs. Lockwood. In all, five men died and thirty were injured.

The railroad follows the Big Sandy River which flows north. Across the river in Pritchard, West Virginia, people could hear the commotion but could not see what had happened, so foggy was the morning.

The wives of those who died, and the injured, sued the railroad for negligence. The C & O lawyers on the witness stand charged that the men on the motor cars had been drunk, and that had caused the

---

(Photo on opposite page) Taken in the fall of 1918, about two months after the freight and section crew wreck, this photo shows the Turman house at Burnaugh, Ky. Train No. 36 rounds the curve once more. The dead and injured men were carried up to the house and laid on both porches to await the train that would carry them to Louisa. In the left foreground, barely visible, are pieces still left from the wreckage of the three motor cars. Bess Turman Lockwood recalls that Paul Diamond's remains lay scattered "just about where the tracks enter the picture." She remembers vividly that on the evening of the day of the wreck, she and her father walked down the track, and came upon a piece of human liver that had been overlooked. *Courtesy Mrs. Ben G. Lockwood.*

Jay Thompson, engineer of the light engine that hit the motor cars on the morning of July 15, 1918. He is on the front row, his wife's arms around him. The man kneeling at the left is Walter Burke. Photo taken in 1922. *Courtesy Elizabeth Burke Fahrson.*

accident, since when the injured men had arrived at the hospital, there had been liquor on the breaths of all of them! Mr. Turman testified that it was he who had given the men liquor, and the families won their suits, Mrs. Lockwood thinks, for $5,000 each.

The Huntington *Advertiser* of July 15, 1918, reports that four men were killed and eighteen injured, that only "about 26" men were on the motor cars, and that the wreck occurred at six-thirty, also that "the motor cars were attached together." But Mrs. Lockwood insists her facts are the accurate ones.

On a clear summer morning sixteen years later, July 7, 1934, Mrs. Lockwood and her husband, Ben, then living in Paintsville, were working in the garden after breakfast, when they heard "a commotion." Bess stayed back, having several small children at home, but people ran by, calling to each other, "36 has wrecked on the overpass!"

Her husband dropped everything and went running towards the wreck, thinking his brother was on the train that morning. In fact, he was not, though it was his usual run.

In a house nearby, Bess Lockwood's friend, Elizabeth "Lib" Burke, was washing her breakfast dishes. Looking out the kitchen window, she could see passenger train No. 36, the same one that Bess Turman had been riding that morning in 1918, maybe half a mile away, approaching the highway crossing about two hundred feet from a bridge. As she watched, the engine "rared up and pitched over" before her eyes. She called to her husband Walter, an engineer who had been out on a night run and was still sleeping. "Walter! Walter! 36's engine went over the bridge!" Together, they "went like wildfire." "That's McDonie and Cheap," Walter told her as they ran towards the locomotive, which was stopped on its left side and practically at right angles to the track, its rear end on the roadbed and its head end down the fill. When they got there, she saw it lacked fifty feet or so of having gone off the bridge onto the highway.

Elizabeth and Walter Burke, 1925. *Courtesy Elizabeth Burke Fahrson.*

FOUR KILLED, EIGHTEEN ARE INJURED AS TRAIN AND MOTOR CARS CRASH

Four men were killed outright and eighteen injured at 6:30 a. m. Monday morning, fifteen miles east of Catlettsburg, on the Big Sandy division of the Chesapeake & Ohio railroad, when three railroad motorcars attached together collided with a freight engine running light, during a heavy fog.

The dead are:

Paul Diamond, single, Louisa, Ky.

John Chapman, married, of Louisa, Ky.

Jack Gillin, married, of Buckhannon Ky.

Harry Lambert, married, of Buchannon, Ky.

The workmen on the motorcars were enroute from Buchannon to Ashland, where they were to work on the construction of the freight depot.

The injured men are not believed to be fatally injured.

About twenty-six men are said to have been on the motorcars. The collision occurred in a heavy fog and on a curve. The injured were rushed to the Chesapeake & Ohio hospital in this city after they had been taken to Louisa, Ky., where they were given temporary treatment. The injured are: Andrew Thompson, Louisa Ky.; Harrison Moore, Buchannon, Ky.; Ira Tabor, Louisa, Ky.; Paul Johnson, Louisa; John Stewart, Buchannon; John Reed (colored), Louisa; Gus Scarberry, Louisa; Hobert Scarberry, Louisa; Virgil Phife, Maize, Ky.; Sherman Bauch, Chapman, Ky.; Charles Stump, Gilda, Ky.; D. D. Hobson, Buchannon, Ky.; John Nolan, Louisa, Ky.; Ben Thornhill, Louisa, Ky.; M. P. Hilton, Buchannon, Ky.; William Belcher, Louisa, Ky.; Ira Carter, Louisa, Ky.

The cause of the accident has not as yet been determined. The case is being investigated by the Kentucky State Railroad Commission and railway officials.

ENEMY COMBINES BLOW AT PARIS AND RHEIMS

The German offensive was resumed this morning on the fifty mile front extending from Chateau-Thierry eastward into the Champagne region.

Early indications are that the enemy is combining a drive toward Paris with a desperate effort to capture Rheims and eliminate that city as an obstacle to the advance.

The Champagne region thus has been linked up with the Flanders, Picardy, Oise and Marne fronts, nil, four miles west of Main de Massiges.

The first news of the resumption of the German offensive was received in this country shortly before eight o'clock this morning, in a dispatch from Fred S. Ferguson, United Press Staff correspondent, on the Marne front. He described a heavy bombardment from Vaux, two miles west of Chateau-Thierry to Jaulgonne, followed by an infantry attack at six a. m.

As they approached they could hear a feeble call from the engine, which emitted clouds of steam. "Help me! Help me!"

Walter Burke and William David "Bub" Cheap, 40–year–old fireman on No. 36, were close, so Walter recognized his friend's voice. From someone who had come to the wreck already Walter borrowed an overall jacket and put it over his head and arm as best he could. He reached into the engine from underneath, unable to see anything at all in the steam, and finally got hold of his friend's arm. But by that time Bub's hand and arm were so badly scalded that the skin slipped off in Walter Burke's grasp. Driven back by the steam, he stood helplessly, listening to the continuing cries of his friend, yelling for help. His calls produced a doctor, Paul B. Hall, out of the

Courtesy Elizabeth Burke Fahrson.

155

crowd, who reached in and gave the suffering man a shot of morphine. Cheap died a few minutes later.

Later the engineer, R. D. McDonie, wounded and confused in the collision, testified that the train, hauled by engine No. 444, a class F-15, 4-6-2 locomotive, built in Richmond in April 1907, was traveling about thirty miles an hour as it reached the crossing. McDonie looked down and, observing track ballast being thrown from under the engine cab, immediately applied the brakes in emergency, at which the engine derailed and then overturned. The time was 9:55 A.M. Conductor John Goodin, unharmed, got off the train at once and examined the crossing; it was filled with loose ballast and crushed stone. "Lib" Burke Fahrson explained that highway workers had put a load of limestone on the crossing.

Section Foreman Allen arrived ten minutes after the accident and observed mashed stone on the track, which was in the process of being repaired and was being carefully and regularly patrolled by trackwalkers, and tamped down frequently. The ICC investigation concluded that the accident "was caused by crossing material on the rails at a highway grade crossing." Mrs. Fahrson remembers well that her husband Walter said after the wreck that "his deepest fear was scalding to death."

Three years and a month later, on August 25, 1937, "Lib" Burke, then living in Paintsville, had her sister-in-law as a houseguest. Walter was out on a night run, carrying empty coal cars to the mines above Paintsville, and returning with loaded ones. He had left about three in the afternoon, with engine 1105, a class K-1, 2-8-2, built in Richmond in 1911. Lib was tired that night, having canned seventeen quarts of tomato juice that day, yet it was too hot to sleep. She wandered into the living room and lay down on the sofa, sleepless in the hot dark. Walter was due back at any time from eleven to four, depending upon how much coal there was to carry and how many cars there were to haul. Lib denies any premonitions of disaster that night, though it was unusual for her to have trouble falling asleep. Finally at midnight a light rain began, wafting coolness into the room, and Lib drifted off.

At four in the morning there was a knock at the front door. Aroused instantly from her drowse, she saw that it was her second-door neighbor. "Are you by yourself?" he asked.

The engine in which "Bub" Cheap died on July 7, 1934, turned almost at a right angle to the tracks. *Courtesy C & O Historical Society, Alderson, W. Va.*

"No, my sister-in-law is here with me," she said. "Why?"

"Go wake her up," he said.

But Lib Burke, a strong woman, stood her ground. "You might as well to tell me now," she told him. "Something's happened."

Her sister-in-law, Louise, woke up at this point, and immediately assumed something had happened to *her* husband, Lib's brother Bob, and emerged from her bedroom screaming.

"Walter got killed last night," the neighbor told her quietly.

"Where is he?" was all she could think to ask.

"At the funeral home," the man replied.

They had been married twenty-four years. Over the next few minutes, she got the story in pieces.

Walter, on the return run from the mines only eight miles east of Paintsville, nearly home, had suddenly seen a rockslide on the track before them near Auxier, and yelled for the fireman and brakeman to jump. The brakeman, E. T. "Doke" Sherman, did. The train crashed into the rock and derailed, at about 12:25 A.M. It turned over down the fill one and one-quarter times, going right over "Doke" Sherman without touching him, and finally landing near the edge of the Big Sandy River. The conductor, Charlie Stapleton, ran at once to the front of the train. He and the fireman, Dave Corder, got Walter Burke, who was calling piteously for help, out of the engine. Conductor Stapleton then ran a mile to the closest C & O telephone to call Paintsville for help. Walter had been hit in the head by the seatbox, and was, in addition, badly scalded. Corder and Sherman, both severely scalded themselves, tried to get Walter up the bank. They would gain one step, then slide back three, as the fill gave way. Walter said, "Lay me down, boys. I'm going to die." He asked them to take his shoes off and to pray with him. When Stapleton got back, he and Walter prayed together "until the last breath left him," twenty-five minutes after the

ENGINEER KILLED IN C. & O. CRASH

Two Other Men Are Hurt When Train Plows Into Slide Near Auxier, Ky.

One man was killed and two others were seriously injured in a train wreck at 12:30 o'clock this morning east of Auxier, Ky., between Prestonsburg and Paintsville.

Walter Burke, 50, Paintsville, engineer, was instantly killed, while Dave Corder, 50, West Van Lear, Ky., fireman, and E. T. Sherman, 40, Paintsville, brakeman, were badly scalded.

The engine, a shifter-extra working out of the coal fields in the vicinity of Paintsville, was pulling a number of empty coal cars from Paintsville along the main line of the C. & O. railroad when it ran into an earth slide, caused, officials said, by heavy rains last night.

Burke was a veteran engineer, having been employed by the C. & O.

accident. Stapleton told Lib that he was conscious until the last minute. The other two, though according to the newspaper accounts "scalded over their entire bodies," survived.

As for engine 1105, the tender remained coupled to it, and the first four cars were scattered down the embankment, badly damaged, while the next three derailed and were slightly damaged. The rock slide, according to the ICC report, consisted of about 150 tons of blue shale, fallen from an almost vertical cut. No reason could be offered for why the slide occurred.

After Walter died, Lib married E. R. Fletcher, the C & O insurance claims agent who settled with her over her husband's death. She recalls sardonically that she "had to marry him to get rid of him," so hard did he press his suit upon her. "Then," she says, "I had to get rid of him all over again." Finally, in 1948, eleven years after Walter's death, she married Frank Fahrson, another C & O engineer, whom she has also outlived. For the years of her three marriages, she had a Gold Pass, which meant she could ride any C & O train free anywhere, anytime.

Lib Fahrson is spry and feisty at eighty-seven, but gets annoyed that she can no longer see well enough to drive at night. Today she still has a free Amtrak pass, which she used recently for trips to Washington and Norfolk.

These photos show Engine 1105 being raised. New track had to be laid for the engine to be set on. The last two show her upright, and in the photo above the Big Sandy River shows in the background. *Courtesy Elizabeth Burke Fahrson.*

Bess Lockwood (left) and Lib Fahrson, 1982. *Photo by Paul Shue.*

Her lifelong friend, Mrs. Ben Lockwood, eighty-five, has painted four of her ceilings this summer of 1982, works her own garden and flower beds, and is proud that she isn't "on any kind of medication." She still lives in the house in Paintsville, Kentucky, that she and Ben bought from the railroad in 1933 for three hundred dollars. She has been connected with the railroad all her life. Her husband worked fifty-three years for the C & O, retired at seventy-three, and lived to be ninety-two. Her three sons all worked for the C & O for at least part of their careers. Her father-in-law was a bridge foreman for the C & O who died on duty at Montgomery, West Virginia, in 1916. The Lockwoods were a close family. Bess's husband had five brothers, all of whom worked for the C & O, and each of them had at least fifty years' service. Today some of their sons still work for the railroad. One of these, Bill Lockwood, forty-four, of the Seaboard Coast Line Railroad, describes Bess as a "beautiful old lady." When Ben died in 1977, Bill rode all night on a motorcycle to Paintsville from Savannah to be a pallbearer at his uncle's funeral. Bess Lockwood says proudly that Lockwoods have given more than 350 years of service to the C & O!

The "Freight and Section Crew Wreck" documents the 1918 accident accurately, which leads me to believe it must have been written by someone close by, certainly someone involved with the railroad. Norm Cohen discovered the song in the Kentucky Folklore Archives, where it was attributed to the Rev. E. J. Shumway. Mrs. Fahrson can't recall who that might have been, but Mrs. Lockwood recalls a "Brother Shumway who was a Methodist minister somewhere around at the time." Norm Cohen sent the ballad to Ron Lane, who published it in the March 1972 *C & O Historical Society Newsletter.* It seems to exist only as a broadside, and perhaps never was a song. Yet it might be tempting to try some of those marvelous old Methodist hymn tunes to see if a "fit" could be found. When I read the words over the phone to Mrs. Lockwood, she said, "That's exactly right. Exactly. It makes me shiver." The song is formulaic, and ends with the usual cautionary message. It is interesting that the facts of the song agree with Mrs. Lockwood's facts rather than with the news stories.

C. & O. FREIGHT AND SECTION CREW WRECK

In the Big Shady Valley of Kentucky, a division of the
   famous C & O,
A section boss gets orders at Louisa, clear block to
   Hampton City, boys, let's go.
With 28 miles before them on their journey, three motor
   cars are speeding on the way,
Not a man had dreamed before they started, that for
   some of them 'twood be a fateful day.

Jay Thompson got his orders at Ashland, with Doc
   Compton he was pulling on an east bound freight,
The operator telegraphed Louisa, but alas he telegraphed
   too late.
"One chance remains to save the boys," said Wellman,
   "if they haven't passed Buchannon they'll not die."
He telephoned, "For God's sake flag those handcars."
But they answered back, "Too late, they've just
   passed by."

The fog was rising thickly from the river, "We're just
   below Buchannon," someone said.
Just then three crashes came which tell the story, and
   five section men are numbered with the dead.
Dear railroad men take heed from one that loves you, be
   careful as you speed along the way.
Remember as you face the many dangers, you too must
   face your maker judgment day.
                    (*Rev. E. J. Shumway, Whites Creek, Ky.*)

Jim Dobbins of Johnson County told Jean Thomas
he made up the song about the wreck of 36, and said
it was (in 1939) still being sung by survivors of the
crew. For this one too, unfortunately, the tune is lost.

THE WRECK OF 36

It was on one July morning
About eight o'clock, they say,
When Thirty-Six left Ashland
And thundered on her way.
McDonney at the throttle,
A man both tried and true
And Bubby Cheap, his fireman,
And a faithful engine crew.

They made good time that morning
Their spirits rolling high.

They had no thought that danger
Was surely lurking nigh.
As Thirty-Six neared Paintsville,
The train began to rock,
A sound of grinding metal
And then a mighty shock.
McDonney did not falter
His trust he did not fail,
And Cheap stood firm and ready
As the engine left the rail.

The story soon was ended;
As on her side she lay,
The scalding steam came hissing;
Someone's life must pay.
For, pinned beneath the engine,
Poor "Bub" he writhed in pain,
McDonney lay there helpless,
His struggles all in vain.

The burning steam came rolling,
But they were forced to lie.
"Bub" Cheap was slowly scalded,
An awful death to die!
But quick, and willing workers
McDonney's life did save,
Poor "Bub" was past all succor,
His precious life he gave.

When tender hands released him,
He was past all mortal pain.
They bore him from the wreckage
Of that ill-fated train.
Long will his friends in service
The story sad relate,
When Thirty-Six turned turtle,
And "Bub" Cheap met his fate.

And finally, Buddy Preston told Jean Thomas he
wrote "The Wreck on the Hunnicut Curve" for his
good friend Walter Burke, and Thomas transcribes it
once again with no tune. This one can be sung to
many of the "other" tunes, and is rather admirable in
its accuracy and grace. I would suggest that a good
tune might be that of "The Freight Wreck of Altoona," though the "1256" tune is nice also.

They called for a train crew at Paintsville,
On a night that was rainy and drear,
And the men started out at the summons
With no thought of the danger so near.

The engineer mounted the engine,
And his fireman was close by his side.
He laughed as he opened the throttle,
And prepared for his last fatal ride.

The flagman waved them his signal
As they paused at the switch light so bright;
And with one final shriek of the whistle
The train headed west in the night.

There were only three men on that "shifter"
Many nights they had worked this same crew;
And poor Walter threw open the throttle
With a hand that was steady and true.

The fireman leaned out from the window,
Watched the sparks from the great drivers fly;
They pulled on the switch and took siding
To let old Thirty-Nine thunder by.

Through the switch, up the main line they started
With their minds on the work to be done;
Gathered cars full of coal from the tipples
With no thought they were on their last run.

They were only eight miles out of Paintsville,
On the Hunnicut Curve, so 'tis said;
When the engine she rocked and she trembled
And then slipped to the deep river bed.

But the brakeman he leaped from the wreckage
And he climbed over slippery coal.
He found Walter still at the throttle,
With a prayer on his lips growing cold.

Now you brave railroad men all take warning,
Make your peace now with God, don't delay.
Let Him strengthen your hand on the throttle,
For it may be your last run today.

Journalism is often imprecise. The news stories about Walter Burke's death all claim that he "died instantly."

Mrs. Fahrson, who was Mrs. Burke, has a copy sent to her by Blanche Preston-Jones that is exactly the same except that in stanza 2 "by" is "at." Lib, oddly, does not know who Blanche Preston-Jones was, but recalls that Buddy Jones was the son of her landlady after Walter died.

```
                        Ashland, Kentucky.

                        Feb. 7th, 1938.


Mrs. Walter Burke,
Paintsville, Ky.

Dear Mrs. Burke:

     I wish to thank you and many other Paintsville Radio
friends for the interest displayed in my regular 8 oclock
broadcasts every Monday night. I take great pleasure in
sending you the words of the song composed on the wreck of
the Hunnicut Curve and assure you that it was written and
is featured with the greatest respect and reverence toward
the brave man who gave his life in the performance of his
duty.

     Will appreciate all comments and requests from my Big
Sandy listners in your vicinity.


                        Sincerely Yours,

                        "Chick" Thomas
                        Signed

"CHICK & HIS GUITAR"
Radio Station W C M I,
Ashland, KY.
```

Courtesy Elizabeth Burke Fahrson.

NOTES

In June 1982, I sent letters to newspapers all over the area where the wreck songs I had found originated. I had an especially gratifying response from the area around Huntington, Ashland, and Paintsville. One day in mid-July I had a response from Quincy J. Milem, Jr., saying that Walter Burke's widow, named "Farson," was still living, in Ashland. The next letter in the pile was from Elizabeth Burke Fahrson! On July 24, Maureen Worth and I visited her, and she shared her memories and photographs of the wreck that killed her first husband. A beautiful and vital woman still, she grows flowers indoors and out, is interested in antiques, and has a "way" with animals. She and her late husband Frank Fahrson actually tamed a cardinal once that lived with them as a house-broken pet, for three years. She has lived with the railroad all her life. Her father worked for the C & O, though he was killed in an accident in 1910 while working for a coal company as foreman of a tipple. When she was a child, her family raised canaries, which were valued not only as pets but as barometers of gas in the coalmines of Kentucky and West Virginia. "Lib" put me in touch with her old friend Bess Lockwood. Another who helped me date the Kentucky wrecks is Burt Allen. Everett N. Young of the C & O Historical Society sent me ICC wreck reports for which I am grateful. Bob Chapman of Huntington sent me xeroxes of clippings describing the wrecks; Huntington *Advertiser*, 15 July 1918; Ashland *Daily Independent*, 7–8 July 1934; 25–6 Aug. 1937. Mrs. C. L. (Jackie) Meek sent information, as did Fay Moore of the Louisa Library.

A copy of this ballad in the Blue Ridge Institute's archives at Ferrum College, Virginia, identifies the author of "The Freight and Section Crew Wreck" as Rev. H. L. Shumway (which is an example of how confusing folk-research can be), a "Big Sandy Circuit Rider, Kentucky Conference, Methodist Church, now of Van Lear, Kentucky." [1940]

In September, Bess Lockwood's nephew William G. "Bill" Lockwood, of Savannah, called me to add his memories to those of his aunt.

On October 1, Paul Shue and I went to Ashland to see Lib Fahrson and meet Bess Lockwood and to pick up a picture Bess had found of her girlhood home and the spot where the 1918 wreck occurred. We were utterly charmed, as Bess and Lib reminisced about their lives with the C & O. As girls, they had even dated some of the same young men. Recalling one, Bess Lockwood asked, "Why didn't you marry him?" Lib grinned. "I'll tell you why. I asked him what he was thinking of doing. He said 'Farming' and that did it!" Clearly, these are serious C & O women. Lib told us that Jean Thomas, who collected the two later songs in this chapter, is still alive at 101, living in Ashland in a nursing home. She called Lib after both her husbands died, though they are only distantly acquainted. When Lib last spoke with her, several months ago, "she was down to seventy pounds, and confided,

'I don't live here. I'm just here temporarily, working for the Courier-Journal.'" Bess Lockwood is indeed, as her nephew had promised, "a beautiful old lady," full of energy and wit and charm. She and Lib spun many a tale in the several hours we were there, but my favorite was of the time she went to buy groceries with one of her babies on her hip. The new storekeeper, being friendly, commented on how much the baby looked like its father. Pleased, Bess Lockwood agreed. When she brought out money to pay for her groceries, the storekeeper protested, asking her why she didn't charge them. "We don't charge," she replied. "Aren't you Mrs. Walter Burke?" he asked. Mrs. Lockwood replied, "No, I'm not. And Walter Burke isn't the father of this baby, either!"

On August 25, 1937, Walter Burke died when his engine turned over on Hunnicutt Curve. When the other crew members tried to carry the dying Burke up the fill, it was impossible because of the steep sides. Here the wrecking crane has arrived to put the engine upright again. *Courtesy C & O Historical Society, Alderson, W. Va.*

The Wreck of the Sportsman

In the dusk of a fair crimson sunset
Near the path of the old Midland Trail
'Twas there that the fast-flying Sportsman
Was wrecked as she swung from the rail.

Homer E. Haskell, of Huntington, West Virginia, had been with the C & O for more than thirty-five years the night he failed to observe the "slow" signal while bringing the Sportsman past the small station at Hawks Nest, West Virginia. The elegant passenger train was on time, due to pass through Hawks Nest at around 8:45. The station lies on an S-curve, thus necessitating that all through trains brake before passing.

On that midsummer's night, June 21, 1930, there was a vivid red sunset streaking the sky in that dramatic and mountainous spot on the New River. In 1868, W. A. Kuper, a surveyor for the C & O railroad, had written of the New River Gorge: "A location is obtained at a cost per mile scarcely to be realized by those who have but the opportunity of seeing it from the verge of its precipitous slopes and cliffs. The foot of man treads this valley but seldom; the toil and danger is such that but few attempt it, certainly not to gratify idle curiosity."

There were an unusual number of spectators at Hawks Nest Depot that Saturday night. Weather reports of that day and the next several indicate record highs. So possibly people preferred to stroll out in the cool of the evening for a breath of air.

The Sportsman was a luxury express, and had been in service only three months, running daily between Old Point Comfort and Detroit. Tom Dixon points out that the name came about because the train connected the Virginia coast resorts and the Virginia-West Virginia spring resorts with the resort and sporting areas of Michigan. Train No. 47 was pulled by engine 474, a class F-17 Pacific, a 4-6-2 locomotive. According to *C & O Power*, the Sportsman engines, "dolled up with polished cylinder and valve head covers, polished air pump jackets and embossed eagles on the Elesco feedwater heaters . . . were always immaculately groomed. . . ."

Between Sewell and McDougal, West Virginia, the New River Gorge is so narrow that the westbound track runs on the north side of the river, and the eastbound on the south side. The Sportsman, train No. 47, was westbound and moving on the north side. Close to Hawks Nest, the Hawks Nest Bridge crosses the river, and the two lines converge on the south side. Where the westbound track curves to cross the river, the speed is restricted to twenty miles per hour for all trains.

The signs, circular eighteen-inch yellow markers with block lettering, are on posts on the right, the engineer's side. The top number designates the speed limit for passenger trains, and the bottom number for freight, but this sign had only the one number: 20. An engineer failing to observe the sign would be in trouble.

VIEW WEST FROM HAWKS NEST.

Courtesy Thomas W. Dixon, Jr.

Courtesy C & O Historical Society, Alderson, W. Va.

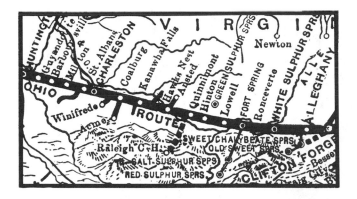

A view from the scenic overlook at Hawks Nest. On the curve just out of the camera's range, Homer Haskell and Henry Anderson lost their lives on the evening of June 21, 1930. This photograph was made by Henry Anderson in June, 1929, almost exactly a year before he died. The Hawks Nest station is the topmost building in the picture, with a spur track leading to it, and three standing cars. *Courtesy Ron Lane.*

Homer E. Haskell, the engineer, was sixty-seven years old. Henry C. Anderson, his fireman, was thirty-four. According to Ron Lane, they had made the Huntington to Hinton run earlier that day and were on the way back, only about two hours away from home. A contemporary timetable shows the train was due into Huntington at 11:18 P.M.

Did Haskell suffer a stroke or a heart-attack? Was he overtired from his long day's journey? Why did he fail to observe the "slow" sign for the curve at Hawks Nest Station? For some reason never determined, he kept his engine at speed going through Hawks Nest that evening. Before a group of horrified observers, the engine, followed by a combination baggage and passenger car, a passenger car, and an express car, went off the rails on the north side of the river just before the bridge, directly in front of the station, and the cars piled up close to the bridge abutment. Before the rescuers could get to the cab, Haskell was dead, his hand actually clutching the throttle. He was caught in the cab as the locomotive buckled up after derailing. His fireman, Henry C. Anderson, was lying free in the cab, alive but burned over three-fourths of his body by steam escaping from the cracked boiler of the locomotive. Hysterical passengers scrambled to safety over the wreckage which lay close to the depot. Lane describes the scene. A frantic search of the damaged cars was made, and it was determined that, miraculously, only three other people were injured: an express messenger, a baggage man, and a black woman who was a passenger. Quickly, Anderson and the other three were driven to Coal Valley Hospital, eighteen miles away. Anderson never regained consciousness, and died at 1:21 A.M. The others all survived. Haskell's body was taken to the Hooper Funeral Home in Montgomery.

At the wreck scene, passengers from the damaged cars were moved to the undamaged ones. The last half of the train, including a passenger car, three

Locomotive No. 1642 blew up with earth-shattering force in Hinton, West Virginia, on June 9, 1953, killing three crew members. The blast demolished the locomotive as it entered the yards with 125 loaded coal cars in tow, and three hundred feet of tracks were torn up. Among the dead was Engineer W. H. Anderson, sixty-two, who more than twenty years before had mistakenly been identified as the Anderson who was killed in the wreck of the Sportsman. C. W. Cabin tower is visible in the background. The cab of the engine was blown one hundred feet into the nearby New River. William J. Lockwood, of The Family Lines, recalls that "a few years ago, pieces of the engine were still visible in the New River." *Photo courtesy William J. Lockwood and C & O Historical Society, Alderson, W. Va.*

Henry Anderson and his son Oscar, 1929. It fell to Oscar to go to the station and collect his father's remains, which arrived in a wicker basket, the day after the wreck of the Sportsman. He recalled to Ron Lane that his father's train pass was wired to the basket as identification. *Courtesy Ron Lane.*

Onlookers gape the next morning at the wreckage scattered across the tracks just west of Hawks Nest Station, West Virginia. *Courtesy C & O Historical Society, Alderson, W. Va.*

sleepers, and a diner, had remained on the track. The engine had been stripped of its appurtenances on the left side, the engine truck torn apart and its wheels deposited in the debris. Wrecking crews working in the darkness cleared the track and enabled the Sportsman, behind another engine, to continue its run after only a three-and-a-half hour delay. The next day, a Sunday, hundreds of visitors came to this out-of-the-way spot, by auto and by train, to visit the crash scene.

Lane adds the following ironic story: the family of the engineer had to be notified first. The second call from Montgomery, to report the later death of Mr. Anderson, mistakenly went to the family of another railroading Anderson, a cousin of the man who had died. Since the other Anderson was also on a run, his family had to live with the terrible news for several hours until their husband and father arrived safely home and the error was corrected. However, in June, 1953, this family was to receive another call saying, this time correctly, that their loved one had been killed, along with his fireman, in a boiler explosion just as engine 1642 was drifting into the yards west of Hinton.

Damage to the locomotive and controls was devastating. On the left stands a somber inspector from Handley, while the workmen pose on the tender gangway.

The tool car men get ready to work on the wrecked baggage car. The brake wheel has been thrown vertically from its normal level position.

Hawks Nest depot, 1935. Photo by William Monypeny. *Courtesy C & O Historical Society, Alderson, W. Va.*

As wrecks go, this was not a very spectacular or devastating one. Yet the relatively minor accident of the Sportsman inspired two songs, including one of the loveliest of all the train disaster ballads. Remembering wrecks in song, though not the exclusive domain of the C & O, seems to have been a special tradition on that line, as has been noted elsewhere. Of course, the C & O runs through particularly rugged and treacherous terrain, with the constant threat of landslides. Certainly the curves and trestles create especially difficult runs, necessitating constant vigilance on the parts of the engineers and their crews. Perhaps Haskell had been at the throttle too long; perhaps his judgment had slipped that night, or overconfidence caused a moment of carelessness costing him his life. He had never been in another accident, which argues for his dependability. He left behind a wife and two children, and Anderson a widow and four children.

The summary of evidence in the ICC report indicates that the train was speeding to make up a few minutes' lost time. Those who testified indicated that Haskell seemed all right just before the wreck, that the brakes were working properly, that a brake application was made just before the train entered the curve, and that the track was in good condition. The conclusion was that the accident was apparently caused by train 47 "entering a sharp curve at a rate of speed considerably in excess of that for which the outer rail was superelevated."

The incident was briefly noted in national newspapers. Even in the state of West Virginia it shared headlines with another story that would end tragically: on June 21, the Lindberghs had a son, 7¾ pounds, and all America rejoiced. But by now we know that the magnitude of a wreck had nothing to do with its memorialization in song.

The Wreck of the Sportsman

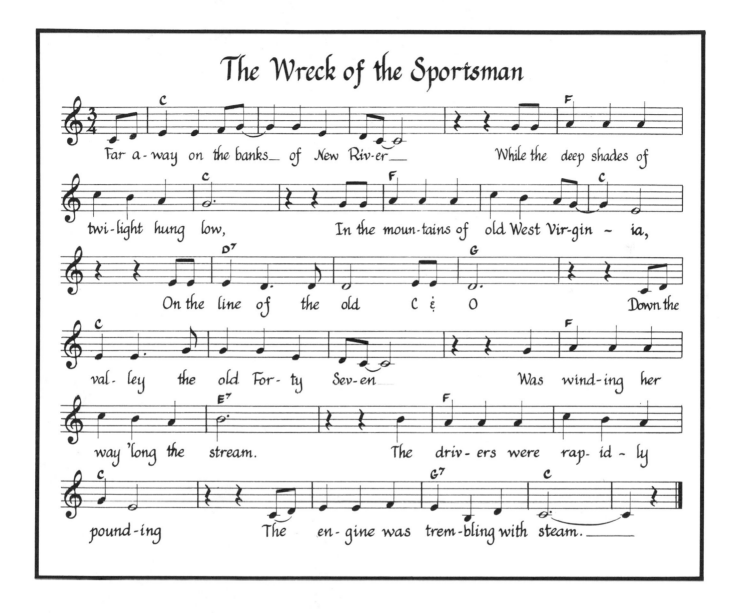

SPORTSMAN ENGINEER KILLED, FIREMAN DIES, THREE HURT

Far away on the banks of New River
While the deep shades of twilight hung low,
In the mountains of old West Virginia,
On the line of the old C & O;
Down the valley the old Forty-Seven
Was winding her way 'long the stream.
The drivers were rapidly pounding
While the engine was trembling with steam.

Haskell firmly held the throttle,
Anderson's fire glowed with red,
And they thought of no danger awaiting
Down the line on a curve just ahead.
In the dusk of a fair crimson sunset
Near the path of the old Midland Trail,
'Twas there that the fast-flying Sportsman
Was wrecked as she swung from the rail.

'Twas there in the dark shades of twilight,
While the bright crimson sky was aglow,
That Haskell and Anderson of the Sportsman
Gave their lives to the old C & O.
Just west of the station called Hawk's Nest
The engine turned over the fill;
The boys were found down near the river
By the engine they loved, lying still.

That night there were loved ones waiting
In Huntington for those boys—in vain,
For God, the Supreme Crew Caller,
Had called them for another train.
The years full of tears may be many,
And sad broken hearts ever burn,
While they think of the "Wreck of the Sportsman,"
And the loved ones who'll never return.

The song is typical of its kind. It is accurate in all but one detail: the body of Haskell and the unconscious Anderson were found in the cab, while the song implies they were thrown from it. Their unfailing nobility and loyalty are implied by the line, "Gave their lives to the old C & O." The deep blood-red sunset provides an appropriate setting for the tragedy, and the religious references in the final stanza are typical. The Midland Trail is Route 60.

"The Wreck of the Sportsman" was on a phonograph record eleven months after the wreck. It was written soon after the tragedy by a lifelong railroad man, Bernice "Si" Coleman, aided by Kyle Roop, a professional musician, both from Princeton, West Virginia. They also composed another song which Mr. Coleman told Ron Lane was about the same wreck. It seems unlikely, as the engineer's name is wrong and the train in the song, No. 4, was going in the opposite direction from the Sportsman. Ron Lane points out, however, that Haskell had engineered No. 4 earlier that day on the trip from Huntington to Hinton. And we have only Mr. Coleman's word on the matter. In July 1982 Mr. Coleman told me that "Ron Lane said this song could apply to the wreck of the C & O No. 5." When pressed, however, he admitted it was written about no wreck at all, that it was "just a story." In my estimation it is one of the loveliest of the wreck songs, historical or not.

The wrecking crane in position to raise the fallen Sportsman from the north bank of the New River. Across the river can be seen the eastbound track. *Courtesy C & O Historical Society, Alderson, W. Va.*

The Dying Engineer

An en-gi-neer one morn-ing___ Had kissed his wife good-bye,___
The sun-light was a-dorn-ing___ A bright and cloud-less sky.___
He stopped to pick a flow-er___ Be-fore he left the gate,___
And when he reached the tow-er,___ He found that he was late.___

THE DYING ENGINEER

An Engineer one morning,
  Had kissed his wife good-bye,
The sunlight was adorning
  A bright and cloudless sky.
He stopped to pick a flower
  Before he left the gate,
And when he reached the tower,
  He found that he was late.

A gentle voice that morning,
  Before he went away,
Breathed tender words of warning,
  "Be careful, Jack, today!"
He climbed into his cabin,
  As oft he'd done before.
A signal from the captain ·
  Highballed old Number Four.

The steam gushed forth with power,
  The wheels began to grind.
And soon the roundhouse tower,
  Was left and far behind.
The train began to quiver,
  The drivers left the rail;
And down beside the river
  Poor Jack lay deathly pale.

And while he lay there dying,
  Upon the stony clay,
He thought of one replying,
  "Be careful, Jack, today!"
"Oh, tell her to remember,
  When she is old and gray,
I kissed her cheek so tender,
  Before I went away."

Bernice B. "Si" Coleman, wearing his Virginian Railroad cap, fiddles happily, July, 1982. *Photo by K. Lyle.*

NOTES

Ron Lane has researched this wreck thoroughly; my thanks to him for so generously sharing his findings with me.

Other information was obtained from the Richmond *Times-Dispatch*, 22–23 June 1930; *C & O Power* by Staufer et al.; *Long Steel Rail* by N. Cohen; "Folkmusic of the C & O—Part 5" by Ron Lane in *The C & O Historical Society Newsletter*; interview with Ben P. Knight, March 15, 1982. Tom Dixon added some interesting observations, and Kuper's quotation is from Wallace's *Chessie's Railroad*. Mr. Robert Chapman, my Huntington correspondent, tried to track down survivors of Homer Haskell in Huntington, but was not able to find any.

Paul Shue comments that the Sportsman left Washington as C & O Train No. 5. Then at Gordonsville it was joined by another section, 47, and became train 5-47. It was known as train 47 also, and was variously called all of these.

I asked at the Hinton *Daily News* in May 1982 about pictures of local wrecks, and Mr. Fred Long of Hinton remembered that when they brought Tokyo Rose to the Federal Women's Reformatory at Alderson some time after World War II, John Faulconer of that paper "went all over the county looking for a camera to photograph her with." Finding none, he decided to buy a camera for the newspaper. Needless to say, I found no pictures of my wrecks at the Hinton paper, as all of my wrecks predated the second world war.

Spikes on the Rail

Ben Dewberry's Engine 1231 lies on its right side in a Georgia cornfield in the rain. We see the engine head-on, with the smokebox door, the endsill and the cowcatcher fully visible. The cab has been twisted off, and the tank and baggage car can be seen behind the engine. *Courtesy Shelby F. Lowe.*

On a bright and sunny day, in the merry month of May,
From Sanford a train pulled out on time,
Was old No. 52, a freight that went on through,
The fastest on the old Southern Line.

This is a true and sad story that has happened more than once. The prelude we can only imagine: a small boy, full of typical exuberant curiosity, is playing one afternoon in a field near a train track. He grows bored with watching the birds, or chewing the sour grass that grows in the field. He has put pennies on the track before, and the train has flattened them to twice their size, made them into formless copper plates. Dimes work even better, but of course they are harder to come by. He wonders what will happen if he puts a railroad spike that he has found along the track bed, on the rail. Maybe the train will flatten that too and he will have a new treasure to show off at school.

He knows from long attention that the train will be along soon now. He looks at the iron spike in his hand. He collects spikes. Maybe he shouldn't put something so big on the tracks. . . . But if it doesn't work, he can find another, as the spikes work their way out of the ties all the time from the vibrations of the trains.

The whistle brings him back. He looks down the track, but the gentle curve prevents his seeing the train. He decides. Quickly, before he can change his mind, he puts the spike across the track, and runs back to a safe distance where he can watch the train loom larger and closer, and wave to the glamorous engineer as he plunges by. . . .

On August 23, 1908, on the Southern Railroad, just a mile south of Buford, Georgia, train 38 (so denigrated in "The Wreck of the Old 97") hit a bolt or spike and wrecked.

It was Sunday afternoon at 12:40 when No. 38 left Atlanta. At the throttle of Pacific engine No. 1237, pulling the northbound passenger train, was a very popular veteran Charlotte Division locomotive engineer, Benjamin Franklin Dewberry. The fifty-year-old engineer had been with the Southern for twenty-five years. He was remembered along his run as tossing apples to children from his engine window. He had a wife of only three years, and each of them had a daughter from their previous marriages. He had sired three children but only one survived infancy.

When Dewberry hit the spike or bolt, he applied the emergency brake, thus saving his train but not himself. The engine toppled completely over on its side, crushing the steam pipes. Neither the engineer nor his fireman, Mayson Wadkins, made any effort to jump, but stayed with their engine.

The Atlanta *Journal* on August 25, 1908, states, "At the cost of his own life, Engineer Dewberry stood at the throttle and fire and scalding water, stood and suffered and died in order that the scores of men and women in his keeping might escape.

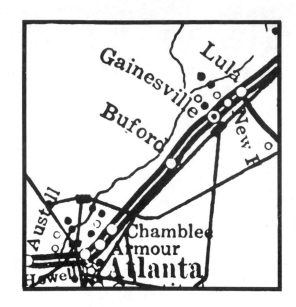

Thereby, many human lives were spared and thousands of dollars of property was saved." The fireman was also fatally injured.

Dewberry's first thought was for his wife. As he was dragged from the engine and laid on the grass, he begged that she be telephoned—"Tell her I'm hurt, but not very much." The Atlanta *Journal* makes the most of this dramatic event, reporting that Dewberry then asked after the passengers, though "the flesh was falling from his arms and a great hole was in his back." Dr. Charles E. Boyston, one of the passengers, obtained olive oil and table linen from the Pullman Car, and dressed the dying man's injuries. Mrs. Dewberry arrived just before he died, and "his eyes lighted up for a moment . . ." as she bent over him, weeping, "and kissed him through the bandages."

Twenty-four hours after the wreck, railroad detectives were at work to find out who had wrecked the train. They had already "heard" that there were "two or three small boys" to blame. On August 26, three days after the wreck, twelve-year-old Lewis Cooksie

ENGINEER BEN DEWBERRY.

Peculiar pathos and regret surround the death of Engineer Ben F. Dewberry, who lost his life in an accident on the Southern railroad on Sunday afternoon. He died, as he had lived, faithful to his duty and faced his end with the calm resignation of one who knew no fear.

When the crucial moment came there was no thought of saving himself, but only of the passengers whose lives were in his keeping, and his latest thoughts were to spare pain and suffering to one who was nearest and dearest to him.

He was one of the veterans of the road. For more than a quarter of a century he has been in the employ of the Southern and he counted his friends by the score, in Atlanta and all along the line of his run. He was recognised as one of the most skilfull and valuable men in the service of the company. In every walk of life he was known as a worthy citizen.

That his life should be snuffed out as a result of what appears to have been the malicious mischief of someone not yet apprehended only adds to the sense of grief with which his sorrowing friends are afflicted.

His name will be held in loving remembrance by a host of those who knew him best and therefore esteemed him most.

was apprehended and charged with having placed the bolt on the track that killed Ben Dewberry and Mayson Wadkins. At that time, it was believed that the lad had not acted alone. On August 30, young Cooksie was bound over to Superior Court and jailed on a murder charge.

From his picture, Lewis Cooksie looks like Tom Sawyer. He readily admitted to the crime, saying "I wanted to see what a train wreck looked like," but steadfastly refused to name his fellow miscreants. Eventually he was released, and charges were dropped on the basis that the boy had "but a slight realization of the enormity of his crime," and that he had "been influenced by two older youths."

There is a touching end to this story: two years later, Effie Lowe Kitchens Dewberry was married for the third time, to a man named Grant S. Martin. But when she died in 1913 she was buried next to Ben Dewberry, indicating, one supposes, that he was her greatest love.

LEWIS COOKSIE.

Ben Dewberry's Final Run

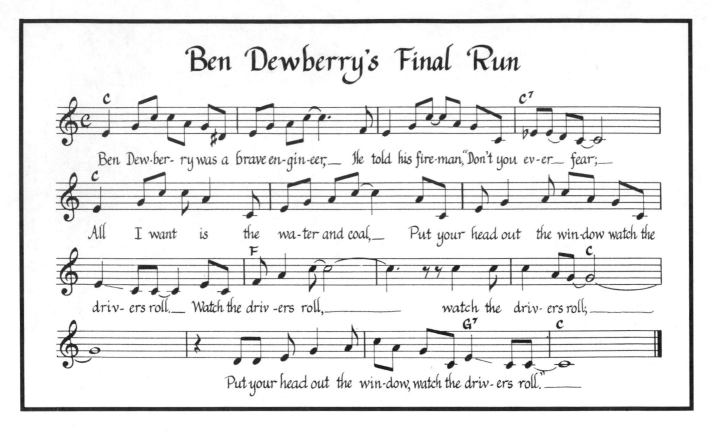

Ben Dew-ber-ry was a brave en-gin-eer,— He told his fire-man,"Don't you ev-er— fear;—
All I want is the wa-ter and coal,— Put your head out the win-dow watch the driv-ers roll.— Watch the driv-ers roll,————— watch the driv-ers roll;——— Put your head out the win-dow, watch the driv-ers roll."———

The Rev. Andrew Jenkins made a song out of this disaster which was recorded by Jimmie Rodgers. It was extremely popular; Norm Cohen reports that it sold 275,000 copies.

BEN DEWBERRY'S FINAL RUN

Ben Dewberry was a brave engineer,
He told his fireman, "Don't you ever fear;
All I want is the water and coal,
Put your head out the window, watch the drivers roll.
  Watch the drivers roll, watch the drivers roll;
  Put your head out the window, watch the drivers roll."

Ben Dewberry said before he died,
Two more roads that he wanted to ride;
His fireman asked him what could they be,
Said, "The old Northeastern and the A and V."
  "The A and V," he said, "the A and V,
  It's the old Northeastern and the A and V."

On the fatal morning it begin to rain
Around the curve come a passenger train;
Ben Dewberry was the engineer,
With the throttle wide open and without any fear,
  He didn't have no fear, he didn't have no fear;
  He had her runnin' wide open without any fear.

Ben looked at his watch, shook his head,
"We may make Atlanta but we'll all be dead."
The train went flyin' by the trestle and switch,
Without any warning then she took the ditch.
  Yeah, she went in the ditch, well, she took the ditch,
  Without any warning then she took the ditch.

The big locomotive leaped from the rail,
Ben never lived to tell that awful tale;
His life was ended and his work was done,
When Ben Dewberry made his final run.
  He made his final run, he made his final run,
  When Ben Dewberry made his final run.

176

The song is somewhat of an anomaly: its tune is cheerful and upbeat, its structure "bluesey." It lacks the usual religious warning so familiar in disaster songs, and it also lacks the usual detail, accurate or not. The A & V railroad was the Alabama and Vicksburg.

It also appears that Andy Jenkins did not know the cause of the wreck; the song implies indirectly that rain caused the disaster. The actual cause of the derailment was not reported in the Atlanta *Journal* until the next day. The ICC report of the wreck a month later listed "malice" as the cause, and indicated that in this accident, "near Suwanee," "1 person was killed and 2 injured." Mayson Wadkins was black; perhaps this explains the omission, for he died before Dewberry. It is tempting to imagine the Rev. Jenkins, writing his song on the very day of the wreck, hoping to cash in on the popular engineer's death. It is Norm Cohen's contention that both "Casey Jones" and "Ben Dewberry's Final Run" derive from earlier models. This may be so, but it seems to me that Ben Dewberry is very close to versions of Casey Jones, which was at that moment perhaps America's most popular song. Its hasty composition seems apparent, and my conclusion is that the song was a slapdash copy.

Another disaster, nearly identical, occurred on May 3, 1933, not quite a mile south of Ruffin, North Carolina, on the Southern Main Line, at four o'clock in the afternoon. Ruffin is just over the state line from Virginia, eleven miles south of Danville. Northbound freight train No. 52, pulling twenty-seven cars full of livestock, appeared to plunge from the rails for no reason. The land is flat, the track on a wide gentle curve. The cars crashed against each other and fell over or piled up, splintering, mashing the contents of other cars beneath them. Within seconds, twenty of the cars were total wrecks. George Allen, of Spencer, North Carolina, was the engineer. In the crash, his engine boiler broke open, and he

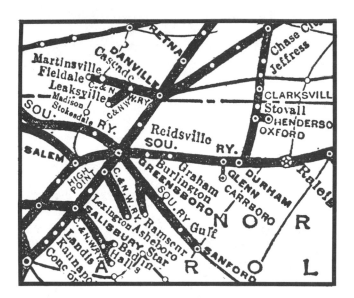

was scalded by escaping steam, along with his fireman, L. O. Woodson, who was less seriously burned. Six other crew members were injured also.

Mr. Woodson later recalled from his hospital bed the anguished animal cries, the neighing, squealing, and bellowing of the helpless hurt animals amid the wreckage. He told police officers that the train had been running at speed, fifty miles per hour, when it left the rails. He first sensed trouble when he felt the train bumping along the cross-ties. Looking ahead, he saw rails fly up into the air, ripped from the track. Then when they stopped, the entire scene was so engulfed with hissing steam that he could not see to get out of the wreckage. He could not find Allen. As he struggled to get out of the cab and away from the steam, he was hit by a flying object and knocked almost senseless. Upon recovering, he started back into the steam to find George Allen, and met a railroad detective and another trainman bringing the unconscious engineer out.

People began to gather at the scene. Allen and Woodson were moved by ambulance to Hughes Memorial Hospital in Danville. The other crew mem-

bers, including Conductor G. H. Miller of Spencer, were treated at the scene of the wreck. Sgt. R. S. Harris of the North Carolina State Police "moved up and down the train killing cows with broken backs and silencing hogs squealing in their agony."

Word quickly spread that there were newly slaughtered animals all over the tracks. People in the area stole hogs and chickens with abandon, and even dragged off several whole beef cattle carcasses before Southern officials could get reinforcements to the scene.

In Danville, Engineer George Allen lay in the hospital fighting for his life. He was scalded over most of his body, and had also inhaled the escaping steam. His wife came during the night, and sitting at his bedside, told reporters that she had heard that a small boy had been seen to place a spike on the track.

Crews from Monroe, Danville, and Spencer labored with the aid of three huge derricks to move the wreckage. By nightfall the tracks were clear, but debris lay piled alongside the tracks, and there were still hundreds of animal carcasses at the scene.

Within hours of the wreck dead animals were being bought and sold in Danville at low rates, for meat and hides. The weather was warm and citizens were offended by the sights and odors they had to endure. Danville city health officials acted quickly.

Cattle lie dead and dying alongside the tracks at Stacey, North Carolina, soon after the wreck of No. 52. Twenty cars were splintered in the wreck, and thousands of hogs and cattle maimed and killed. *Photo by Eugene Rice. Courtesy Elizabeth Rice.*

On May 5, they banned the bringing of killed animals into the city.

Two days after the wreck, George Allen expired from pneumonia, victim of the scalding both outside his body and inside his lungs and nasal passages. The Richmond *Times-Dispatch*, May 6, 1933, in the same article that reported his death, related that "fewer people this morning went to the wreck, and those who did so stayed to windward."

Mr. Woodson, the stricken fireman, according to the Danville *Bee* of May 7, wanted to see the small boy who caused the wreck. Unable to move from his hospital bed because of extensive burns on his legs, he conversed with friends, and said he would like to speak to the boy.

Railroad detectives had lost no time in confirming the rumor. They said Junior Cardwell, age seven, admitted to what he had done. Mr. Woodson was apparently moved by a generous and forgiving impulse in wanting to see the boy. I have been unable to discover whether the meeting ever took place.

People in Ruffin today have their memories. Mrs. B. M. Ellis, who with her husband ran a store right near the wreck site, recalls that she was standing out on her front porch watering flowers, her house just across the highway from the track. Used to the normal sounds of the trains that went by all day and all night, she raised her eyes at a different sound—a lick up the way—just in time to see the steam coming up—"twenty-seven boxcars folded up just like an accordion, and it was a week or two before the wreckage was cleared away." Their store sold out of everything that night. The authorities spent days, she says, talking to Junior Cardwell. She does not know whether the child laid the spike on the track, but it was a million-dollar accident, and a man killed, and she reckons it would have been easier on the railroad to place the blame on the child. Annie and Frank Cardwell, parents, say he did not do it, but that "someone" paid him money to say he did.

Jim Worsham's daddy, Leon "Lyn" Worsham, was a deputy sheriff at the time, and more or less in charge of rounding up the strays from the wreck. Wild cattle they were, right off the range, with no sense at all. "They didn't know what barb' wire was, just went right on through 5 strands like it wasn't even there." The red, white-faced cattle and wild horses damaged nearby property, and ranged over fifteen or twenty square miles before they were caught. A Warrenton, Virginia, rancher who knew how to rope wild cattle was brought in along with a colored fellow called "Lucky" to round them up.

A "big old pit" was dug to bury all the dead animals, Mrs. Ellis remembers. Worsham recalls that "it was the Depression, and everyone was hungry, and they'd just catch a pig and cut off its hind legs for hams and leave it lie out in the fields."

Mrs. Ellis explained that train No. 52, "The Bean Man," as it was affectionately called, was respected and feared in Ruffin. It hauled produce and livestock out of Florida every day. "The law required them not to haul those cattle but so many hours without stopping for water, so it had to go real fast." Jim Worsham, ten at the time, says he "lit out running. The engine was lyin' in the field. There were people running hogs down and turning cows loose—it was a regular rodeo. The car behind the engine was full of fine horses headed for New York for breaking and training. My daddy wound up with one, but it never had any sense at all. . . ."

I asked Mrs. Frank Cardwell, Junior's mother, if he had ever met with L. O. Woodson, the fireman; she said, "They took him to Salisbury."

"To meet the fireman?"

"I don't know. To meet someone."

"Not Danville?" I asked.

"Maybe it was," she said.

Cliff Carlisle wrote and recorded a song about the wreck shortly after it occurred.

The Wreck of No. 52

On a bright and sun-ny day, in the mer-ry month of May, From San-ford a train pulled out on time, Was old Num-ber Fif-ty two, A freight that went on through, The fast-est on the old South-ern line.

THE WRECK OF NO. 52

On a bright and sunny day, in the merry month of May,
From Sanford a train pulled out on time,
Was old No. 52, a freight that went on through,
The fastest on the old Southern line.

George Allen was the name of that engine of fame,
Who rode with that train that fated day,
When he left his wife alone, and his wife there alone,
He thought he'd return to her next day.

The train was loaded down, with stock northern bound
And little did they think they'd out delay,
Oh, little did they know just what fate would bestow
Before they had ever gone halfway.

No one was to blame for the wrecking of that train
But a little boy who was out at play,

He put a spike on the rail; the next train could not fail
To wreck that came along that way.

Everyone knows the tale, how the train left the rail,
And the cattle they were dying everywhere,
Mr. Allen thought of home and his wife there alone
When the steam from the engine filled the air.

On his deathbed Allen lay from the burns he got that day,
His wife and his children by his side,
Then he heard the Master call, and he left them one
    and all,
For Allen had taken his last ride.

There is not much new about the song. Carlisle continues to depend on the tried-and-true formula. The poem has one slightly more sophisticated characteristic than most: there is internal rhyme in the first and third line of each stanza, as if modeled on the ballad "Jesse James," whose tune it fits. The errors in rhythm, the extra syllables or syllables omitted, are puzzling; it would have been so simple to rewrite the lines slightly for accurate rhythm. The only conclusion is that this song, and others like it, were composed hastily and carelessly for an uncritical public.

NOTES

Newspaper sources were the Atlanta *Journal*, 24–30 Aug. 1908; The Danville *Bee*, 4 May 1933; Richmond *Times-Dispatch*, 4 May 1933 and 6 May 1933.

Great thanks to Norm Cohen, who provided me with a tape of the recording by Carlisle of "The Wreck of No. 52," and to my friend Hugh Agee of Athens, Georgia, who sent me the clippings from the Atlanta *Journal*.

Thanks also to Norm Cohen for putting me in touch with Eugene Wiggins of Dahlonega, Georgia, and to Gene Wiggins, who sent me information about Ben Dewberry, and to Robert D. Jacobs and Sidney A. Dewberry of Atlanta for their help, and to Shelby F. Lowe of Douglasville, Georgia, for a picture.

Pick Temple recalls a childhood incident that shows the universality of boys' putting objects on the tracks. He and a couple of friends one day went up past Mt. Royal Station in Baltimore and "climbed a fence and sat on a grassy slope looking down at the trains in the maze of tracks north of the station. The grass sloped down to the top of a stone wall where we stood and looked down about six or eight feet to the tracks, with a stream of water trickling by in a ditch. There was the Third Rail, guarded by a sort of wooden trough, open at the top so the shoes of the electric locos could slide along them. We found a piece of wire, a sort of hoop from an old barrel, and tossed it down on the tracks to see what it would do. It landed on the Third Rail and, at the same time, partly in the trickle of water running beside the tracks. It sizzled and popped and sparked and scared us half to death. We thought we had shorted out the entire railroad and stopped every train for miles in each direction! Of course we hadn't, but we felt responsible. I climbed down the wall and kicked the wire off the rail, thus allowing the B & O to function again!"

Lyle's Law states that once learned, or heard of, a new word or fact will be encountered again within a very short time. On the day after I was writing this essay, Friday, July 9, 1982, the Roanoke *Times* reported an incident in Fair Lawn, New Jersey, in which five teenagers were charged with tripping a switch that sent a commuter train roaring into a factory, killing the engineer and critically injuring a passenger.

Responses to requests for information of this wreck came from David Luther, my dear mother-in-law Frances S. Lyle, Adelle Clement, Chris Sutphin, Mrs. Donald Breedlove, and the people mentioned in the article. My special thanks to Elizabeth Rice of Danville for the photograph of No. 52, and to Marvin Black of Greensboro, North Carolina, for his loan of the photograph of Ben Dewberry's wrecked engine. Proving that these old wreck songs still have viability, Willie 'n' Waylon's "Luckenbach, Texas," contains the line: "Between Hank Williams' pain songs, and Dewberry's train songs. . . ."

The Wreck of
Old 85

On June 30, 1937, "the worst freight wreck in the history of the Pocahontas Division of the Norfolk and Western" occurred at Maybeury, West Virginia, when a runaway train met a dramatic and tragic end. Nos. 85 and 86 were N & W's crack trains, running from Norfolk to Columbus, Ohio, and back again. They were nicknamed "the million dollar trains."

It was the second such wreck on the same section of track. On December 5, 1893, Engineer W. F. Stocker and Fireman Mann Haynes were killed when their westbound coal train ran wild from Coaldale, and wrecked just east of the 580-foot Maybeury trestle, spilling several laden coal cars and trapping Stocker and Haynes beneath the overturned engine.

Some who recalled the first accident saw the second as a spooky replay.

The events of early Wednesday night, June 30, were recalled to his doctors by head brakeman James C. Ball, before he died of his injuries the next day in the Bluefield sanatorium. "I knew the train was running away . . . I kept saying, 'Why don't they

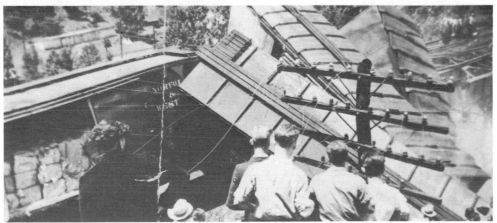

These four views show the devastation that occurred when the big N & W Mallet engine No. 2092 plunged 105 feet off the Maybeury trestle on June 30, 1937, carrying with it fifty-three laden cars of merchandise. Steam was still visible a day later, and the wreck burned for forty-eight hours. Here the steam can be seen rising to the top of the trestle and above it. In the top photo, a wrecker works to extricate the engine. *Courtesy Edgar Shew.*

put on the brake?'" He broke down, sobbing, but recovered enough to continue. "I knew he was bound to wreck if we didn't put the brakes on. . . . Then I felt myself in the air. It seemed I would never land any place, and then after that I just don't know what happened."

What happened, officially, was that the brakes failed as train No. 85, hauled by a single Mallet engine, No. 2092, a 2-8-8-2 built in Richmond, turned down Elkhorn Creek in McDowell County, West Virginia. The manifest freight consisted of eighty-nine cars, most of them sealed cars of merchandise.

Aside from Ball's statement, neither workers nor officials could offer any explanation for the wreck. Eyewitnesses, residents of Maybeury, agreed that "something was wrong with the train."

The big engine, weighing "just shy of a million pounds," according to Edgar Shew of nearby Pocahontas, hit the east end of the trestle at 6:59 P.M. and plunged 105 feet into the valley below, carrying with it fifty-three cars. Thirty-one more stayed on the track, as the train lost momentum at the end of the bridge. Oscar Duff, an off-duty Mill Creek Coal and Coke Company employee, saw the whole thing from the ground. As he watched the engine approaching faster than usual he saw sparks fly from 2092's driving wheels, and then the big Mallet shivered, left the rails, and went off the side "as though riding on air."

The crash was heard at least five miles away. Then came a second crash, the locomotive boiler exploding and being hurled 893 feet. Fragments flew more than a quarter of a mile. For several hundred yards house windows were broken and debris scattered about, causing widespread property damage. An entire home, that of Oscar Ratliff and his family, was leveled, though the family miraculously ran free of the destruction. The fifty-three cars splintered as they crashed, and a conflagration broke out at once, fed by the contents of one of the cars, a gas tank, and another, a boxcar holding six hundred cases of liquor. Other flammable merchandise fed the flames, which soon leapt two hundred feet into the evening sky.

It was known immediately that Engineer W. W. "Willie" Snead, fifty-four, and Fireman Ezra Mc-Haffa, forty-three, must be dead, for the engine was buried beneath burning debris. Brakeman J. C. Ball, thirty-two, had been riding in the tender cupola of the locomotive. He was thrown clear but fatally injured. An ambulance took him to a Bluefield hospital. The conductor, Al Gilbert, seventy-two, escaping without injury, vowed never to make another run.

Firetrucks arrived quickly from Bluefield, Bramwell, Keystone, and Pocahontas, and poured water on the fires for forty-eight hours without stopping.

About the time late the next morning that James Ball succumbed to his injuries, the family of Clark Maxey, twenty, an employee of the Lick Branch Mine of the Pocahontas Fuel Company, officially reported him missing. At first, they had assumed that he had been somehow detained by the wreck, but when he did not come home all night long, they became more and more apprehensive. His father, a section foreman, was at the site when his body was found beneath the wreckage. "That is my son," he said quietly. Friends remembered watching Clark, just before the wreck, making his way up a path towards the top of the trestle. He had left work at six, had stopped to talk with friends at Cecil Moore's Esso Station just below the trestle, then left to head home. He had been, unluckily, directly underneath the last cars to leave the track. The death toll now stood at four.

Engineman Snead was buried so deep that it took workmen three hours to get to his body, crushed beyond recognition at the bottom of an eight-foot deep, forty-foot diameter crater blasted out by the force of the engine when it hit.

Daily Telegraph

WEATHER

WEST VIRGINIA: Generally fair
with slowly rising temperature
Friday and Saturday.

Bluefield, W .Va., Friday Morning, July 2, 1937. —Fourteen Pages

Price, Five Cents

Finding Of Youth's Body Beneath Train Wreck, Brakeman's Death Send Maybeury Disaster Toll To 4

Stark Wreckage At Maybeury Trestle

WRECK SAID WORST FOR POCA DIVISION

Clark Maxey, J. C. Ball Added To Victims

RUINS STILL SMOULDER

Traffic Rerouted As Rescue Crews Strive To Clear Up Twisted Wreckage

A father peered beneath a shattered freight car while flames still flashed close by yesterday morning, and said:

"That is my son."

The unexpected discovery of the body of 20-year-old Clark Maxey—caught by death as he walked unsuspectingly homeward—and the death of James C. Ball, in Bluefield sanitarium, brought to four the victims of the Norfolk and Western freight train which wrecked at Maybeury bridge early Wednesday night.

The body of young Maxey lay on the bank near the top of the trestle, sheltered from the worst part of the wreck.

J. J. Maxey, himself a section foreman living at Maybeury, had feared for his son, since word of the spectacular train wreck reached him, and when he did not return home during the night the parents were convinced that he had been trapped by the piling cars.

Seen On Path

Witnesses saw the young man as he made his way up a pathway toward the top of the trestle. Several persons at a filling station just below the trestle said young Maxey had just left them, and was directly under the last cars that left the track.

185

The clearing-away was very slow because of the fire. It was Saturday before traffic could again operate over the bridge. During the days, cars were lined up for miles along both sides of Highway 52, over which the trestle goes.

The accident is still clear in the memories of local people. J. H. Harmon was staking tomatoes near the trestle and recalls that Engineer Snead blew a blast of his whistle as his runaway locomotive plunged towards the bridge. Edgar Shew of Pocahontas remembers that the crash and explosion as the boiler blew shook the earth for several minutes "just like it was an earthquake." An eighteen-year-old black youth was walking under the trestle as the train approached. "It made such a loud, unusual noise, I looked up. I could see the front wheels of the engine were off the rails as it came onto the bridge." He was hit by a piece of flying metal and his arm was broken.

The N & W station agent at Maybeury ("that would have been Mr. Duff," according to Edgar Shew) sent a ballad to James Taylor Adams soon afterwards. It is not clear whether Duff composed the ballad or not. No music accompanied it.

Old Eighty-five
Had a brave engineer.
To make up twenty minutes
He had no fear.
He went down Bluestone River
In old Eighty-five;
And when he reached the tunnel
He was doing ninety-five.

Chorus
Old Eighty-five
Going down the river;
Old Eighty-five
To Williamson on time;
Old Eighty-five
Trying to make up twenty minutes,
A manifest freight train
Which must go on time.

When he climbed upon his engine,
Starting down the line,
He said to his brakeman:
"I am feeling fine.
And if I blow the whistle
You will know right then,
I'm going to be in Williamson
At half past ten."

When he reached the mountain,
He tried his brake;
Manifest freight
And lives were at stake.
When he tried his air
The fire began to fly;
It seemed to his brakeman
Someone was going to die.

His fireman and buddy
Was his dearest friend;
"Unless this brake can hold her,
It's our journey's end!"
He said "Goodbye,"
And he shook his hand:
"I'll meet you over yonder
In the promised land."

It is fairly unusual for a wreck ballad to have a refrain and the internal repetition that this one has. The song suggests that excessive speed was the cause of the wreck, but the later investigations do not confirm this. Otherwise the ballad is quite conventional.

NOTES

When I sent out letters of inquiry to newspapers, several people in the Princeton-Bluefield area offered information on this wreck, which I did not use as I then had no song about it. On September 24, 1982, I came across the song or ballad at the Blue Ridge Institute at Ferrum College. On September 30, Paul Shue and I visited Edgar Shew of Pocahontas, who had written me at length about this wreck. He supplied me with photographs and yellow, frail newspapers from the days following the wreck, which he let me carry away to copy. Shew played old Vernon Dalhart records for us on his wind-up Victrola as the sun went down on southwest Virginia and a harvest moon rose. Leaving Shew's house after dark, we got hopelessly lost on the winding mountainous dirt roads and stopped to ask directions of an old woman who was enjoying the evening breeze on the front porch of her log cabin. "How do we get back to Pocahontas?" I called. She mentioned a turn to the left, then one to the right. "Then you go straight on down the mountain," she said. She paused, then added philosophically, "Course you can't go straight, 'cause the road curves." Mrs. Elizabeth Lilly of Princeton, West Virginia, also sent information on this wreck.

Others

If it isn't an old saying, it ought to be: *you got to stop somewhere*. It will serve for trains and books as well.

I began this project fearing there would not be enough material for a book; I end it by having to cut everywhere, to leave out stories and songs I have come to love. Some songs I could not ever date. Some wrecks I could find no pictures of. Some letters of inquiry sent to newspapers either were not printed, or elicited no information. Some ballads were not coherent enough to give me even a thread to grasp to begin the unravelling. Appalachia has fuzzy edges.

I admit to cavalierly including what suited me, and omitting what, for whatever reasons, did not.

California, Florida, and Nebraska, for example, were clearly out of my area, but then I never came upon a single train wreck song from any of those states. Richmond is probably not Appalachia, but the Church Hill Tunnel story was too good to omit. Therefore, this final chapter includes a few other songs and stories which did not merit whole chapters, but which I could not bear to leave out.

In November 1903, only two months after the wreck of Old 97, there occurred a wreck on the Lebanon Branch of the L & N Railroad, not far from Louisville, Kentucky. Seven men were killed between two small towns, New Hope and Gethsemane, in a head-on collision. L & N switchman "Blossom" Johnson, born in 1870, recalled the wreck in a

A wreck occurred between the towns of New Hope and Gethsemane, Kentucky, in November of 1903, on the Lebanon branch of the L & N Railroad. At a "fearful speed between midnight and day," a double-header engine collided with a single engine, killing seven, including all three engineers. Parts of two of the engines appear still on the track, but badly telescoped, while the third is overturned down the fill. The people of New Hope and Gethsemane have arrived to see the wreck. Steam still issues from at least one of the engines. *Courtesy Charles B. Castner and the L & N Railroad.*

letter to Randy Atcher in 1958 when Atcher and Charles Castner, then of Station WHAS, were trying to track down the background of a song they'd heard. "The southbound train failed to get its orders at New Hope, Kentucky," he recalled. Also in 1958, Kincaid Herr wrote to Castner that "two freight trains, one of them double-headed, collided as a result of an operator's mistake (not possible today incidentally because of centralized traffic control)." Chief Dispatcher W. R. Fowle named the engineers who were killed Sturgis, Graves, and Cannon, in his letter. Charles Castner, today publicity director for the L & N, kindly shared this information and a picture with me.

The song was copyrighted in 1936 by "Karl and Harty [who were Karl Davis and Harty Taylor] and Doc Hopkins." The song differs from other wreck songs somewhat. It has a chorus, which the music indicates is to be repeated after every stanza. On the record, by Doc Hopkins, the chorus is sung only twice, after the second stanza, and again after the fourth. The song has no moral tag. This absence alone pushed the song towards the category of traditional British and Scottish ballads, in which the narration is absolutely objective. Stergin (Sturgis) is also treated objectively, whereas most of the songs treat the engineer who dies sympathetically. As usual, despite there having been three dead engineers, the story focuses on just one of them.

The Wreck between New Hope and Gethsemane

Once two trains with might-y power run-ning six-ty miles an hour 'Twas a fear-ful speed be-tween mid-night and day Ster-gin must have been a-sleep Passed the point he had to meet And it caused an aw-ful wreck a-long the way. Dark was the night Men worked with all their might In that wreck a-bout two o'-clock or three. 'Twas a morn-ing in No-vem-ber long to be re-mem-bered That wreck be-tween New Hope and Geth-sem-a-ne.

1. Once two trains with mighty power running sixty
     miles an hour
   'Twas a fearful speed between midnight and day
   Stergin must have been asleep
   Passed the point he had to meet
   And it caused an awful wreck along the way.

Chorus

Dark was the night
Men worked with all their might
In that wreck about two o'clock or three
'Twas a morning in November long to be remembered
That wreck between New Hope and Gethsemane.

2. Stergin the engineer was brave, saw his train he could
     not save
   Saw a headlight 'round the curve like lightning flash
   Another train was heading on
   He soon saw that he was gone
   And they came together with an awful crash.

3. When the morning light it came all around the
     burning train
   Many friends and many loved ones gathered there
   Fast beneath that burning train
   They saw their friends they could not save
   So they turned away almost in sad despair.

4. Many lives of men were lost and most fearful was the
     cost
   That the L and N Company did sustain
   'Twas the darkest hour that night
   People gathered to that fright
   But they could not save them from that burning train.

On December 23, 1903, the Flyer Duquesne wrecked and inspired a song. Edward Keefer, twenty-three, told this story the next day to the Pittsburgh *Post*: "Between twelve and twenty men were in the aisle [of the smoker], and every seat was filled . . . we were going fast. . . . She jumped . . . I can't tell it as fast as it happened. The light went out . . . a scalding stream struck me . . . swinging arms hit me. . . . Every person was screaming. At last I reached a win-dow. I half fell, half leaped, through the splintered glass. . . . My throat is burning way down. Get me some cold water. I guess it's the steam. . . ." Keefer died that night. The evening before, at Dawson, Pennsylvania, on the Youghiogheny River, there had occurred the B & O's worst disaster in history. The Duquesne Limited, eastbound passenger train, left Pittsburgh at 6:30, jammed to capacity with holiday crowds, pulled by B & O Engine No. 1465, with Engineer William Thornley at the throttle. Behind the engine, which the Pittsburgh *Post* describes as "one of the new monster machines," were a laden baggage car, a packed smoker, a day car, and three Pullman sleepers, all full. At 7:44, just out of Laurel Run, she crashed, and more than sixty people died. The big engine hit some ties that had fallen across the eastbound track off a westbound train. The engine fell on its side, and the tender was propelled up over the locomotive and traveled thirty feet down the bank to the side of the river. The baggage car went over the locomotive top, and the heavy packed Pullmans forced themselves relentlessly forward; "like egg shells" the day coaches in front were twisted and crushed, the rails "torn up like paper." Dust and smoke camouflaged the scene, defying and blinding all who attempted to help with the rescue efforts. Thieves stole jewelry and money off the bodies of the dead and injured. "All the horrors of hell can only be likened to last night," R. J. George told the Pittsburgh newspaper. "Every poor fellow in that front car was pinned in and boiled to death. The sight of their steaming faces and arms through the broken windows was frightful. When we drew the bodies out they were so completely boiled that the flesh fell from their bones.

"One of the horrors . . . was the effect of those who first inhaled the steam. Death did not come instantly. They ran from the scene speechless, pointing piteously to their mouths for water, ran on again and were afterwards found dead in the bushes."

Of the many sad individual stories of this wreck, one apparently caught the attention of Ernest B. Lydick. He wrote a song for this story and had it copyrighted in the next week, before the year was out: "Robert Davidson, 31," reported the *Post*, "was to have been married tomorrow, and was on his way to meet his bride when the unforeseen accident caused his death." He told his "pitiful story" to the surgeon attending him on the relief train, Dr. Thomas Echard: "'Christmas was to have been my wedding day,' he said, between spasms of pain. 'I was to marry Hanna Wietman, a stenographer. . . . Write to her, doctor; tell her I am dying. My last words were of her. It is awful to die thus, but tell her I was brave.'

"The last words uttered while lying on a cot in the hospital were the saddest incident of any of the harrowing scenes," the *Post* editorialized.

"The Wreck of the Flyer, Duquesne" gives no historical details, but typically ignores the enormous number of deaths to focus on just one.

THE WRECK OF THE FLYER, DUQUESNE

1. The heart of a maiden was beating with pleasure,
   As the day of her wedding drew near,
   She sang as she placed holly wreaths in the window,
   Tomorrow my love will be here,
   This message he sent me brought joy to my heart,
   Yet seems to be haunting my brain,
   "If I am alive,
   My dear, I'll arrive
   On the limited flyer, Duquesne."

   Chorus
   On the limited flyer, Duquesne,
   Like a dart it speeds over the plain,
   May the angels above
   Watch over my love
   On the limited flyer, Duquesne.

2. While tying one wreath with a bow of red ribbon,
   She heard a commotion outside,
   It seemed all the newsboys were running with papers,
   "An awful disaster," they cried;
   She listened intently to hear something more,
   She heard, but the hearing brought pain,
   One "newsie" ran by,
   And loudly did cry,
   "The wreck of the flyer, Duquesne."

   Chorus
   The wreck of the flyer, Duquesne,
   My God! and my love on that train,
   Not a moment I'll wait,
   I must know the fate
   Of my love on the flyer, Duquesne.

3. A special train chartered, was quickly conveying
   Her nearer that heart-rending scene,
   Where death and destruction had wrought awful
      havoc,
   And corpses were strewn o'er the green;
   Arrived at the place, soon her lover she found,
   Her coming had not been in vain,
   On a cot he was lying,
   Well, not dead, but dying,
   Near the wreck of the flyer, Duquesne.

   Chorus
   Near the wreck of the flyer, Duquesne,
   She was clasped to his bosom again,
   But she ne'er was his bride,
   For her lover there died
   Near the wreck of the flyer, Duquesne.

SIXTY LIVES LOST IN WRECK OF FAST B. & O. TRAIN.

The Wreck of the Flyer, Duquesne

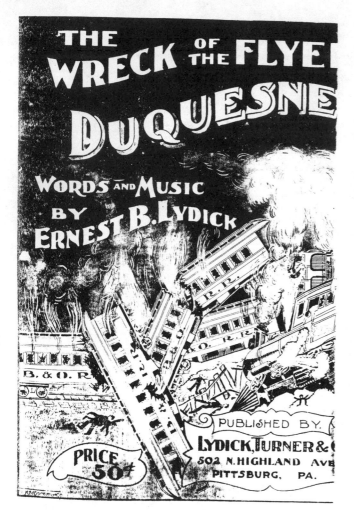

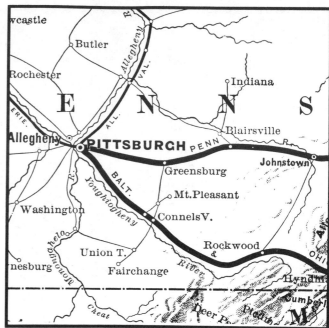

Geneva Anderson relates a ballad about a wreck that occurred near Townsend, Tennessee, on June 30, 1909. Local residents still recall that the song was sung to the tune of "Redwing."

Vic Weals of the Knoxville *Journal* has investigated "The Wreck of No. 3" thoroughly, and the following information comes from his series of articles published in June 1979.

The "outsiders" hired by Little River Lumber Company in Townsend, Tennessee, were regarded by the natives as rowdies. Gordon A. "Daddy" Bryson, fifty-five, was aware enough of local opinion to do something to try to overcome it when he hired on there in 1904. Fat, popular with his fellow loggers, he courted local youngsters by buying them ice cream, and in the end won local favor. So when he was killed June 30, 1909, there was much sadness in the neighborhood, and he is honored with a song that local residents still sing.

He was engineering a log train to the new saw mill in Townsend when the wreck occurred. Robert P. Headrick, a brakeman on the train who survived the crash, told Vic Weals in 1965, "We had just loaded five flatcars with logs. I had just tied down the hand brakes . . . as the train started rolling down the 9.5 grade so fast it was like falling out of a tree." Fireman "Hoot" Foster, Conductor Aaron Jones, and brakeman Bob Headrick jumped and escaped unhurt, but the other two men on the train, brakeman Charles Marion Jenkins and Engineman Bryson, were crushed by enormous logs falling from the wrecked train. Bryson was killed instantly, but efforts were made to save the dying Jenkins. Whiskey was brought as they waited for a rescue train, but his jaws were so tight-clenched with pain that none could trickle down his throat. He died about four hours later.

Some supposed the train lost its brake air. Engine No. 3, a Shay, ran away two other times, too, once before, once after, this wreck. Perhaps the sand box, which trickled sand onto the rails to increase friction on a steep grade, was empty. To this day, no one knows for sure.

THE WRECK OF NO. 3

1. On the thirtieth day of June,
   In the year nineteen hundred nine,
   Daddy Bryson climbed in his engine
   And pulled her out on line;
   He left his home and loved ones,
   His fatal run to make,
   But little was he thinking,
   His own life would he take.

   Chorus
   How the cinders from the stack are flying.
   The brakesman trying the train to stop;
   Still Daddy stood bravely at his post of duty,
   Till his soul was called to meet his God.

2. The morning run was finished,
   The logs were tied on well;
   And that which was to happen,
   No one could tell.
   Fireman Foster stood at the window,
   And the highball did obey,
   Daddy blew the whistle,
   And the train was on its way.

3. The air it had been tested,
   And the handbrake was all right;
   The trainmen they were anxious,
   To get home soon that night.
   Poor brakeman Charlie Jenkins,
   The last word did relate,
   "I hope nothing happens
   On the last run that I make."

4. Down the hill on Jakes' Creek,
   This wicked train did run;
   Conductor and the brakeman
   Saw something must be done,
   But one thing was lacking,
   The most important one,
   When Daddy pulled the lever,
   The sand refused to run.

5. The lightning speed increasing,
   Foster picked his place and jumped;
   Then came an awful crashing
   As he landed in the stumps;
   Old 3 spot she turned over,
   The tank by Daddy passed,
   The logs they fell on him,
   Then poor Daddy breathed his last.

"The Wreck of the 444" was copyrighted in 1942 by Bess McReynolds. Edward L. "Buck" Henson of Clinch Valley College, Virginia, sent me this brief conversation between himelf and J. M. Buchanan, retired N & W engineer, from August 19, 1974:

Henson: (Reading from material provided by Mr. Buchanan)
This goes back to June 8, 1913, train number 85 wrecked at Cleveland [Virginia], killed the engineer, A. F. Gillespie and fireman Stuart. . . .

Buchanan: Stuart?

Henson: Yes, sir.

Buchanan: They run through and killed two women, didn't they?

Henson: Engine 444 and Pusher engine 498, H. Porterfield, engineer, and Oder [maybe Omer] Miller, fireman.

Buchanan: Yep, that's right.

Henson: So 498 was in back of the whole train then?

Buchanan: Was what?

Henson: 498 was in back of the . . .

Buchanan: He was the pusher engine. The two engines were together. The 44—the 444 was the head engine and 498, H. Porterfield was the engineer on that, and he got hung in his legs in them coils[?] and stuff and they give him up to burn up. He burned part of his face. And there was an old Combs boy . . . he went down in there and got ahold of that fellow, locked his hands around his knees, and give a surge or two and pulled him out. Miller went on to the C & O later on and I don't know where he is at now.

The Richmond *Times-Dispatch* of June 9, 1913, reports on this wreck on the Clinchfield division of the N & W, west of Bluefield at Cleveland, Virginia. The home of forty-year-old Mrs. Fannie Owens was destroyed; she and her daughter Winnie, seventeen, were scalded to death by steam when both engines of double-header freight No. 85 (pp. 000-000) left the track on a curve at around 4:00 A.M., plunging down a steep bank onto the house. The leading engine, No. 444, was a class M, 4-8-0 engine built in Richmond in 1907. Twenty-five cars were derailed; eleven caught fire and burned, and both engineer Frazier Gillespie, thirty-eight, and Fireman Stewart, twenty-seven, were killed. The bodies of the dead were burned so that it was "nearly impossible to tell the women from the men." The body of Gillespie lay

SCALDED TO DEATH IN THEIR OWN HOME

Mother and Daughter Die and Locomotive Engineer and Fireman Killed.

ENGINE PLUNGES INTO HOUSE

Eleven Loaded Freight Cars Leave Track Catch on Fire and Are Destroyed

[Special to The Times-Dispatch]
Roanoke, Va. June 7. As a result
of a freight wreck on the Winnifield
division of the N . . . and Western
near Eleven . . . . . . ng the home
of . . . . the . . .
. . . da ghte . . . g . . . . cate
a . . . .
. . . . We . . . .
. . . .

under the wreckage for two days before it could be recovered.

The song itself is somehow askew: nearly impossible to play or sing, it is oddly reminiscent of Gilbert and Sullivan, or John Philip Sousa, or both. Its beginning is like the beginning of a British train song collected by Roy Palmer called "Newcastle and Carlisle Railway," which begins "On the ninth day of March in the year thirty-five, The railway was crowded with people alive . . ." though this may of course be nothing more than coincidence.

Though I risk being labeled "sexist," I would venture that this song reads (and sings, if one dare try) like a song written by a woman, and a giddy one at that. To compare a locomotive to a kingfisher . . . to romanticize out of nothing a lover sleeping under his sweetheart's roof . . . to assert cheerfully that the N & W so "perfected a plan" that there would never again be an accident . . . and then to top it all off with a sort of inflated military chorus—why, who else but a woman could have done all that?

The Wreck of 444

THE WRECK OF 444

On a lovely June morning at "five thirty five"
The crew of two engines were all glad and alive,
But old "Four forty four" made time, she was late,
on the broad Cleveland track, 'Twas here met her fate.
There was nothing to warn them that grim death lurked
  nigh
As down the Clinch Valley Gillespie and Stuart did fly,
It all happened so quickly In the twinkling of an eye,
As the iron mass toppled over, Fate decreed that four
  should die.

Chorus
Old "4-4-4" could you but know all the agony you
  caused,
As you spun around that fatal curve, In your speed you
  would not have paused!
Had you held true to your course westward, As true as
  a Kingfisher's flight!
You would have been in Norton, Soon after it was
  daylight.

Near the track in a cottage three lay sound asleep,
Mother, daughter, lover, the last two dreaming deep
Of their near wedding day, But death made them part,
for she gave up her life, It broke Walter's heart,
For he loved his dear Willie, and she loved him too,
For soon was their wedding and it left him there, oh,
  so blue,
Then they buried his darling Right there by her
  mother's side,
For fate ruled that she should leave him, Never be his
  own sweet bride.

No new accident ever happened again
For the N and W have perfected a plan
And they know the worth of a true soldier tho'
he serves as a railroad man engineers.
Hold your throttles steady, firemen! hand them a
  helping hand!
Railroad men! All be alert to your duty
and don't forget the fate of the 4-4-4 and your
  fellow men
nor ever forget Combs to whom honor is due!

A man named Talmadge Osborne is remembered in song, but whether such a man ever lived is problematical.

In the early days of railroading, this new and outrageous mode of travel was very suspect. Early on, the railroads complained that public opinion was such that in legal cases, juries nearly always found in favor of the individual against the iron dragons that traveled at such breathtaking speed and tore up the landscape.

According to James Osborne, attorney at law (and no relation to Talmadge that he knows of), in law as in other areas of American life there are ebbs and flows, reflecting changing public needs. At present, we are in a phase when human rights are valued more highly than corporate rights. Certainly at no other time in history have individuals recovered such large amounts in damages as they presently do. A case in point: in Fincastle, Virginia, in 1979, a railroad employee named Sligh recovered $150,000 after losing his hand in a railroad-related accident. This was the highest jury verdict ever for personal injury in Botetourt County, according to W. T. "Pete" Robey, who was the attorney for the defendant.

But this was not always so. During the late decades of the nineteenth century, and well into the twentieth, courts tended to afford protection to the developing vital industry that railroads were. Certainly this was no "conspiracy," as the following song suggests, but rather a reflection of the public attitude that the industry was more important than the life or safety of an individual. If an engine went by a house every day and threw cinders off, and one day that house burned down, the onus was on the house owner to prove that it was the railroad's fault, which he could hardly do, since a house might burn for any number of reasons. And what did one poor house owner count for against the vital movement of mail, passengers, and goods?

On January 16, 1890, E. E. Johnson, a C & O

brakeman in the Huntington yards, lost most of one hand and the entire use of that hand while uncoupling two cars of a train while the train was in motion. In May of 1890 he sued the C & O for his losses, but the courts ruled that in going between the cars to uncouple them while they were in motion, he willfully violated a company rule that specifically forbade this action, that he knowingly acted in a dangerous manner, that he was therefore guilty of carelessness, and that furthermore he knew of the printed company policy that a brakeman violating the rule could not recover for injury.

Locally, this ruling, which set a legal precedent for other similar cases, became known as the "Johnson Law." Naturally it was unpopular with railroad employees.

Album notes on *Virginia Traditions*, subtitled Native Virginia Ballads, made at the Blue Ridge Institute at Ferrum College (Release No. BRI004) tell us that Ernest Stoneman, who died in 1968, wrote to folklorist Alfred Frankenstein on August 6, 1929, identifying Talmadge Osborne as a young man from Grayson County who went to West Virginia to work in the coal mines to enable him to make payment on a piece of land in his native Grayson County. Osborne apparently habitually bummed rides on trains while drunk, and in this instance he tried it once too often, in or near Williamson, West Virginia. According to West Virginia Law of 1923, Chap. 145, Sec. 31, a trespasser on a train was considered a "disorderly person." Conductors had the right to act as constables, to carry guns, and to throw hobos off the trains. Thus when Talmadge Osborne lost his hands and died, the railroad took no responsibility, and the law was on the side of the railroad. Here is the song as sung by Ernest Stoneman, and recorded for Victor on May 19, 1927.

Would you please to listen, to a story often said,
Of a young man Talmadge Osborne who was deemed to
  have no dread,
The people all took notice of the screams heard once or
  twice,
They believed he had a warning of a calling of his life.

He was born in Grayson County, here paying for some
  land,
Now he's in eternity, and in judgment he will stand,
He saw the engine coming, amoving down the road.
Some boys said, "Look out, Osborne," but upon it he did
  load.

The engine it was backing up, when Osborne caught the
  ride,
He got off with his hands cut off, and he lost his life
  besides.
They stopped the engine quickly, with a signal it was
  given,
I do not know who was the engineer, but his engine was
  497.

They took him back to Grayson in an unexpected way,
When his casket reached his home, you could hear the
  people say:

There's many a man's been murdered by the railroad,
There's many a man's been murdered by the railroad,
There's many a man's been murdered by the railroad,
And laid in his cold lonesome grave.

You may think it's jolly, but it's really good advice,
If you're having lots of fun, and living mighty nice,
Be careful how you're walking on the company's
  right-of-way,
The Johnson law will get you and your dues you'll have
  to pay.

For they have a kind of a law out there, it's a mighty
  secret thing,
You'll get all that's coming if you're not in the ring;
Put a pistol in your pocket when riding on a train,
Six months upon a county road will be your final doom.

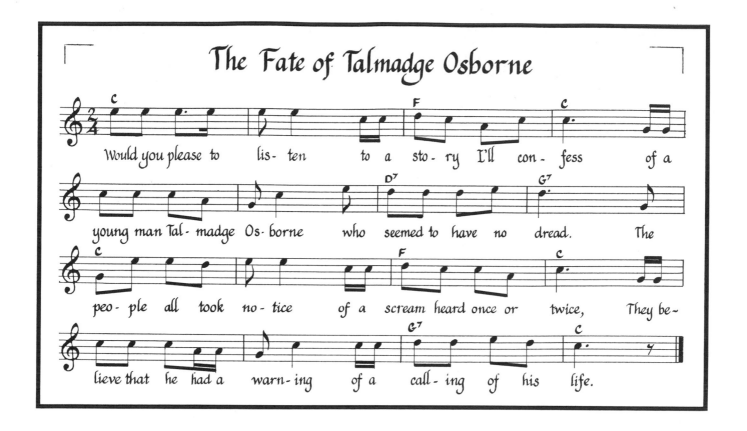

The Fate of Talmadge Osborne

Would you please to lis-ten to a sto-ry I'll con-fess of a young man Tal-madge Os-borne who seemed to have no dread. The peo-ple all took no-tice of a scream heard once or twice, They be-lieve that he had a warn-ing of a call-ing of his life.

"The Fate of Talmadge Osborne" has not lasted as a folk song. Its story line is vague, its time sequence unclear. The first stanza appears to suggest that perhaps Osborne had had some kind of warning: probably he had been thrown off trains before. What surfaces in the song is a deep, if unjustified, anger at the law of the time. But it might fairly be said that Americans lack a sense of proportion when it comes to their folk heroes. Never mind that Osborne was on the train illegally, and if Stoneman's comments were accurate, drunk besides. In the battle between individual and institution, American society in general has long tendered a romantic notion that the individual ought to win. When he in fact loses, his loss is seen as a threat to the "freedom" of us all.

The Blue Ridge Institute at Ferrum College has conducted an exhaustive search for facts or dates about the life of Talmadge Osborne, and even searched birth and death records for decades in Grayson County. To date, they have found no evidence of his existence.

"The Powellton Labor Train Explosion" is a ballad that has been catalogued by the Blue Ridge Institute of Ferrum College, Virginia. It tells of a tragedy that occurred on December 27, 1934, on the company-owned railroad of the Elkhorn Piney Coal Mining Company. The Richmond *Times-Dispatch* related on December 28 that "just as the morning sun was peeping over the mountain into this little mining community" near Charleston, West Virginia, the lo-

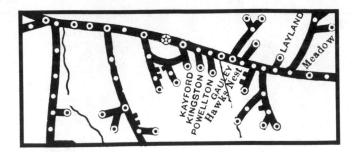

comotive boiler suddenly exploded violently, scattering victims over a wide area, and literally *shaking* the isolated settlement of Powellton, in Fayette County. "When the great barrage of steam cleared, the dead and dying lay sprawled over an area of more than 100 square yards." The engine landed on the first of the four cars that had just stopped to pick up workers before continuing on to the mine. The force of the blast tossed the engine cab through the roof of a nearby house, almost killing a mother and two sleeping children. All of the men killed were riding in the front coach. When the steam cleared, ambulances and private cars carried the dead and dying to nearby Montgomery. The wreckage so cluttered the narrow right-of-way that rescue was very difficult, and that night, reported the *Times-Dispatch*, "children cried in their mining homes for fathers who did not return." In all, seventeen persons were killed and forty-three severely injured. Charles A. Hudson of Pulaski, Virginia, composed the following ballad about the disaster, which his mother, Mrs. Elizabeth Hudson, sent to James Taylor Adams in March 1940. The poem is an excellent example of what Laws refers to as "sincere sentimentalism." The facts are correct; the words seem to have been written by an eyewitness; the correct rules have been followed, the song ending with the usual sober warning. And yet the song stands up better as history than as literature, as is true of so many of the songs in this book.

THE POWELLTON LABOR TRAIN EXPLOSION

It was a cold December morn,
The hour was about six o'clock,
There came a vast explosion
All MacDunn was filled with a shock.

Chorus
The explosion of the Powellton labor train,
  On Armstrong Creek that day;
Leaving orphaned children and wives so dear,
  Most to the poor house strayed.

The boiler of the labor train,
Was hurled into the air,
And crashed down through the man-filled coach,
Burning, killing miners there.

The air was filled with death cries,
And was clouded with hot blinding steam;
They knew not what had happened
When they heard their comrades scream.

The fireman was dashed against the rocks,
The engineer was hurled into the air,
They found them in a tangled mass;
Blood chilling, lying there.

It was an awful, horrible wreck,
One we never shall forget,
Those sixteen cold, perished men,
Made all eyes misty wet.

The hospital it was crowded,
The nurses and doctors had no rest;
They were soothing the blistered miners
They gave the live ones the best.

The lives of sixteen miners were taken
As I have told you before,
And many others wounded;
Forty-some, or more.

Those that were uninjured,
On that unforgotten day,
Remained to help their work mates
Who in the wreckage lay.

The wreck scene was heartbreaking,
Crowds came from miles around,

To gaze upon those blood smeared caps,
And love letters that were found.

On the Twenty-seventh day of December,
The people's hearts were filled with cheer;
They knew not of their impending doom,
Bringing both misery and fear.

Neither do we know what day or hour,
Death may claim our soul,
Be kind and good to all you meet
As onward the years do roll.

Fathers, sons, husbands and sweethearts,
Your train sometime might explode,
So be prepared at any time
And stay on the righteous road.

And finally, this ballad, by Denver Stull, appeared
in the West Virginia *Hillbilly* on April 10, 1982,
commemorating a wreck that occurred in the early
twenties; a cousin of the author, Vinson McKean,
was the engineer killed in the wreck. Mr. Stull says
the 1923 date in the poem is only a guess, and that
he changed Smithburg, West Virginia, to Smithton.
He recalls that the McKean boys, Vince, Peter, and
George, all engineers for the B & O, had reputations
as highballers. This wreck, of a fast freight hauling
cattle and produce, had a mystery about it: just before the wreck, a hobo was seen on the train by several people. After the wreck, no sign of him could
ever be found, dead or alive, except for his hat.
Though this ballad has not yet been set to music, the
tradition lives on!

THE RIDE TO HELL

Vince was a railroad engineer,
His train a daily freight
That roared through hills at mighty speeds,
Insanely testing fate.

From Parkersburg to Grafton Town
He was quite widely known;
The folks in towns along the track
All knew his whistle's tone.

One day in nineteen twenty-three
While driving a fast freight,
A hot box caused a long delay
And Vince was running late.

He told the fireman, "Give me steam;
We've got to ball the jack;
I'll be in Parkersburg on time
If she'll stay on the track."

They went through Smithton at a speed
They'd never seen before;
The agent at the depot laughed,
"It's Vince again," he swore.

"Please slow down Vince," the fireman yelled,
"There's a bad switch ahead;
The entire train may jump the track.
Then we will all be dead."

Vince pulled the throttle out some more;
The fireman heard him yell
"I'll be in Parkersburg on time,
Or ride this train to hell."

His whistle's artful whippoorwill
Echoed through hill and dell,
And at top speed they hit the switch
And rushed right into hell.

Now friends still living in these parts
Say when the nights are still
They sometimes hear the distant wail
of Vince's whippoorwill.

NOTES

Charles B. Castner of the L & N Railroad, not content to answer my inquiry and let it go at that, took up my banner, dug around in company files, and sent reams of information about four or five L & N wrecks, many xeroxed railroad songs, maps, and newspaper clippings. Every researcher should be so lucky! He begs me to add that railroads are constantly at work to improve safety. In fact, I would be remiss if I did not add here, at the end of this book about railroad disasters, the happy information that today railroads are the safest general transportation in America. The Department of Transportation reports that in 1980 there were only 667 fatalities in American railroads, the lowest number since 1891, which was the first year of accident statistics.

The Pennsylvania Railroad kindly lent me information on "The Wreck of the Flyer Duquesne." Lorene Smith of the Maryville, Tennessee, library took up my cause as if it were her own, and covered the area for me in search of information about "The Wreck of No. 3," even starting a file about the wreck for her own library. She has my gratitude. After months of searching N & W files for something about the strange song "The Wreck of the 444," both Arthur Bixby of the Roanoke Transportation Museum and Everett N. Young of the C & O Historical Society concluded that on the basis of what we knew about Locomotive 444 I ought to look in the years between 1907 and 1913. As I was engaged in doing so, E. L. "Buck" Henson of Clinch Valley College, Virginia, came up with information out of his own local history files, which he generously shared with me. I am grateful to Roddy Moore of the Blue Ridge Institute, and Mrs. H. B. Eller, Grayson County historian, for help with Talmadge Osborne. Dan Riley, a law student at Washington and Lee University, kindly helped me find the law pertaining to this song. I found "The Powellton Labor Train Explosion" at the Blue Ridge Institute. In addition to the newspaper articles cited, I found material on this wreck in Reed's *Train Wrecks*. My thanks to Denver Stull for permission to reprint his ballad, "The Ride to Hell," and for passing on what information he had about the wreck upon which he based the song.

Bibliography

Only books and magazine articles are listed here; newspaper articles, interviews, and personal debts are acknowledged at the end of each chapter.

Adams, James Taylor. *Death in the Dark*. Big Laurel, Virginia: Adams-Mullins Press, 1941.

Alvarez, Eugene. *Travel on Southern Antebellum Railroads, 1828–1860*. University: University of Alabama Press, 1974.

Ames, Russell. *The Story of American Folk Song*. New York: Grosset & Dunlap, 1955.

Anderson, Geneva. "A Collection of Ballads and Songs from East Tennessee." Master's thesis, University of North Carolina, 1932.

Anderson, Roy B. "Wreck of the 1256." *C & O Historical Society Newsletter*, 1 July 1969.

Belden, Henry M. *Ballads and Songs Collected by the Missouri Folk-Lore Society*. 2d ed. Columbia: University of Missouri Press, 1955.

Botkin, B. A., and Alvin F. Harlow. *A Treasury of Railroad Folklore*. New York: Bonanza Books, 1953.

Bower, Suzanne. "Collapse on Church Hill," *Richmond Mercury Magazine*, 5 March 1975.

Brown, Frank C. *The Frank C. Brown Collection of North Carolina Folklore*. Vol. II. Folk Ballads. Belden and Hudson. Durham, North Carolina: Duke University Press, 1962.

Brunnings, Florence E. *Folk Song Index*. New York: Garland Publishing Company, 1981.

Burford, Cary Clive. *The Chatsworth Wreck*. Fairbury, Illinois: Blade Publishing Company, 1949.

Cambiaire, Celestin Pierre. *East Tennessee and Western Virginia Mountain Ballads*. London: Mitre Press, 1934.

Chase, Richard. *American Folk Tales and Songs*. New York: Book of NA Library of World Literature, 1956.

Cohen, Norm. *Long Steel Rail*. Urbana: University of Illinois Press, 1981.

Combs, Josiah H. *Folk-Songs du Midi des États-Unis*. Paris: Presses Universitaires de France, 1925.

Cox, John Harrington. *Folk-Songs of the South*. 1925. Reprint. Hatboro, Pennsylvania: Folklore Associates, 1963.

———. *Traditional Ballads and Folk-Songs Mainly from West Virginia*. 1939. Reprint. Philadelphia: American Folklore Society, 1964.

Cyporyn, Dennis. *The Bluegrass Songbook*. New York: Macmillan, 1972.

Davis, Arthur Kyle, Jr. *Folk-Songs of Virginia*. Durham, North Carolina: Duke University Press, 1949.

———, ed. *Traditional Ballads of Virginia*. Charlottesville: University Press of Virginia, 1929.

Dixon, Thomas W. "Billy Richardson's Last Ride." *Railroad Magazine*, 83 (Oct. 1968): 32–33.

———. "The Story of the FFV," *C & O Historical Society Newsletter*, 11 (Dec. 1979).

Flanders, Helen Hartness, and George Brown. *Vermont Folk-Songs and Ballads*. Hatboro, Pennsylvania: Folklore Associates, 1968.

———, Elizabeth Flanders Ballard, George Brown, and Phillips Barry. *The New Green Mountain Songster*. Hatboro, Pennsylvania: Folklore Associates, 1966.

Fountain, Clara Garrett. *The Wreck of Old 97*. Danville, Virginia: Womack Press, 1976.

Fox, Pat. *The Wreck of Old 97*. Danville, Virginia: Fox Publishers, 1969.

Gerould, Gordon Hall. *The Ballad of Tradition*. Oxford: Oxford University Press, 1932.

Gregory, Howard. *History of the Wreck of the Old 97*. Danville, Virginia, 1981.

Gordon, Robert W. *Folksongs of America*. New York: National Service Bureau, 1938.

Greenway, John. *American Folksongs of Protest*. Philadelphia: University of Pennsylvania Press, 1953.

Grissim, John. *Country Music: White Man's Blues*. New York: Paperback Library, 1970.

Harris, William H., and Judith S. Levy. *The New Columbia Encyclopedia*. New York & London: Columbia University Press, 1975.

Heart Songs. Boston: Chapple Publishing Company, 1909.

Heite, Edward. "The Tunnels of Richmond." *Virginia Cavalcade*, 14 (Winter 1964).

Holbrook, Stewart H. *The Story of American Railroads*. New York: Crown Publishers, 1947.

Hubbard, Freeman H. *Railroad Avenue*. New York: McGraw-Hill, 1945.

———. *An Encyclopedia of North American Railroading*. New York: McGraw-Hill, 1981.

Journal of American Folklore. American Folklore Society, 1888–1982.

Kincaid, Bradley. *Favorite Mountain Ballads and Old Time Songs*, No. 8. New York: Southern Music Publishing, 1937.

Korson, George. *Coal Dust on the Fiddle*. Hatboro, Pennsylvania: Folklore Associates, 1965.

———, ed. *Pennsylvania Songs and Legends*. Baltimore: Johns Hopkins University Press, 1949.

Lambie, Joseph T. *From Mine to Market*. New York: New York University Press, 1954.

Lane, Ron S. "Folk Music of the C & O." A continuing series in the *C & O Historical Society Newsletter*: Part 1 [general introduction], 1 (Oct. 1969): 4–5; Part 2 ["C & O Wreck"], 1 (Dec. 1969): 9–10; Part 3 ["Wreck of C & O #5"], 2 (Feb. 1970): n.p.; Part 4 ["Wreck of C & O *Sportsman*"], 2 (Mar. 1970): n.p.; Part 5 ["Engine 143"], 2 (June 1970): "Historical Section"; Part 6 [Billy Richardson], 2 (July 1970): n.p.; Part 7 ["Wreck of 1256"], 2 (Aug. 1970): n.p.; Part 8 ["C & O Excursion"], 4 (Aug. 1972): 7; Part 9 ["Wreck of C & O *Sportsman*"], 4 (Oct. 1972): 8–9; Part 10 ["The Dying Engineer"], 4 (Nov. 1972): 8–9; Part 11 ["The Clifftop Train"], 6 (Mar. 1974): 6–7; Part 12 ["The Wreck of the C & O #5—A Sequel"], 6 (Apr. 1974): 14–15; Part 13 ["The C & O Blues"], 6, (Oct. 1974): 10; Part 14 ["John Henry"], 6 (Nov. 1974): 10–15.

Laws, G. Malcolm, Jr. *Native American Balladry*. Rev. ed. Philadelphia: American Folklore Society, 1964.

Leisy, James F. *The Folk Song Abecedary*. New York: Hawthorn Books, 1966.

Locomotive Engineers' Monthly Journal. Cleveland, 1868–. Published as *Locomotive Engineers' Monthly Journal*, 1867–71; *Brotherhood of Locomotive Engineers' Journal*, 1872–73; *Engineers' Monthly Journal*, 1874–82; *Brotherhood of Locomotive Engineers' Journal*, 1883–1906; *Locomotive Engineers' Journal*, 1907–59; *Locomotive Engineer*, 1960–.

Lomax, Alan. *The Folk Songs of North America*. Garden City, New York: Doubleday, 1960.

———, and John Lomax. *Our Singing Country*. New York: Macmillan, 1941.

Lomax, John. *The Adventures of a Ballad Hunter*. New York: Macmillan, 1947.

Malone, Bill C. *Country Music, U.S.A.* Austin: University of Texas Press, 1968.

McIntosh, David S. *Folk Songs and Singing Games of the Illinois Ozarks*. Carbondale and Edwardsville: Southern Illinois University Press, 1974.

Murray, Robert K., and Roger W. Brucker. *Trapped!* New York: Putnam, 1979.

O'Brien, Patrick. *The New Economic History of Railways*. New York: St. Martin's Press, 1977.

Palmer, Roy. *Strike the Bell*. London: Cambridge University Press, 1978.

Pepper, Brooks. *'Ritin and Railin'*. Richwood, West Virginia: Jim Comstock, 1973.

Peters, Harry B., ed. *Folk Songs Out of Wisconsin*. Madison: State Historical Society of Wisconsin, 1977.

Phillips, Lance. *Yonder Comes the Train*. New York: A. S. Barnes, 1965.

Porterfield, Nolan. *Jimmie Rodgers*. Urbana: University of Illinois Press, 1979.

Railroad Man Magazine 8 (Jan. 1909), 9 (September 1909).

Reed, Robert C. *Train Wrecks: A Pictorial History of Accidents on the Main Line*. Seattle: Superior Publishing, 1968.

Reid, H. *The Virginian Railway*. Milwaukee: Kalmbach Publishing, 1961.

Robertson, James I. "The Wreck of Old 97," *Virginia Cavalcade*, Autumn 1958.

Sandburg, Carl. *The American Songbag*. New York: Harcourt, Brace, 1927.

Scholes, Robert, and Robert Kellogg. *The Nature of Narrative*. New York: Oxford University Press, 1966.

Shaw, Robert B. *A History of Railroad Accidents, Safety Precautions, and Operating Practices*. N.p.: Vail-Ballou, 1978.

Shellans, Herbert. *Folk Songs of the Blue Ridge Mountains*. New York: Oak Publications, 1968.

Sherwin, Sterling, and Harry McClintock. *Railroad Songs of Yesterday*. New York: Shapiro, Bernstein, 1943 .

Shue, Paul. "Railroad Wrecks in Story and Song." *Augusta Historical Bulletin*, 9 (Fall 1973).

Shuster, Phil., Gene Huddleston, and Al Staufer. *C & O Power: Steam and Diesel Locomotives of the Chesapeake and Ohio Railway 1900–1965*. LC #65-26713, 1965.

Silber, Fred and Irwin. *Folksinger's Workbook*. New York: Oak Publications, 1973.

Temple, L. P. "Pick." "A Folksinger Rides the C & O." *C & O Historical Society Newsletter*, 1975.

Turner, Charles W. *Chessie's Road*. Richmond: Garrett & Massey, 1956.

Wallace, Conley, and Aubrey Wiley. *The Norfolk and Western Handbook*. Goode, Virginia: W-W Publications, 1980.

Wallace, George Selden. "Chessie's Railroad." N.p., n.d., courtesy of Mr. Ben P. Knight.

West Virginia Centennial Committee on Folklore. *The West Virginia Book of One Hundred Songs, 1863–1963*. © Patrick W. Gaines, 1963.

Index

Aberdeen, N. C., 79
Adams, James Taylor, 33, 186, 202
Adams, Joshia, 65
Agee, brakeman, 143
Alderson, W. Va., 12, 39, 41, 46, 182
Aldrich, E. G. ("Dad"), 142–49
Allegheny Tunnel, 2, 96
Allen, George, 177–81
Alley, Capt. Leonidas Salathiel, 34
Alley, George W., 34–49, 70, 115, 145
Alley, Leonidas S., Jr. ("Lon"), 36, 41
Altoona, Pa., 125–31
Amtrak, 158
Anderson, Ada Legge, 91
Anderson, David, Jr., 118
Anderson, Geneva, 194
Anderson, Henry, 165–72
Anderson, Oscar, 166
Anderson, Roy B., 107, 114
Anderson, Sam M., 103–109
Anderson, W. H., 76, 167
Appalachia, 3, 5, 114, 188
Arizona Wranglers, 28
Armistead, Wentworth, 17, 21
Armstrong Creek, W. Va., 202
Ashland, Ky., 151, 153, 160
Atlanta, Ga., 15, 16, 19, 174, 176

Atlantic Coast Line—see Railroads; see also Engines
Auxier, Ky., 157

Ball, James C., 182
Beauvallet, Leon, 5
"Ben Dewberry's Final Run," 11, 176
Bernhardt, Sarah, 15
Big Bend Tunnel, 47, 96, 100
Big Ivy, The (McCague), 9
Big Sandy River, 153, 157
"Billy Richardson's Last Ride" (song), 74–76, 98
Blair, J. Thomas, 21
Bluefield, W. Va., 27, 184, 196
Blue Ridge Institute, 33, 113, 162, 187, 200 ff.
Blue Ridge Mountains, 3
Boggs, Dock, 113
Bolton, James, 118
Boulding, B. R., 21
Boyston, Dr. Charles E., 174
Bramwell, W. Va., 184
"Brave Engineer, The" (song), 46, 109
Brentlya, A. H., 34
Brewer, W. H., 136
Brightwell, foreman, 86

Bristol, Tenn., 59
Broady, Joseph A. ("Steve"), 9, 16–33, 111
Brockman, Polk C., 140
Brown, Frank C., 80
Brown, John, 59
Bryan, Tom, 94
Bryan, William Jennings, 97
Bryson, Gordon A. ("Daddy"), 194–95
Buchanan, J. M., 196
Buchanan, Ky., 151, 160
Buckeye Park, O., 5
Buena Vista, Va., 2
Buford, Ga., 174
Burke, Elizabeth—see Fahrson, Elizabeth Burke
Burke, Walter, 154–62
Burnaugh, Ky., 151
Byrd Street Station, Richmond, Va., 118

"C & O Freight and Section Crew Wreck" (song), 160
Caldwell, Bill, 59–67
Calhoun, Ga., 115
Cannon, engineer, 189–91
Cannonball, N & W, 50–56
Cardwell, Junior, 179
Carlisle, Cliff, 49, 179, 181

"Casey Jones" (song), 14, 34
Castner, Charles B., 189, 204
Cattlettsburg, Ky., 88, 150
Chapman, Ky., 151
Chappell, weaver, 22
Charleston, W. Va., 93, 143, 201
Charlotte, N. C., 77–82 passim
Charlottesville, Va., 95, 96, 107
Chatham, Va., 18
Chattanooga, Tenn., 115
Cheap, W. D. ("Bud"), 154–55, 160
Chesapeake and Ohio Railway—see Railroads; see also Engines
Chidsey, Walker, 133–40
Church Hill Tunnel, Richmond, Va., 116–24, 188
Clapp, Albion G. ("Buddy"), 16–33, 111
Cleveland, Va., 196
Clifford, Captain, 41
Clifton Forge, Va., 34–49, 92, 96, 104, 107
Clinch Valley College, Va., 66, 196
Coaldale, W. Va., 182
Cohen, Norm, 5, 13, 24, 29, 43, 45, 49, 100, 102, 111, 114, 129 ff., 137, 140, 149, 159, 176, 177, 181
Coleman, Bernice B., 142, 145, 149, 170
Collins, Floyd, 97, 111, 140
Combs, Josiah H., 88
Columbus, O., 182
Compton, "Doc," 152, 160
Conner, Charles, 72
Cook, fireman, 90
Cooksie, Lewis, 174–75
Corder, Dave, 157
Corrie, A. M., 132–40
Cotton Hill, W. Va., 74
Coulter, J. A., 88
Country Music, U.S.A.—see Malone, Bill
Cousins, W. C., 53
Covington, Harry, 9, 51–56
Covington, Robert, 52–56
Covington, Va., 2, 96
Cox, John Harrington, 150, 152

Dalhart, Vernon, 1, 25, 26, 31, 46, 95, 109, 129, 137, 187
Damron, Jerry, 113–14
Dan River, 18, 31
Danville, Va., 2, 14–33, 177–81
Davidson, Robert, 192–93
Davis, Karl, 189
Davis, Mary E., 103, 104
Dawson, Pa., 191
"Death of Jerry Damron, The" (song), 113–14
Deepwater, W. Va., 141
Detroit, Mich., 164

Dewberry, Benjamin F., 174–77
Dewberry, Effie Lowe, Kitchens, 175
Diamond, Paul, 152, 153
Dickinson, Jack, 45, 49
Dillard, Sidney M., 103–109
Dixon, Jack, 49
Dixon, Thomas W., Jr., 5, 12, 37, 41, 59, 69, 70, 75, 76, 91, 100, 101, 115, 149, 164, 172
Dobbins, Jim, 160
Dodge, Robert, 16–33 passim
Donnelly, Shirley, 49
Douglasville, Ga., 115
Dry Fork, Va., 18
Duff, Oscar, 184
Duff, station agent, 186
Duncan, John A., 32
Dunlap, Jennings J., 17, 23, 64
Dunlop, Va., 50–56
Durham, N. C., 77–82 passim
"Dying Engineer, The" (song), 171

Echard, Dr. Thomas, 192
Eckles, Robert S., 53
Elkhorn Creek, W. Va., 184
"Engine 143" (song)—see "The Wreck on the C & O"
Engines: Atlantic Coast Line, No. 335, 50; Chesapeake and Ohio, No. 70, 68; No. 134, 38–41; No. 137, 92–101; No. 161, 73; No. 183, 92; No. 231, 120; No. 444, 156; No. 474, 164–70; No. 820, 85–90; No. 1105, 156, 158; No. 1120, 88; No. 1256, 102–109; No. 1642, 167; No. 2767, 106, 115; Norfolk and Western, No. 6, 51; No. 29, 50–56; No. 444, 196; No. 497, 200; No. 498, 196; No. 2092, 182–87; Pennsylvania, No. 1262, 125–31; Southern, No. 1051, 59–65; No. 1061, 56–57; No. 1102, 14–33; No. 1219, 132, 137; No. 1231, 173; No. 1237, 174; No. 1256, 132, 137; Virginian, No. 102, 141–43; No. 212, 141–43

Fahrson, Elizabeth Burke, 154–62
Fahrson, Frank, 158
"Fast Mail," 14
"Fatal Run, The" (song)—see "The Wreck on the C & O"
"Fate of Talmadge Osborne, The" (song), 200
Faulconer, John, 172
Ferrum College—see Blue Ridge Institute
Fetner, Harry, 77–78
FFV, the, 24, 37–38, 68, 69, 72
"FFV, The" (song)—see "The Wreck on the C & O"

Fincastle, Va., 199
Flannagan, John, 40
Fletcher, E. R., 158
"Flyer Duquesne, The" (song), 191–94
Font, Dr. George E., 53
Fort Spring, W. Va., 36
Foster, "Hoot," 195
Foster, Robert, 38
Fowle, W. R., 189
Frankenstein, Alfred V., 45, 200
Franklin Junction, Va., 17–33 passim
Freeman, Chesley, 83
"Freight Train" (song), 111
"Freight Wreck at Altoona" (song)—see "The Wreck of 1262"
Fries, Va., 25

Gaffney, S. C., 64
Gardner and Chickering, 89
"George Allen" (song)—see "The Wreck on the C & O"
"George Alley" (song)—see "The Wreck on the C & O"
George, David Graves, 17, 24–33
George, R. J., 191
Gethsemane, Ky., 188–91
Gibson, Henry, 62
Gilbert, Al, 184
Gilbert and Sullivan operettas, 197
Gillespie, Frazier, 196
Gladstone, Va., 103
Glen Wilton, Va., 103
Goodin, John, 156
Gordon, Robert W., 29
Gordonsville, Va., 172
Grafton, W. Va., 203
Graves, engineer, 189
Great Bend Tunnel—see Big Bend Tunnel
Greenbrier River, 39, 45
Griggs, Walter S., 118, 123
Gulley, Charles H., 93–95
Guyandotte Bridge, 69, 83–91
"Guyandotte Bridge Disaster," 88–91
Guyandotte River, 84–91
Guyan River—see Guyandotte River

Hall, Dr. Paul B., 155
Hamilton, conductor, 143
Hamlet, N. C., 77–82
"Hamlet Wreck, The" (song), 80–82
Hampton City, Ky., 151
Handley, W. Va., 70
Hanger, E. Sterling ("Tod"), 12, 42
Harbin, Dr., 140
Hardy, Mrs. George, 134
Harmon, J. H., 186
Harris, R. S., 178

Harvey, Roy, 46, 145, 148
Haskell, Homer, 9, 163–72
Hawks Nest, W. Va., 163–65
Haynes, Mann, 182
Headrick, Robert P., 195
Henry, John—see John Henry
Henson, E. L. ("Buck"), 196, 204
Herr, Kincaid, 189
Hill, Lee, 64
Hinton, W. Va., 34–49 passim, 69–73 passim, 92, 100, 165, 167, 170
Hodge, John Madison, 33—See also Robert Dodge
Hodges, Tenn., 59–67
Holbrook, Stewart, 14
Hopkins, Doc, 189
Horseshoe Curve, Pa., 125–31 passim
Hubbard, Freeman, 102
Hudson, Charles A., 202
Hunnicut Curve, Ky., 161
Huntington, Collis P., 117
Huntington, W. Va., 70, 71, 93, 141, 163, 165

Ingleside, W. Va., 144–49

Jackson River Depot, Va., 34
James, Jesse, 181
James River, 3, 103–108, 118
James River Railroad Bridge, Lynchburg, Va., 17
Jenkins, Andrew, 11, 137, 140, 176, 177
Jenkins, Charles Marion, 195
Jerry's Run, Va., 2, 96
"Jesse James" (song), 181
John Henry, 98, 124
Johnson, "Blossom," 188
Johnson, E. E., 199–200
Johnson, Rev. Henry E., 53
Johnson, W. G., 106
Jones, Aaron, 195
Jones, Casey, 98

Kane, William, 59–67
Keefer, Edward, 191
Keith, S. J., 136–40
Kelly, Katherine, 143
Kellysville, W. Va., 144
Kelso, C. S., 120–22
Keystone, W. Va., 184
Kinney, William, 29
Kittanning Point, Pa., 125–31
Knight, B. P., 12, 32, 38, 53, 69 ff., 105–106, 114, 124, 131, 141, 172
Knoxville, Tenn., 57–67
Kuper, W. A., 163

Lane, Ron S., 12, 34, 36, 43, 49, 68, 94, 100, 104, 159, 165, 167, 170, 172
Laurel Run, Pa., 191
Laurinburg, N. C., 79
Laws, G. Malcolm, 10, 97, 102
Lawyers, Va., 29
Lester, James, 23
Lewis, Llewellyn, 123
Lewis, Lloyd D., 142, 148 ff.
"Life's Railway to Heaven" (song), 9
Lima, Va., 18, 27
Lindbergh, Charles, 168
Lively, Cecil, 73, 76
Lockwood, Ben G., 151 ff.
Lockwood, Bess Turman, 150–62
Locomotives—see Engines
"Lonesome Whistle" (song), 111
Long Steel Rail—see Cohen, Norm
Lord, Albert, 5
Lotz, Given, 127–29
Louisa, Ky., 153, 160
Louisville, Ky., 188
Louisville and Nashville Railway—see Railroads
Lowe, Shelby F., 115, 140, 181
Lydick, Ernest B., 194
Lyle, Harry, 102–115
Lynchburg, Va., 16–33 passim

"McAfee, Carlos B.," 109, 114—see also Carson Robison
McCague, James, 9
McCrory, Charlie, 2
McDonie, R. D., 154–56, 160
McDougal, W. Va., 164
MacDunn, W. Va., 202
McGhee, John, 145, 146
McHaffa, Ezra, 184
McIvor, W. E., 23
McKean, George, 203
McKean, Peter, 203
McKean, Vinson, 203
McReynolds, Bess, 196
McWaters, John, 15
Malone, Bill, 5, 24, 25, 109
Malone, Will, 78
Mann, Judge W. H., 52
Marrowbone, Ky., 114
Mason, Tom, 120–23
Maxey, Clark, 184
Maybeury, W. Va., 182–87
Meadows, Rufus, 85–91
Meeks, Cleburne C., 11, 53–56, 69, 74, 95, 98
Meyer, A. R., 135
Midland Trail, 163, 170
Miller, G. H., 178

Miller, Mrs. Alexander McVeigh, 41
Miller, Oder (Omer?), 196
Miller, Samuel, 79
Mills, Jim, 59–63
Monroe, Va., 16–33, 178
Montgomery, W. Va., 159, 165
Moore, Cecil, 184
Moore, Roddy, 204
Morgan, David, 4
Morristown, Tenn., 59
Mosby, B. F., 121–23
Moss, H. R., 136
Myers, "Happy," 2
Myrick, Eliza, 56

"N & W Cannonball Wreck" (song), 98
Nashville, Tenn., 115
"Newcastle and Carlisle Railway" (song), 197
New Hope, Ky., 188–91
New Market, Tenn., 59
"New Market Wreck, The" (song), 64–67
New River, 9, 45, 163, 170
New River Gorge, 70, 73, 163, 164
New River Highway Bridge, 69
"Nine Hundred Miles Away From Home" (song), 111
Noonan, Mayor, 37
Nordica, Lillian, 107, 115
Norfolk and Western Railway—see Railroads; see also Engines
Norfolk, Va., 50, 141
Notasulga Hill, Ala., 15

Ohio River, 3, 88
Ohio Valley, 88
Old Point Comfort, Va., 164
"On A Cold Winter's Night" (song), 109
O'Neal, Frank M., 143–49
"Only A Brakeman" (song), 102
Oostanaula, Ga., 115
Opelika, Ala., 15
Orr, Hal, 107
Osborne, Talmadge, 199–200
Owens, Fannie, 196
Owens, Winnie, 196

Page, W. Va., 143
Paintsville, Ky., 151–61 passim
Parent, Brad M., 85
Parkersburg, W. Va., 203
Parrott, E. M. ("Dick"), 57–63
Pence Springs, W. Va., 45
Pennsylvania Railroad—see Railroads; see also Engines
Perry, W. E., 127
Petersburg, Va., 50, 54

Phillips, Wallace, 23
Pierce, Billy, 123
Pierce, Robert M., 136–40
Pikeville, Ky., 114
Pinckney, W. F., 22
Pincuspy, G. M., 127
Pleasant Valley, Pa., 126
Pocahontas, Va., 184
Ponce de Leon, the, 132–40
Poole, Charley, 148
Porterfield, H., 196
Poteet, Charles T., 92–101
"Powellton Labor Train Explosion, The"
    (song), 202
Preston, Buddy, 160–61
Prichard, Dr. Alan, 152
Princeton, W. Va., 144, 170
Pritchard, W. Va., 153

Quinn, Michael, 40

Railroads: Alabama and Vicksburg, 177;
    Atlantic Coast Line, 18, 50; Baltimore
    and Ohio, 2, 88, 191–93, 203; Chicago,
    Cincinnati and Louisville, 83; –Chesa-
    peake and Ohio, passim—see esp. 34–
    49, 68–76, 83–91, 92–101, 102–15,
    116–24, 150–62, 163–72; Columbus,
    Hocking Valley and Toledo, 5; The
    Family Lines, 166; Hocking Valley, 84;
    Kanawha and Michigan, 84; Louisville
    and Nashville, 188–91; Norfolk and
    Western, 2, 16, 50–56, 182–87, 196–99;
    Pennsylvania, 125–31; Seaboard Air
    Line, 18, 77–82; Southern, 14–33,
    57–67, 132–40, 173–81; Virginia
    Central, 34, 71, 117; Virginian, 141–49
Ramey, Linda, 66
Ratliff, Oscar, 184
Reed, Alfred, 145, 146–47
Reed, Robert, 83, 102, 114, 204
Richardson, Billy, 1, 9, 68–76
Richardson, Frank, 71
Richardson, George, 71
Richardson, Will, 71, 73
Richmond, Va., 50, 73, 116–24, 196
"Ride to Hell, The" (song), 203
Riddle, Morton, 52
Roanoke, Va., 141–49 passim
Robison, Carson, 31, 95, 109, 114
Rockingham, N. C., 79
Rockmart, Ga., 132–40
Rodgers, Jimmie, 176
Rogers, Henry Huttleston, 141–42
Rogersville, Tenn., 59
Rome, Ga., 133–40 passim
Ronceverte, W. Va., 93

Roop, Kyle, 170
Rorrer, Kinney, 33, 149
Rorrer, Posey, 148
Royal Palm Express, 132–40
Ruffin, N. C., 177–79

Sanford, N. C., 180
St. Alban's, W. Va., 73
Salt Petre Cave, Va., 115
Saltville, Va., 16, 23
Scary, W. Va., 73
Scheline, F. C., 9, 126–31
Seldom Scene, the, 2
"Seno Wreck, The" (song), 89
Sewells Point, Va., 141
Sewell, W. Va., 44, 164
Sharpsburg, Pa., 126
Shaw, Robert, 115
Sherman, E. T. ("Doke"), 157
Shew, Edgar, 184, 186
"Ship That Never Returned, The" (song), 46
Shockoe Bottom, Richmond, Va., 118
Shue, Paul, 4, 11, 12, 23, 30, 31, 53, 55, 72, 75,
    95 ff., 106, 114, 123, 149, 162, 172, 187
Shumway, Rev. E. J., 159
Slaughter, Marion Trye, 109—see also
    Vernon Dalhart
Smithburg, W. Va., 203
Snead, W. W., 184–86
"Soldier's Joy" (song), 149
Sousa, John Philip, 197
Southern Railway—see Railroads; see also
    Engines
Spencer, N. C., 16, 23, 27, 29, 177, 178
Spencer, Samuel, 29
Spies, Lewis, 21
Sportsman, the, 163–72
Stacey, N. C., 178
Stapleton, Charlie, 157
Starcher, Buddy, 49
Staunton, Va., 92, 96
Stevens, George W., 86
Stergin, engineer—see Sturgis
Stewart, fireman, 196
Stillhouse Creek, Danville, Va., 18, 28
Stillhouse Trestle, Danville, Va., 18
Stocker, W. F., 182
Stockyard, W. Va., 45
Stoneman, Ernest, 200
Sturgis, engineer, 189–91
Sugar Valley Station, Ga., 115
Swaen, F. W., 135

Tabor, Ira, 153
Tait-Douglas, Fred, 129
Taubler, H. F., 127
Taylor, Harty, 189

Temple, L. P. "Pick," 10, 12, 33, 49, 94, 100,
    114, 124 ff., 181
Thomas, Jean, 160, 162
Thompson, Jay, 152, 160
Thompson, J. Harris, 18, 23
Thompson, J. L., 21
Thompson, John, 17
Thompson, Ralph, 17, 21
Thornley, William, 191
"Three Drowned Sisters, The" (song), 95
Thurmond, W. Va., 74
"Titanic, The" (song), 91
Tokyo Rose, 172
Townsend, Tenn., 194
Tracy, Ben, 115
"Train That Will Never Be Found, The"
    (song), 123–24
Train Wrecks—see Reed, Robert
Trendeman, Peter, 118
"True and Trembling Brakeman, The" (song),
    112
Turman, Samuel, 150, 153–54
Twyford, Warner, 21

Union Station, Lynchburg, Va., 17

Vaden, Mary Booth, 21–22
Valentine, James E., 100
Vann, Dr. L. L., 22
Virginia Military Institute, 71
Virginia Central Railway—see Railroads
Virginian Railway—see Railroads; see also
    Engines

Wadkins, Mason, 174–77 passim
Waldon, Tim, 79
Warman, Cy, 4
Warter, Thomas, Jr., 133–40 passim
Washington, D. C., 16–33 passim, 96
Weaver, J. L., 144
Webb, B. B., 16, 23, 64
Webber, C. B. ("Ed"), 9, 85–91
Weeks, John Boyd, 142–45 passim
Westinghouse airbrakes, 15, 125–26
Whitcomb, Col. H. D., 118
Whitcomb, W. Va., 93
White Oak Mountain, Va., 18, 24
White Sulphur Springs, W. Va., 93
Whitsett, N. C., 16
Whitter, Henry, 25
Wickham, Williams C., 118
Wietman, Hanna, 192
Wiggins, Eugene, 181
Wiggins, W. Va., 40
Williamson, W. Va., 186, 200
Withrow, Lewis, 38, 41
Womack, R. D. ("Dolly"), 92–101

Woodson, L. O., 177–79
Worsham, Leon ("Lyn"), 179
"Wreck at Altoona, The" (song), 130–31, 160
"Wreck at Latona, The" (song), 131
"Wreck Between New Hope and Gethsemane, The" (song), 6–7, 188–91
"Wreck of No. 52, The" (song), 45, 180–81
"Wreck of Old 85, The" (song), 186–87
"Wreck of the C & O No. 5, The" (song), 1, 95–101
"Wreck of the FFV, The"—see "The Wreck on the C & O"
"Wreck of the Flyer Duquesne, The" (song), 193

"Wreck of the 444" (song), 196–99
"Wreck of the N & W Cannonball" (song), 54–56, 98
"Wreck of the Number Nine, The" (song), 109, 111, 115
"Wreck of the Old 97, The" (song), 1, 11, 14, 25–33, 34, 64, 174, 188
"Wreck of the Royal Palm, The" (song), 11, 139–40
"Wreck of the Sportsman, The" (song), 149, 163–72
"Wreck of the 1256, The" (song), 1, 108–109, 160
"Wreck of the 1262, The" (song)—see "The Wreck at Altoona"

"Wreck of the Virginian No. 3, The" (song by Roy Harvey), 148
"Wreck of the Virginian No. 3, The" (song by John McGhee), 145–46
"Wreck of the Virginian No. 3, The" (song by Alfred Reed), 146–48
"Wreck of 36, The" (song), 160
"Wreck on the C & O, The" (song), 11, 34–49, 89
"Wreck on the Hunnicut Curve, The" (song), 160–61

Youghiogheny River, 191
Young, Everett N., 204